Craig Pritchett

play the
English

EVERYMAN CHESS

Gloucester Publishers plc   www.everymanchess.com

First published in 2007 by Gloucester Publishers plc (formerly Everyman Publishers plc), Northburgh House, 10 Northburgh Street, London EC1V 0AT

British Library Cataloguing-in-Publication Data
A catalogue record for this book is available from the British Library.

ISBN: 978 1 85744 5459

Distributed in North America by The Globe Pequot Press, P.O Box 480, 246 Goose Lane, Guilford, CT 06437-0480.

All other sales enquiries should be directed to Everyman Chess, Northburgh House, 10 Northburgh Street, London EC1V 0AT
tel: 020 7253 7887 fax: 020 7490 3708
email: info@everymanchess.com; website: www.everymanchess.com

EVERYMAN CHESS SERIES (formerly Cadogan Chess)
Chief advisor: Byron Jacobs
Commissioning editor: John Emms
Assistant editor: Richard Palliser

Typeset and edited by First Rank Publishing, Brighton.
Cover design by Horatio Monteverde.
Printed and bound in the UK by Clays, Bungay, Suffolk.

Contents

Bibliography

Books

Beating Unusual Chess Openings, Richard Palliser (Everyman Chess 2006)
Chess Explained: The English Opening, Zenon Franco (Gambit 2006)
English ...e5, Alex Raetsky & Maxim Chetverik (Everyman Chess 2003)
English Opening: Classical & Indian, Vladimir Bagirov (Everyman Chess 1994)
English Opening: Symmetrical, Vladimir Bagirov (Everyman Chess 1995)
How to Play the English Opening, Anatoly Karpov (Batsford 2007)
Starting Out: The English, Neil McDonald (Everyman Chess 2003)
Symmetrical English, David Cummings (Everyman Chess 2001)
The Dynamic English, Tony Kosten (Gambit 1999)
The Dynamic Reti, Nigel Davies (Everyman Chess 2004)
The Gambit Guide to the English Opening: 1...e5, Carsten Hansen (Gambit 1999)
Winning with the English, Zoltan Ribli & Gabor Kallai (Batsford 1992)

Databases

Correspondence Database 2006
Mega Corr 4
Mega Database 2007
The Week in Chess

Periodicals and Online Resources

Chess Informant, Chess Today, ChessPublishing.com, New in Chess Magazine, New in Chess Yearbook and *Schach Magazin 64*

Acknowledgements

I acknowledge the contribution of the multitude of players who appear in the pages of this book. They have created the theory and continue its development. Many great players and writers have inspired me, not least John L. Watson who wrote a landmark Batsford series on the English over 35 years ago and still writes on the opening with undiminished vigour and insight.

I have a special fondness for a personally inscribed copy of one of the late Vladimir Bagirov's volumes on the English, going back to the days when we both played in the Schachklub Zehlendorf team in the Bundesliga.

As always, thanks are due especially to Elaine, Katie and Sally for their support and forbearance. Thanks, too, to my Everyman editors, John Emms and Richard Palliser, for their eye for detail and the big picture, as well as for their patience.

I would finally like to dedicate this book to Harald and Edelgard Lieb for their warm friendship and generous hospitality over the years and to many fond memories of battles fought in Berlin and elsewhere for Schachklub Zehlendorf.

Introduction

This book aims to provide a no-nonsense, straightforward introduction to key strategic ideas and developments in the English Opening. It is aimed primarily at the club and tournament player and is repertoire based. In writing this book, I hope that my readers will not just be entertained by the many great games it contains, but that they will also be inspired to play the English.

The Repertoire

Apart from the variation 1 c4 e5, which should be regarded as a 'reversed' form of the Sicilian Defence, very broadly there are two main ways to play the English. Either White plays his central pawns, particularly his d-pawn, with restraint in the centre, usually combining this approach with a kingside fianchetto and slow manoeuvring, or he combines 1 c4 with 2 ♘f3 and plays for a space-gaining break in the centre with an early d4 (with or without a kingside fianchetto).

This book covers both 'reversed' Sicilians and lines which combine 1 c4 and 2 ♘f3 with d4 in mind. This is my preferred way of playing the English. Thus this book does not include many lines based on c4, g3 and d3 systems, except in the reversed Sicilian lines, where this is a necessary and major exception. The book's main exclusion is those slow symmetrical English lines, where both sides fianchetto on the kingside and play c4/...c5 and d3/...d6. You don't have to play them.

Our approach is a full-blooded way to play the English. It perhaps suits players, like me, who have migrated to the flank openings from 1 e4. We like that early d4 idea. It reminds us of our aggressive roots in open 1 e4 play. Apart from that, playing the English this way offers a flexible bonus. We can enter all the lines in this book by playing 1 ♘f3, except for the 1...e5 systems. If not in the mood to play the reversed Sicilian lines, opening with 1 ♘f3, of course, rules out these lines altogether.

More on the Power of the d4 Pawn Break

Quite simply the English Opening is utterly sound and dangerous. All the world's great players play it and it is probably at its most popular in many of the more direct c4, ♘f3 and d4 push or break lines, which take up a good deal of this book. The reasons for the popularity of this direct approach are very clear:

1) If Black doesn't contest the centre after c4 and ♘f3 with early pawn moves to the fourth rank, an early d4 push by White, perhaps combined with an eventual e4, will result in an impressive c4, d4 and e4 centre.

2) Against an early ...c5 by Black, d4 followed by an exchange of pawns on that square will establish the basis for nagging Maróczy Bind pressure, based on a c4 and e4 pawn centre.

3) Against an early ...e5 by Black, d4 followed by an exchange of pawns on that square functions rather like it does in many 1 e4 openings, creating free central piece play and releasing potential for further space-gaining advances into Black's position.

4) And finally, if Black plays ...d5, without support by ...c6 or ...e6, White can eventually expect to exchange his c-pawn for Black's d-pawn, establishing an extra white pawn in the centre.

Of course, it is all much more complicated than that, but White can clearly press in all these lines. So you get the picture!

An Overview of the Main Chapters

Chapters 1-3 deal with the positions arising after 1 c4 e5 which lead to a huge variety of reversed forms of the Sicilian Defence. Chapters 1 and 2 focus on The English Four Knights with 4 g3, the main modern battleground and my repertoire choice. Chapter 3 deals with set-ups for Black that seek to avoid this tough as nails White system. A tempo up on 'real' Sicilians, White has the initiative. Black daren't risk the sharpest options open to White after 1 e4 c5 and must play with considerable care.

Chapter 4 addresses the many lines that can arise after the symmetrical response 1 c4 c5 2 ♘f3 ♘f6 3 ♘c3 ♘c6, 3...d5 and the Keres-Parma Defence. Black plays more cautiously in these ...c5 systems, aiming for gradual equality. White's steady ♘f3/d2-d4 repertoire approach, however, offers good long-term chances of obtaining a pull.

Chapter 5 covers the main line ...e6/...d6 and double fianchetto Hedgehog defences that can arise after a variety of move orders. Hedgehogs famously give up much of the centre to fight from a position of coiled potential on the first three ranks. White's extra space, active pieces and early initiative, however, allow him to play well into the middlegame in search of a genuine edge.

Finally, Chapter 6 addresses certain hybrid forms of the Nimzo-Indian and Grünfeld Indian Defences. White can battle for the advantage against these defences along purely English lines based on holding back any advance by White's d-pawn in the earliest stages. However, I have explicitly excluded Queen's Gambits and Slav, Dutch and King's Indian Defences. How to confront these essentially unavoidable lines, should Black insist on playing into them, is a matter of wide personal taste. Most 1 c4 and 1 ♘f3 players transpose to (1 d4) main lines.

Making Practical Use of the Repertoire

All opening books writers are positively deluged by data. I couldn't have covered the English sensibly in one book without adopting a repertoire approach and heroic summarization. It's the same for you, dear reader. All of us, these days, fight a losing battle if we try to take on board 'everything'. So my first point is simply to stress what we all know – don't expect to be spoon-fed by this or any other book. Look for ideas, explanations and ways to play, rather than immutable variations. Then release your inner artist and work hard to find your own way when you work on your game and particularly when you actually play.

Secondly, I'm young enough at heart to stress just how important it is simply to enjoy the game. Chess is not a static art. It's an ever-changing adventure. That's one reason why I invariably try to write opening theory into fully annotated games. Chess theory develops through play. In writing books on such vast subjects like these, I'm always struck by the phenomenal creativity of all those players, at all levels, who have ever played the opening. I feel connected to all these minds and it inspires me. I trust that it also inspires you, as the book's title suggests, to play the English!

Thirdly, use this book as a starting point. I am sure most readers will gain value by reading it without access to computer engines and databases. But at whatever level you play and whether you use or do not use computers, watch out for new ideas in lines you like and note them. If you use computers, you can do this much more effectively, of course. Whatever you do, enjoy it.

I will finally emphasize that I have written this book from the standpoint of a practical player and can assure you that the repertoire is not just reliable but a good one. I have perhaps paid slightly more attention to ensuring that the reader understands how to play the white side well, but in doing so I have not consciously tried to underplay Black's chances. Like you, sometimes I also play Black and against the English!

Craig Pritchett,
Dunbar,
November 2007

Chapter One

The Four Knights: 4 g3 ♗b4

This chapter considers the main lines arising after the moves **1 c4 e5 2 ♘c3 ♘f6 3 ♘f3 ♘c6 4 g3 ♗b4**.

From this position, White generally plans to complete his kingside development and exert pressure on the h1-a8 diagonal, particularly the d5-square. He will use this light-square restraining strategy as a basis to seek greater control of central and queenside space, by gradually advancing his central and queenside pawns and perhaps occupying d5 with his queen's knight.

For his part, Black generally plans to bolster his e5-strongpoint and seek opportunities to disrupt the logical flow of White's plans, by means of further sensible piece and pawn play, with moves such as ...d6, ...♖e8 and ...h6. Black should be constantly alert to any dynamically unbalancing opportunity to double White's c-pawns by playing ...♗xc3, perhaps combined with ...e4.

Play now commonly continues **5 ♗g2 0-0 6 0-0 e4** reaching one of the main lines in this variation. White can then choose to continue with Gary Kasparov's dynamic favourite **7 ♘g5 ♗xc3 8 bxc3 ♖e8 9 f3**.

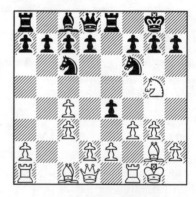

This was Kasparov's 1987 reinterpretation of a line that had been long established but thought neutralized, and it remains a serious test of Black's resources. Game 1 reveals what may be his most splendid discovery in response to **9...exf3** in this most promising and complex of combinative labyrinths. Game 2 investigates Black's radical gambit alternative **9...e3**. White has good chances of obtaining an edge in both lines. But if White wants to play 'safe', he can also seek to gain a (very modest) minimal pull with **7 ♘e1 ♗xc3 8 dxc3 h6 9 ♘c2** (Game 3).

As a result of concern about the strength of Kasparov's line, although the theoretical jury may not yet have reached an entirely final conclusion, many Black players subsequently returned to other 'older' lines for the defence, such as **6...♖e8** (Game 4) and **6...♗xc3** (Game 5). Black constrains his ambition but retains a very sound and solid position. White may obtain a slight pull, but breaking down these defences is far from easy.

Many White players, conscious of the potentially disruptive effect of the exchange ...♗xc3, have also recently dabbled with another older move, **5 ♘d5**, which is still worth a try, in an attempt to rule out Black's exchanging opportunity altogether (Game 6).

Game 1
G.Kasparov-V.Ivanchuk
USSR Championship,
Moscow 1988

1 c4 e5 2 ♘c3 ♘f6 3 ♘f3 ♘c6 4 g3 ♗b4 5 ♗g2 0-0 6 0-0 e4

This is Black's most energetic choice, staking a claim to some serious space in the centre.

7 ♘g5

White doesn't shirk the challenge.

He forces an immediate exchange on c3, which strengthens his central pawn mass. He then plans to undermine Black's hold on e4 with an f3-break, leading to positions where White has a potentially mobile pawn centre supported by potentially lethal bishops and promising play down the half-open f-file.

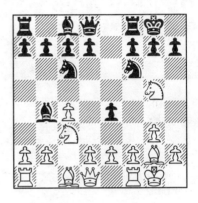

7...♗xc3 8 bxc3

White can also play the quieter 8 dxc3 with the idea after 8...♖e8 9 ♘h3 (or 9 ♕c2 ♕e7) of re-centralizing White's knight via f4 to d5. This line is similar to, though perhaps a little less flexible than, lines arising after 7 ♘e1 (Game 3). Black retains his strong e4-pawn and can develop comfortably after 9...h6 10 ♘f4 d6 (or 10...♘e5 11 b3 b6 followed by ...♗b7) 11 ♘d5 ♗f5 when it is hard for White to make the theoretical advantage of his bishops count due to Black's solidity.

8...♖e8 9 f3

Black cannot maintain his pawn on e4 after this move. White can achieve the same undermining effect after 9 d3 exd3 10 exd3, but without establishing the same dynamic potential in the centre. R.Hübner-R.Kasimdzhanov, Bad Wiessee 1997, continued 10...h6 11 ♘e4 b6 12 ♖b1 ♗b7 13 ♘c5 ♗c8 14 ♘b3 ♗b7, while H.Hernandez-Y.Quezada, Havana 2004, saw 10...d6 11 ♖b1 h6 12 ♘e4 ♘xe4 13 ♗xe4 ♕f6 14 ♗d2 ♗f5 15 f3 ♖ab8, in both cases with a satisfactory game.

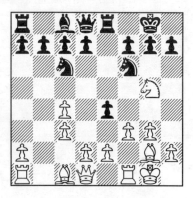

9...exf3

See Game 2 for the radical gambit alternative 9...e3.

10 ♘xf3 d5

This line had been considered satisfactory since the mid-1970s. No doubt sensing an improvement, Karpov instead tried 10...♕e7!? 11 e3 ♘e5 (*see diagram*) against Kasparov in Game 4 of their 1987 World Championship match. Most previous games had gone 11...d6 which doesn't directly contest White's pawn centre, leaving White with chances of developing long-term attacking chances, as in, for example, V.Smyslov-P.Peev, Cienfuegos 1973, which continued 12 d3 ♗g4 13 h3 ♗d7 14 e4 h6 15 ♖b1 ♖ab8 16 ♘h4 ♘e5 17 ♗e3 b6 18 ♘f5 ♗xf5 19 ♖xf5 ♘fd7 20

♕f1 ♘f8 21 d4 ♘ed7 22 ♕d3 ♘h7 23 ♖bf1, with a clear advantage.

Kasparov, however, met Karpov's idea with the brilliant gambit 12 ♘d4! when Black's best move may be to revert to 12...d6. Instead Karpov chose to eliminate the bishop-pair, but without stemming the flow of White's forces. After 12...♘d3 13 ♕e2 ♘xc1 14 ♖axc1 d6 15 ♖f4 c6 16 ♖cf1 ♕e5 17 ♕d3! ♗d7 18 ♘f5 ♗xf5 19 ♖xf5 ♕e6 20 ♕d4 ♖e7 21 ♕h4 ♘d7 22 ♗h3 ♘f8 23 ♖5f3 ♕e5 24 d4 ♕e4 25 ♕xe4 ♖xe4 26 ♖xf7 ♖xe3 27 d5, White won.

Note too that accepting the gambit is risky. C.Leotard-M.Vigneron, correspondence 1996, continued 12...♘xc4 13 ♘f5! ♕e6!? (or 13...♕e5 14 e4! and if 14...d6 15 d4 ♕a5 16 ♘h6+ gxh6 17 ♖xf6 ♕xc3 18 ♗xh6 ♘e3 19 ♕h5 ♕xa1+ 20 ♗f1, winning – Franco) 14 d3 ♘e5 15 e4 d5 16 d4 ♘xe4!? (Leotard's notes mention 16...♘c4 17 exd5 ♘xd5 18 ♕g4 g6 19 ♘h6+ ♔g7 20 ♕h4! f5 21 ♘xf5+! gxf5 22 ♗xd5 ♕xd5 23 ♗h6+ and wins) 17 ♗xe4 dxe4 18 dxe5 ♕xe5 19 ♘d4, and White eventually won.

Returning to 10...d5:

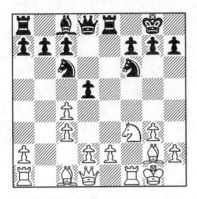

11 d4!

One year after the Seville match, Kasparov reveals one of his world championship secrets. Theory still considers that Black has good dynamic chances after 11 cxd5 ♕xd5! 12 ♘d4 ♕h5! and he established dangerous light-square threats in P.David-A.Gipslis, Bardejov 1991, which continued 13 ♘xc6 bxc6 14 e3 ♗g4 15 ♕a4 ♗e2 (strong too is 15...♖e6, and if 16 ♖b1 ♗e2 17 ♖e1 ♘g4 18 h3 ♕f5) 16 ♖f4 ♘g4 17 h3 ♘e5 18 d4 ♘d3 19 ♖h4 ♕f5 20 ♕xc6 ♕f2+ 21 ♔h2 ♖ab8 22 ♗d2 g6 23 ♖g1 ♖e6 24 ♕xc7 ♖b2, and Black won.

11...♘e4

Declining the c-pawn which White offers with a view to mobilizing his pawn centre. Instead S.Kramer-C.Pauwels, correspondence 2002, continued 11...dxc4 12 ♗g5 (White can also consider 12 ♕c2 and 12 ♖b1, aiming after ...♘e4 to transpose into the main game continuation) 12...♕d6 13 ♗xf6 ♕xf6 14 e4, with an edge. In such positions, not only is White's centre secure, but Black's c4-pawn is clearly vulner-

able in the long term. This explains Ivanchuk's 11th move, delaying any capture on c4.

12 ♕c2!

White can also offer a different, but less clear gambit 12 cxd5 ♘xc3 13 ♕d2 ♘xd5 14 e4 ♘f6 15 e5, as he did in A.Vaisser-L.Janjgava, Uzhgorod 1988. However, Kasparov's move, continuing to offer the c4-pawn, is more consistent.

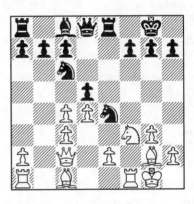

12...dxc4!?

If Black is going to take this pawn he is best doing it now. Practice has also seen 12...♗f5!? 13 ♘h4 and now:

a) 13...♗g6 14 ♘xg6 hxg6 sees Black having to battle with two knights against an active bishop-pair. Black's knights can occupy good central squares, but White can chip away at Black's support for them, often after a later ...f5, by playing g4, and has a nagging edge. G.Baiocchi-H.Rittner, correspondence 1995, continued 15 ♖b1 (White can also fight for the initiative with 15 ♕d3 ♘a5 16 cxd5 ♕xd5 17 ♖f4 f5 18 g4, as he did in J.Benjamin-J.Kurth, Berlin 1989) 15...♘a5 16 cxd5

♕xd5 17 ♗f4 ♘c4 18 ♕d3 f5!? (18...♖ac8 19 ♖b4 b5 20 a4 a6 21 axb5 axb5 22 g4 is also better for White) 19 ♗xc7 ♖ac8 20 ♗f4 ♖e6 21 ♖b4 b6 22 a4 a6 (after 22...♖ee8 both 23 h3 and the immediate 23 g4 maintain a pull) 23 g4 ♖ec6 (or 23...fxg4 24 ♗g3, threatening ♖f4, and if 24...g5 25 ♗e5, winning an exchange) 24 ♗g3 ♖e8 25 h4 b5 26 axb5 axb5 27 h5 ♕d7 28 gxf5 gxf5 29 ♖xb5 ♘cd2 30 ♖c1 ♖h6 31 ♗f4 ♖xh5 32 ♗xd2! ♘xd2 (32...♕d6 fails to 33 ♖e5! ♖xe5 34 ♗f4) 33 ♖e5 ♘b3 34 ♖xe8+ ♕xe8 35 ♖b1 ♕b8 36 ♗d5+ and White won.

b) 13...♗g4!? doesn't fully convince. According to Raetsky and Chetverik White retains a plus after 14 e3 ♘a5 15 cxd5 ♘d6 (or 15...♕xd5 16 ♖f4 f5 17 h3 g5 18 ♖f1) 16 e4 f6 17 ♗f4.

13 ♖b1!

Kasparov turns the queenside screw a further notch before switching his attention to more direct central action. The immediate 13 ♘e5 ♘xe5 14 ♕xe4 ♘g6 15 ♕d5 ♕e7 16 e4 is also playable, but White can play for more.

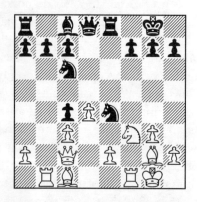

13...f5

With his bishop consigned to de-fence on c8, Black can only support his knight on e4 with this potentially weakening pawn move. Against other moves, White quickly dominates the centre: for example, I.Brooks-J.Neves, correspondence 1995, continued 13...h6 (13...f6 14 ♘e5 fxe5 15 ♗xe4, and if 15...♗h3 16 ♖d1, is no better; neither was 13...♕e7 14 ♘d2 ♘g5 15 e4 ♗h3 16 ♗xh3 ♘xh3+ 17 ♔g2 ♘g5 18 h4 ♘xe4 19 ♘xe4 ♕xe4+ 20 ♕xe4 ♖xe4 21 ♖xb7, and White won the endgame in J.Hodgson-I.Naumkin, Amantea 1995) 14 ♘e5 ♘xe5 15 ♗xe4 ♘g4 16 ♗h7+ ♔h8 17 ♖xf7, and White won.

14 g4!

Kasparov was ready for Black's 14th move. This superb discovery sustains further undermining pressure against e4.

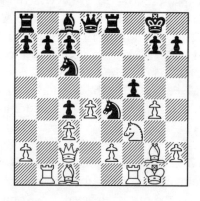

14...♕e7?!

Ever since this game, few players have wished to defend this position. While all its secrets may not have been teased out yet, it is hard for Black to counteract White's obvious pressure on e4. Ivanchuk's choice fails, but other choices also have downsides:

a) 14...fxg4 15 ♘e5 ♘xe5 (15...♘d6 16 ♘xc6 bxc6 17 e4 is better for White but may be Black's best choice according to Kasparov) 16 ♗xe4 ♘g6 17 ♗xg6 hxg6 18 ♕xg6 gives White good play for a pawn and clear attacking chances, in large part due to the influence of his dark-squared bishop. The game A.Lesiege-I.Zugic, Montreal 2001, concluded 18...♕e7 (instead 18...♕d7 19 ♖b5, and if 19...♕xb5 20 ♖f7, or 19...♗e6 20 ♕h5 ♕e8 21 ♗a3, is good for White according to analysis by Raetsky and Chetverik) 19 ♖b5! ♕e6 20 ♕h5 g6 21 ♕h6 and 1-0.

b) 14...g6 has also been tried, but after 15 ♗f4 intending ♘e5, Black remains on the defensive. I.Smirin-B.Avrukh, Groningen 1996, continued 15...♗e6!? (15...♘d6 16 ♘e5 is also better for White) 16 ♖xb7 ♗d5 17 gxf5! ♘xd4 18 cxd4 ♗xb7 19 fxg6 hxg6 20 ♘e5, and White won.

c) 14...♘d6 may be Black's best practical chance. White then threaded his way through great complications in P.David-T.Polak, Olomouc 1995: 15 ♗g5 ♕d7 16 ♘h4 (Stohl's 16 ♗f4!?, intending ♘e5, may be best) 16...♘f7 17 ♖xf5 ♘xd4 18 cxd4 ♕xd4+ 19 e3 ♕xg4 20 ♖xf7 ♔xf7 21 ♘f3 ♗f5 22 ♕f2, and White won.

15 gxf5 ♘d6?!

Already clearly in trouble, Black should perhaps have tried the alternative 15...♗xf5, but after the reply 16 ♘g5! g6 17 ♘xe4 ♗xe4 18 ♗xe4 ♕xe4 19 ♕xe4 ♖xe4 20 ♖xb7, White has a pronounced endgame advantage. Play might continue 20...♘e7 (20...♖c8 fails

to 21 ♗h6! and if 21...♖h4 22 ♖xc7) 21 ♖xc7 ♘f5 22 ♖xc4, with excellent winning chances.

16 ♘g5 ♕xe2 17 ♗d5+ ♔h8 18 ♕xe2 ♖xe2

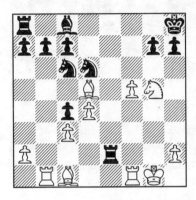

White now has overwhelming attacking and positional advantages. The game ended abruptly:

19 ♗f4 ♘d8 20 ♗xd6 cxd6 21 ♖be1! ♖xe1 22 ♖xe1 ♗d7 23 ♖e7 ♗c6 24 f6! 1-0

After 24...♗xd5, the game would have concluded 25 ♖e8+ ♗g8 26 f7 ♘xf7 27 ♘xf7 mate.

Game 2
H.Elwert-H.Tiemann
correspondence 2004

---

1 c4 e5 2 ♘c3 ♘f6 3 ♘f3 ♘c6 4 g3 ♗b4 5 ♗g2 0-0 6 0-0 e4 7 ♘g5 ♗xc3 8 bxc3 ♖e8 9 f3 e3

This very sharp gambit is critical. If White accepts, he seriously weakens his pawn structure and clearly has much to do to straighten out his piece development and mobilize his kingside pawns. If he declines, he retains health-ier pawns but Black's far-advanced e-pawn affects communications between White's flanks.

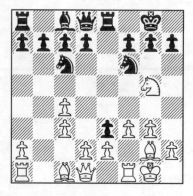

10 d3

Declining is probably best. Garry Kasparov played this way, after very lengthy thought, when he first faced this position in Game 2 of his 1987 World Championship match. White can also take Black's pawn, following up with ♘h3-f4, keeping d5 under con-trol and planning kingside expansion with g4. However, White then has a lot of unravelling to do and Black has counterplay. After the alternative 10 dxe3 we have:

a) 10...♕e7!? 11 ♘h3 ♕c5 12 ♘f4 ♕xc4 13 e4 d6 (a risky pawn grab is 13...♕xc3!? allowing 14 ♖b1 followed by ♗b2) 14 ♕d3 ♘e5 15 ♕xc4 ♘xc4 16 g4 ♖b8 17 ♖d1 b6 18 g5 ♘d7 19 ♘d5, and although White had a pull, Black held in G.Kasparov-D.Sadvakasov, Astana 2001.

b) White made a speculative knight sacrifice in V.Topalov-B.Gelfand, Nov-gorod 1997, after 10...b6 11 e4 h6!? 12

♘xf7!? ♔xf7 13 f4 ♔g8 14 e5 ♘h7, and now 15 f5 is best.

c) Perhaps Black should drive away White's knight immediately: Cu.Han-sen-S.Brynell, Malmö 1998, continued 10...h6 11 ♘h3 b6 (11...♘e5 12 e4 ♘xc4 13 ♘f4 is also possible) 12 ♘f4 ♘a5 13 c5!? ♕e7!? 14 cxb6 axb6 15 e4 ♕c5+ 16 ♔h1 ♗b7 17 ♘d3 ♕c4 18 ♗f4 d6 19 ♕c2 ♘d7, with an unclear game.

10...d5

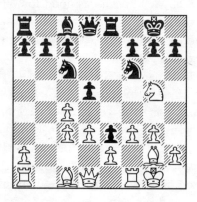

11 ♕b3

Both sides race towards move 14 and the first really critical decision point. Black aims to concentrate his forces in the centre and support his game-cramping e-pawn. White's two bishops promise long-term power, but he must seek to constrain Black's pieces, while at the same time prepar-ing the eventual advance of his c- and f-pawns. Instead 11 cxd5 ♘xd5 12 ♕b3 (if 12 ♘e4, then 12...f5) 12...♘a5 (or 12...♕xg5 13 f4 ♕h5!? 14 ♗xd5 ♗g4) 13 ♕a3 b6 14 f4 ♗b7 15 c4 ♘f6 releases the central tension too soon, achieving nothing.

11...♘a5 12 ♕a3 c6 13 cxd5 cxd5 14 f4

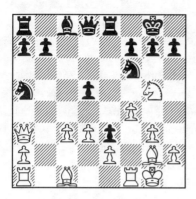

14...&g4

The placement of this bishop is a key issue for Black. White's last move prepares a retreat for his knight on f3, heightening his pressure against d4 and e5. On g4, Black's bishop attacks e2, provides the possible option of a minor piece exchange on f3, and in the event of h3, provokes a weakening in White's kingside pawn defences.

Black can also re-centralize his queen's knight, postponing the bishop's development. G.Kasparov-A.Karpov, World Championship (Game 2), Seville 1987, continued 14...&c6 15 &b1 &c7 16 &b2 &g4, which despite Black's connected rooks and harmonious development, Karpov nevertheless considered preferable for White after 17 &fe1 (17 &f3 is also possible). However, Kasparov actually played 17 c4!? dxc4 18 &xf6 gxf6 19 &e4 &g7 20 dxc4?! (20 &c3 and if 20...&d8 21 &xb7 was probably best) 20...&ad8 21 &b3 &d4 22 &xe3 &xc4, and with a clear initiative, Black won.

We should also note that defending passively in S.Mamedyarov-S.Papa,

Lausanne 2004, saw Black demolished after 14...&c6 15 &f3 &d7 16 &b1 b6 17 c4 &c8?! (17...dxc4 was essential) 18 cxd5 &xd5 19 &b2 a5 20 &fc1

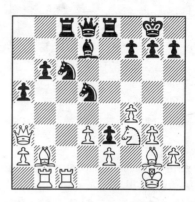

20...&cb4 21 &a1 h6 22 &b2 &f6 23 a3 &bd5 24 &e5 &e6 25 &xc8 &xc8 (instead 25...&xc8 is met by 26 f5! &xf5 27 &xd5 &xd5 28 &xf7! – Mamedyarov) 26 &d4 &e6 27 &c4 &f8 28 &b5 &b7 29 &xd5 1-0.

15 &f3

This flexible retreat is probably more accurate than the alternative 15 &e1. Although that move echoes Karpov's recommendation on move 17 in his game against Kasparov (see the previous note), the analogy isn't direct, not least because Black's queen hasn't yet committed to c7 and can play more ambitiously to d7 in support of a possible kingside attack. Indeed, J.Lautier-M.Illescas Cordoba, Dos Hermanas 1995, continued 15...h6 16 &f3 &c6 17 &b1 &d7 18 d4?! (18 &b3 or 18 &b2 were both better) 18...&h3! 19 &h1 (or 19 &xh3 &xh3 20 &xb7 &g4 21 &f1 &e6 with dangerous threats) 19...&h5! with a serious attack.

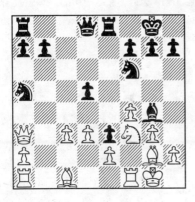

15...♘c6

After 15...♗xf3?!, 16 ♖xf3! puts great pressure on Black's e-pawn. John Watson then gives 16...d4 17 ♗b2 ♘c6 18 ♖ff1, with good chances.

16 h3!?

This ambitious move seeks to improve on some earlier correspondence games. White gains space at the cost of slightly weakening his kingside pawns, which could provide potential targets for Black if he could train his forces against them. The earlier postal games had concentrated on the line 16 ♖b1 ♕d7 17 ♕b3 b6 18 ♗b2, which also seems good. White plans ♖fc1 and c4, hoping to open up the position to the advantage of his active pieces, particularly his bishop-pair, or in the event of ...d4, to have enough room to play round Black's d4/e3 central pawn wedge (often involving a c5 break), seeking to undermine Black's position from the queenside. One thematic example continued 18...♗h3 (Black has also failed to equalize after 18...♖ac8 19 ♖fc1 when White retains the upper hand after 19...♗xf3 20 ♗xf3 ♘a5 21

♕b4, and if 21...♘c6 22 ♕a4 ♘e5 23 ♕xd7 ♘xf3+ 24 ♔g2 ♘h4+ 25 gxh4 ♘xd7 26 ♔f3) 19 ♖fc1 ♗xg2 20 ♔xg2 ♖ac8 21 h3 ♘h5 22 c4 ♖e6 23 ♔h2 ♖g6 24 ♖g1 ♘f6 25 f5 dxc4 26 ♕xc4 ♖h6 27 g4 ♘d5 28 g5 ♖d6 29 f6 ♘ce7 30 ♘e5 ♕e6 31 ♕a4 gxf6 32 gxf6+ ♘g6 33 ♖bf1 ♖dd8 34 ♘xg6 1-0, I.Brooks-A.Kazoks, correspondence 2001.

16...♗d7

Black should probably retreat his bishop. Even with h3 played, White's position still looks promising after 16...♗xf3 17 ♖xf3 d4 18 ♗b2 ♖c8 19 ♖b1.

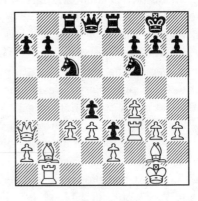

Both sides then wobbled in B.Gulko-O.Korneev, Montreal 2006, which continued 19...a5!? 20 cxd4?! (20 ♖ff1 may be best) 20...♘b4 21 ♖c1? (now 21 ♖ff1 and if 21...♘bd5 22 ♖fc1 was essential), when instead of 21...♖xc1+? Black could have won an exchange with 21...♘c2 22 ♕a4 ♘xd4 23 ♖xc8 ♘xf3+ 24 ♗xf3 ♕xc8.

17 ♔h2 ♕c7 18 ♖b1

White's kingside seems secure and he again prepares for a c4-break.

18...b6 19 ♗b2 ♖ad8

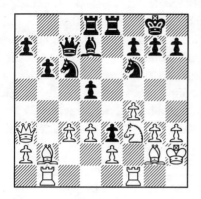

20 c4

White might consider the further preparatory move 20 ♖fc1 but the sharper text move, which is based on a tactical justification, also has obvious merits.

20...dxc4 21 ♖bc1

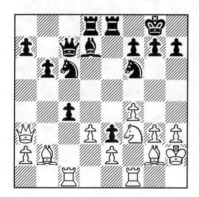

21...♗e6

White stands well too after 21...cxd3 22 ♗e5! (but not 22 ♗xf6? d2! and if 23 ♖xc6 ♗xc6 24 ♗xd8 ♖xd8 25 ♖d1 ♗xf3 26 ♗xf3 ♕c2 27 ♕b3 ♕xb3 28 axb3 ♖c8, which is better for Black) 22...♕b7 (or 22...♕c8 23 ♕xd3) 23 ♗xf6 gxf6 (not 23...d2? 24 ♗xd8 dxc1♕ 25 ♖xc1 ♖xd8 26 ♘e5 ♖c8 27 ♕d6, and White wins)

24 ♕xd3.

Black is also somewhat worse after both 21...♘a5 22 ♗e5, and if 22...♕c8 (22...♕c5? 23 ♕xc5 bxc5 24 ♗c7 loses) 23 dxc4 ♘xc4 24 ♗xf6 gxf6 25 ♕xa7, and 21...b5 22 ♗xf6 gxf6 23 dxc4, intending 23...b4 24 ♕b2.

22 ♘g5 ♗d5

The fundamentals tell against Black, not least the raking power of White's fearsome bishop-pair: for example, a hidden bishop fork decides after 22...♘a5 23 ♘xe6 ♖xe6 24 dxc4 ♖d2 (or 24...♘xc4 25 ♕b4 b5 26 ♗xf6 ♖xf6 27 ♕xb5 ♖c8 28 ♗d5) 25 ♗e5 ♕c5?! (25...♕e7 26 ♕xe3 ♖xa2 27 c5 is better but still good for White) 26 ♕xc5 bxc5 27 ♗c3.

23 ♗xd5 ♘xd5 24 ♖xc4

Black has managed to exchange off one of White's bishops and avoid the worst, but White remains better. Black has little real counterplay and must grimly defend in all sectors.

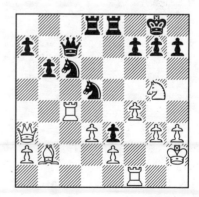

24...♕d7 25 ♖fc1 f6 26 ♘f3 ♖e6 27 ♖e4 ♖de8 28 ♖xe6 ♖xe6 29 ♕a4 ♖d6!?

Black has great difficulty forming an active plan. Ideally he'd like to mobilize his queenside pawn majority, but White controls too many key squares, particularly the queenside light squares, whose domination eventually leads to Black's demise in the endgame.

30 ♗a3 ♘cb4 31 ♕b3 a5 32 ♘d4!

White plays with great skill in this technical phase. The strong central position of this knight, combined with two subsequent pawn moves (f5 and a4), put a powerful light-square clamp on Black's game.

32...♔h8 33 ♗b2 h6 34 ♕c4 ♘e7 35 ♕f7 ♘bd5 36 f5

One pawn is in place.

36...♘c7 37 a4

Now the other: Black's pieces are so trussed up that he can find nothing better than to exchange queens and head for a dubious endgame.

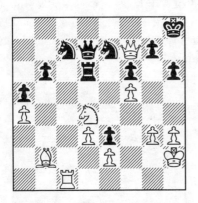

37...♘ed5 38 ♕xd7 ♖xd7 39 ♔g2 ♔g8 40 ♔f3

The final key point: in the endgame, White's king can join in the central battle, putting additional, game-winning pressure on Black's e-pawn.

40...♔f7 41 ♖c6 h5 42 ♘e6 ♘e8 43 ♗a3 ♘ec7

Black loses material. Another fine finish is 43...♔g8 44 ♖c8 ♔f7 45 ♘xg7, and if 45...♘xg7 (or 45...♔xg7 46 ♖xe8) 46 ♖f8 mate.

44 ♘xc7 1-0

Following 44...♖xc7 45 ♖xc7+ ♘xc7 46 ♔xe3 b5 47 ♔d4! bxa4 48 ♔c5, followed by e4, White dominates Black's knight and a-pawns, with an easy win.

Game 3
L.Portisch-I.Farago
Hungarian League 1993

---

1 c4 e5 2 ♘c3 ♘f6 3 ♘f3 ♘c6 4 g3 ♗b4 5 ♗g2 0-0 6 0-0 e4 7 ♘e1

This older and more modest knight move used to be White's main choice. White will re-centralize his knight via c2 to e3. If Black exchanges his bishop for White's knight on c3, White usually recaptures with his d-pawn, and then plays to exchange pawns on f3, opening lines for his bishop-pair. Black's game is solid, but in skilled hands, such as Portisch's, this line can still be effective, though White must frequently be prepared to battle long into the endgame to achieve anything.

7...♗xc3

Black generally exchanges immediately. Delaying the exchange with 7...♖e8!? invites the promising, space-gaining 8 ♘d5 (8 ♘c2 usually transposes into main lines after 8...♗xc3 9 dxc3 h6). If Black now retreats his bishop, White has a pleasant game by breaking in the centre with d3. Retaining Black's bishop on b4, with a view after d3 to simplifying by a minor piece exchange on e1, also has drawbacks, which were revealed by some virtuosic endgame play in another game by Portisch and by a great attacking idea introduced in a game by Smyslov:

a) 8...h6 9 d3 ♗xe1 10 ♖xe1 ♘e5 11 dxe4 ♘xc4 12 ♘xf6+ ♕xf6 13 ♕c2 ♕c6 14 ♗f4 ♘e5 15 ♖ac1 ♕xc2 16 ♖xc2 c6 17 ♖d1 b6 18 f3 (White has extra space, active bishops, a lead in development and opportunities to fix Black's backward pawns) 18...a5 19 ♗h3 ♖a7 20 ♗f5 f6 21 ♔f2 ♔f8 22 h4 ♔e7 23 ♗xe5 fxe5 24 ♖cd2 ♖f8 25 h5 ♖c7 26 f4

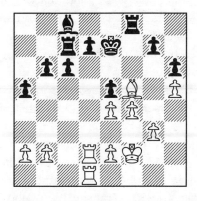

26...exf4 27 gxf4 d6 28 ♗xc8 ♖cxc8

29 ♔e3 ♖f6 30 ♖g1 ♔f8 31 f5 ♖e8 32 ♔f4 ♖e5 33 ♖c1 c5 34 ♖cd1 ♔e7 35 a4 (White has a light-square bind and promising activity on the d-, g- and b-files) 35...♔d7 36 ♖g1 ♖e7 37 e5! (achieving a winning passed f-pawn and an entry square on g6) 37...♖xe5 38 ♖xg7+ ♖e7 39 ♖g6 ♖ef7 40 e4 ♔c7 41 ♖dg2 b5 42 axb5 a4 43 ♖xf6 ♖xf6 44 ♖g7+ ♔b6 45 ♖g6 ♖f8 46 ♖xd6+ ♔xb5 47 e5 c4 48 e6 a3 49 bxa3 c3 50 ♖d1 1-0 was the instructive encounter, L.Portisch-R.Hübner, Tilburg 1983.

b) V.Smyslov-J.Mestel, Hastings 1972/73, varied with 8...d6, but after 9 d3 ♗xe1 10 ♖xe1 exd3 11 ♗g5! dxe2 12 ♖xe2 ♖xe2 13 ♕xe2 ♗e6 14 ♘xf6+ gxf6 15 ♗h4 ♘e5 16 ♗xb7 ♗xc4 17 ♕h5 ♖b8 18 ♗e4 ♘g6 19 b3 ♗a6 20 ♖e1, White enjoyed a strong attack.

8 dxc3

Recapturing towards the centre with White's knight on e1 rather than g5 is no longer convincing as Black needn't relinquish his hold on e4, and after 8 bxc3 ♖e8 9 f3 d5 10 cxd5 ♕xd5 with ...♕h5 in mind, Black has good chances.

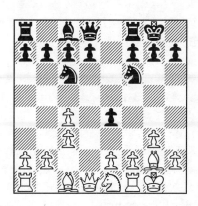

8...h6

Black usually plays this to prevent ♗g5. Although this pin isn't always effective, it often has extra bite in positions with Black's pawn on e4: exchanging Black's knight on f6 weakens Black's hold on e4 and d5; due to the potential weakness of Black's e4-pawn, Black's bishop remains slightly more defensive than its White counterpart; and White controls the half-open d-file, can occupy d5 and play to advance his pawns on either or both flanks. White should never lightly give up the bishop-pair, of course, but in such positions, at any rate, White has frequently made concrete progress after ♗g5, despite many seemingly solid features in Black's game.

A particularly shocking example of what can go wrong for Black occurs after 8...♖e8!? 9 ♗g5 ♖e5? (9...h6 is much better) when 10 f4! establishes a clear attacking advantage, as Black can't allow 10...exf3 11 ♘xf3, catastrophically opening the f-file. L.Portisch-T.Warakomski, Warsaw 2005, concluded 10...♖e6 11 ♘c2 ♕e7?! 12 f5 ♖d6 13 ♕c1 ♘e5 14 ♘e3 h6 15 ♗xf6 ♖xf6 16 ♘d5 ♕c5+ 17 ♔h1 ♖d6 18 f6! g5 19 ♖f5 ♖xd5 20 cxd5 d6 21 ♖xg5+! 1-0.

More common is the sequence 8...d6 9 ♘c2 (9 ♗g5!? ♗f5 10 ♘c2 h6 11 ♗xf6 ♕xf6 12 ♘e3 may give White a very slight edge, but the pin has less obvious effect with Black's rook on f8, which leaves e8 more naturally for Black's queen's rook) 9...♖e8!? 10 ♗g5 h6 11 ♗xf6 ♕xf6 12 ♘e3.

Black's position clearly has defen-

sive strength but White has chances:

a) 12...♖e5 13 ♕b3! ♖b8 14 ♖ad1 b6 15 ♕c2 ♗f5 16 ♖d5 ♖be8 17 ♖fd1 ♗d7?! 18 ♖xe5 ♘xe5 19 ♕xe4 saw White win in W.Uhlmann-S.Reshevsky, Skopje 1976.

b) Y.Averbakh-R.Rodriguez, Polanica Zdroj 1975, was clearly good for White after 12...♗f5 13 f4! ♘e7 14 g4 ♗d7 15 ♕e1 ♗c6 16 h4 ♖ad8 17 ♕g3, followed by g5.

c) 12...♖e6 13 ♕d2 ♕g5 14 ♖fe1 ♖e8 15 ♖ad1 ♗f5 16 f4 exf3 17 exf3 ♗e6 18 f4 ♕c5 19 b4 ♕b6 20 ♕f2 ♘e7 21 f5 ♘xf5 22 c5 dxc5 23 ♘xf5 cxb4 24 ♘d4 ♗c4 25 cxb4 ♕xb4, and Black was a little worse in T.Petrosian-V.Korchnoi, Tbilisi 1976.

Returning to 8...h6:

9 ♘c2 b6

Black can complete his queenside development either by fianchettoing his queen's bishop or developing it on the c8-h3 diagonal. Both approaches offer good equalizing chances due to Black's sound development and structural strength. Transpositions abound and both players must understand broad plans. Black will usually open the centre at some point by exchanging pawns on f3 (though there are some lines where he can offer his e-pawn as a positional gambit). Both players must then fight hard for control in that sector. Three key positions tend to arise often after 9...♖e8 10 ♘e3:

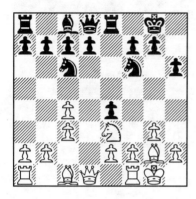

a) 10...d6 with a further divide:

a1) 11 ♕c2 enables White to continue with the ambitious plan ♗d2, ♖ae1 and f4, so that after Black exchanges pawns on f3, his pieces have maximum punch in the centre. Black certainly remains on the board, but White can undoubtedly push a little. I.Ibragimov-A.Zakharov, Novgorod 1997, continued 11...a5 (White also kept an edge after 11...♗d7 12 ♗d2 a5 13 ♖ae1 a4 14 f4 exf3 15 exf3 ♘e7 16 ♘g4 in J.Timman-A.Mestel, Las Palmas 1982, and after 11...♖e5 12 ♗d2 ♘e7 13 f4 exf3 14 exf3 ♘f5 15 ♖ae1 c6 16 f4 ♘xe3 17 ♗xe3 in S.Mikhailuk-D.Kuljasevic, US online League 2006) 12 ♗d2 ♕e7 13 f4 exf3 14 exf3 ♕e5 15 ♖ae1 ♕c5 16 ♔h1 ♗d7 (16...♗e6?! 17 f4! ♖e7?! 18 f5 ♗d7 19 ♘d5 ♘xd5 20 ♗xd5

♖xe1 21 ♗xe1 is bad for Black, and while 17...a4 18 b4 axb3 19 axb3 improves, 17...♗xc4? 18 b4 doesn't) 17 f4 ♘g4 18 ♕d3 ♕h5 19 ♘xg4 ♗xg4 20 ♕d5 ♕xd5 21 cxd5 with a bishop-pair endgame pull.

a2) More fluid is 11 b3. White remains alert to the possibility of playing f4, but won't rush things. He may play an eventual ♘d5, freeing e3 for his bishop and supporting possible queenside action, based on a4 and/or b4, and he may place a rook on d1, with c5 in mind. Playing like this puts a premium on both players' manoeuvring skills. Black must play well to remain active. L.Portisch-Z.Izoria, Warsaw 2005, continued 11...a5 12 ♕c2 a4 13 ♖b1 axb3 14 axb3 ♘e7 (or 14...♕e7 15 ♘d5 ♘xd5 16 cxd5 ♘b8 17 ♗e3) 15 ♖d1 ♗d7

16 c5 (if 16 ♗xe4 ♘xe4 17 ♕xe4 ♕c8 with good play) 16...dxc5 17 c4 ♖a6 18 ♗b2 ♕c8 19 ♖a1 ♖xa1 20 ♗xa1 ♘f5 21 ♕d2 ♘d4 22 ♗xd4 cxd4 23 ♕xd4 c6 24 ♕b6, with a slight edge.

b) 10...♘e5 gambits Black's e-pawn and after 11 ♕c2 (declining the gambit seems better; R.Barcenilla-I.Shliperman,

New York 2000, for example, continued 11 b3 d6 12 ♕c2 ♘eg4 13 h3 ♘xe3 14 ♗xe3 ♕e7 15 ♖ad1 ♗f5 16 ♕c1 a5 17 ♖fe1 ♘d7 18 ♕d2 ♗g6 19 f4 and White went on to win) 11...d6 12 ♗xe4!? ♘xe4 (12...♘xc4 13 ♗g2 ♘xe3 14 ♗xe3 is also playable) 13 ♕xe4 ♘g4 14 ♕d3 ♘xe3 15 ♗xe3 ♕e7 16 ♖fe1 b6 17 ♗d2 ♗b7 18 f3 ♕e6 19 e4 ♕h3, White found it impossible to make any real impression on Black's position in F.Berkes-Z.Gyimesi, Hungarian League 2003.

Returning to 9...b6:

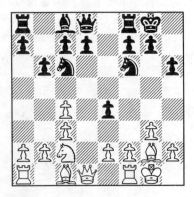

10 ♘e3 ♗b7 11 ♘d5

This is White's simplest and possibly best move. It clears a path for the development of his queen's bishop and by closing the h1-a8 diagonal prepares to play f4 without allowing Black's bishop easy access to play in the resulting open centre.

White can also play in a more complex way: E.Vasiukov-A.Gipslis, USSR 1981, continued 11 ♕c2 ♘e5 12 h3 ♖e8 13 ♗d2 d6 14 f4 exf3 15 exf3 ♕d7 16 ♖ad1 ♖ad8!? (16...a6, and if 17 ♗c1 ♕e6 18 b3 b5, is better – Gipslis) 17 ♗c1 ♕c8 18 b3 a6 19 g4! ♘g6 20 ♘d5! ♘h7?! 21

f4, with a strong attack. Note White's 19th move which is a common preliminary to a general kingside pawn advance in such positions: White controls f5 and avoids simplification on the long light-square diagonal.

11...♘e5 12 b3 ♖e8

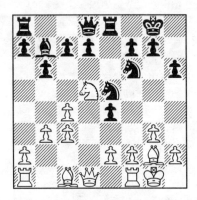

13 f4

White achieved no more than equality by avoiding this move in V.Korchnoi-A.Karpov, 9th matchgame, Moscow 1974, which continued 13 a4 d6 14 ♖a2 ♘ed7 15 h3!? a5 16 ♗e3 ♘xd5 17 cxd5 ♕f6 18 c4 ♕g6.

Much more interesting was the continuation of V.Malakhov-S.Ivanov, Sochi 2004: 13 f3 ♗xd5!? (an idea of Salov's) 14 cxd5 exf3 15 exf3 ♕e7 16 d6!? ♕xd6 17 ♕xd6 cxd6 18 f4 ♘c6 19 c4 d5! 20 cxd5 ♘b4 21 d6 ♖ac8 22 ♗d2 ♘d3 23 ♖f3 ♘c5 24 ♗b4 ♖e4, and Black's active knights held. Declining the pawn with 16 ♕d4!?, and if 16...c5 (or 16...♕c5 17 ♕xc5 bxc5 18 ♗a3 d6 19 ♖ad1 c4 20 ♖d4 cxb3 21 axb3 ♖ab8 22 b4 ♘ed7 23 ♔f2 ♘b6 24 c4 ♖e5 25 ♖fd1 ♖be8 26 ♗f1) 17 ♕d2 d6 (or 17...c4 18 d6 ♕e6 19 f4 ♘c6 20 f5) 18 c4 b5 19 ♕c2 bxc4 20 bxc4 ♖ab8 21 ♗d2, may be better for White, but needs a test.

13...exf3

Black almost always exchanges pawns on f3 in such positions. Otherwise, with his pawn on f4, White can generally look forward to developing kingside pressure, based on advancing his kingside pawns. Black has no obvious counterplay in the centre, due to White's powerful blockading grip on e3 and control down the d-file.

14 exf3 ♘xd5

This is the natural recapture, but note that 14...♗xd5 15 cxd5 ♕e7 transposes into Malakhov-Ivanov above. Black can also play Makarychev's largely untested 14...♖b8!? leaving White with his strong knight intact on d5 but with doubled c-pawns. White may keep an edge after 15 f4, and if 15...♘g6 16 ♕d4 c5 17 ♕d3 d6 18 ♗d2.

15 cxd5

15...♕f6

Playing this way stems from a game between Seirawan and Salov (Brussels 1988), with the only slight difference that each side had already played a4

and ...a5. This line allows Black to achieve further rapid simplification in the e-file. Also playable is 15...d6 though White retains similar slight long-term bishop-pair chances after 16 ♕d4 (or perhaps 16 f4!? ♘d7 17 c4 ♕f6 18 ♖b1) 16...♕f6 17 ♗b2 followed by c4.

16 f4 ♘g6 17 ♗b2 ♖e3 18 ♕d2 ♖ae8 19 ♖fe1 ♕e7

Salov had earlier pointed to the alternative defence 19...♖xe1+ 20 ♖xe1 ♖xe1+ 21 ♕xe1 ♕d8 (in the position with pawns on a4 and a5). This hasn't been tested.

20 ♕xe3 ♕xe3+ 21 ♖xe3 ♖xe3 22 ♔f2 ♖e8 23 c4 a5 24 a3

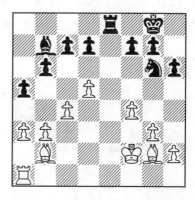

Not having played a4 earlier allows White a little more flexibility in pushing forward his queenside pawns. The side with the bishop-pair generally has to be able to gain squares with mobile pawns to hope for any tangible advantage in such endgames, often, as here, on both sides of the board. White aims both to restrict the scope of Black's remaining pieces and to get his pawns nearer to the queening squares, so that any opportunity to create a passed pawn may then pose winning threats.

24...d6 25 b4 ♖a8 26 ♗h3 axb4 27 axb4 ♖xa1 28 ♗xa1 b5!?

Black takes a tough decision to go active. He might have remained passive by playing 28...♘e7 29 ♗d7 f5 followed by ...g6 and ....h5, with f8 and f7 available to his king, leaving White still a long way from any decisive breakthrough.

29 cxb5 ♘e7?!

Black plans to retake on d5 with his knight, but this may be the losing idea as it walks into a surprisingly effective temporary pin on the long diagonal. Better was 29...♗xd5, and while White can obtain a dangerous outside passed pawn after 30 ♗d4 ♗f8 31 b6 cxb6 32 ♗xb6 ♔e7 33 ♗c7 ♗c4, Black's well-centralized forces might still defend.

30 ♗d4 ♘xd5 31 ♗g2

Now, however, the awkward position of Black's knight and decentralized king allow White time to make further serious ground on the kingside.

31...♔f8 32 h4 f6 33 g4 ♔e7 34 h5 ♗a8 35 g5 ♘b6

While Black has been rushing his king to the centre and trying to free his awkwardly placed bishop and knight, White has achieved a game-winning break on the kingside. Black is lost after 35...hxg5 36 fxg5 fxg5 (or 36...♔f7 37 g6+ ♔f8 38 ♗a7, threatening ♗b8) 37 ♗xg7 ♔f7 38 h6 ♔g8 39 ♔g3, and if 39...♘b6 then 40 ♗xa8 ♘xa8 41 ♔g4 ♘b6 42 ♔xg5 ♔h7 (or 42...♘d5 43 ♔g6 ♘f4+ 44 ♔f6 ♘d5+ 45 ♔e6 ♘xb4 46 ♔d7 ♘d5 47 ♔c6) 43 ♔f6 ♘d5+ 44 ♔e6 ♘xb4 (or 44...♘b6 45 ♔e7 d5 46 ♔d8) 45 ♔d7 d5 46 ♔xc7.

36 gxf6+ gxf6 37 ♗xa8 ♘xa8 38 f5!

White fixes h6 as a target, condemning Black's king to abject kingside defence.

38...♘b6 39 ♗e3 ♘d5 40 ♗d2!

White's final refinement: he controls Black's knight and holds on to both b-pawns prior to bringing his king into play to decide.

40...♔f7 41 ♔f3 ♘e7 42 ♔e4 ♔g7

Black also loses after 42...d5+ 43 ♔d4 threatening ♗f4, and if 43...♘xf5+ 44 ♔xd5 ♘e7+ 45 ♔c5, when ♗f4 can no longer be prevented.

43 ♗f4

43...♔f7

By giving up his h-pawn and allowing White to obtain a powerful outside passed h-pawn, Black effectively capitulates. But both 43...♘c8 44 ♔d5 ♘e7+ 45 ♔e6 ♘c8 46 ♔d7 ♘b6+ 47 ♔xc7 ♘d5+ 48 ♔xd6 and 43...d5+ 44 ♔d4 ♘xf5+ 45 ♔xd5 clearly also lose, while the end only comes more interestingly after 43...♔h7 44 ♗xd6! cxd6 45 b6 d5+ (or 45...♘c6 46 b7 ♔g7 47 b5 ♘b8 48 ♔d5 ♔f7 49 ♔xd6 ♔e8 50 ♔c7) 46 ♔d4 ♘c6+ 47 ♔c5! and if 47...d4 (or 47...♘b8 48 ♔xd5 ♔g7 49 ♔d6 ♔f7 50 b5 ♔e8 51 ♔c7) 48 ♔xc6 d3 49 b7 d2 50 b8♕ d1♕ 51 ♕c7+ ♔g8 52 ♕c8+ ♔g7 53 ♕d7+.

44 ♗xh6 d5+ 45 ♔d3 ♘xf5 46 ♗f4 ♔e6 47 h6 ♘e7 48 ♗xc7 ♔d7 49 ♗h2 ♔c8 50 h7 ♘g6 51 ♔d4 ♔b7 52 ♔xd5 ♔b6 53 ♔e4 1-0

Game 4
J.Timman-R.Hübner
5th matchgame, Sarajevo 1991

---

1 c4 e5 2 ♘c3 ♘f6 3 ♘f3 ♘c6 4 g3 ♗b4 5 ♗g2 0-0 6 0-0 ♖e8

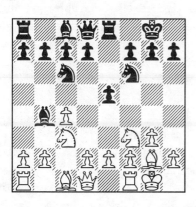

If Black is not going to play the immediate ...e4, this very logical and solid developing move is a major option. Its one possible drawback is that it invites White to occupy d5, gaining central space and avoiding doubled pawns in the event of a minor piece exchange on c3. For 6...♗xc3, which cuts out this possibility for White, see Game 5.

7 ♘d5

White probably can't hope to achieve much by not occupying d5, but he can aim for an edge with 7 d3, and if 7...d6 8 ♗d2, followed by a3. Nowadays Black generally prefers 7....♗xc3, leading back into lines that usually arise after 6...♗xc3 in Game 5.

7...♘xd5

With this exchange Black signals his intention to give no ground in the centre and to advance his own remaining knight to a forward outpost (d4). Black's main alternatives are:

a) 7...e4 8 ♘e1 d6 9 d3 transposes into a line considered in Game 3 (see note 'b' to Black's 7th move).

b) 7...♗f8 is a little passive and allows White time to consolidate his spatial edge. Play usually continues 8 d3 h6 9 ♘xf6+ (9 b3 and 9 e4 are also good) 9...♕xf6 10 ♘d2 and now 10...d6 11 ♘e4 ♕d8 12 ♘c3 ♗e6 13 b4 a6 14 ♖b1 ♕d7 15 a4 ♖ab8 16 b5 ♘e7 17 ♕b3 axb5 18 axb5 ♗h3 19 e4 ♗xg2 20 ♔xg2 ♘g6 was R.Kasimdzhanov-I.Sokolov, Wijk aan Zee 1999, when Ribli's recommendation is 21 f4 exf4 22 ♗xf4.

c) 7...a5 is livelier, but weakens b5, allowing White to develop around Black's dark-squared bishop. Cu.Hansen-A.Raetsky, Reykjavik 1996, continued 8 d3 h6 9 b3 d6 10 ♗b2 ♗c5 11 e3 ♗g4 12 h3 ♗h5 (White was also better after 12...♗f5 13 a3 ♗a7 14 ♘c3 ♗h7 15 ♔h2 ♘d7 16 ♘e1 ♘c5 17 ♘d5 in V.Chuchelov-A.Raetsky, Münster 1998) 13 a3 ♗a7 14 ♘c3 ♕d7 15 ♔h2 ♗g6 16 ♕d2 ♗f5 17 ♖ae1 ♗e6 18 ♘b5 ♗b6 19 e4 ♘h7!? (or 19...a4 20 b4 ♘h7 21 ♕c1) 20 d4, with advantage.

d) 7...♗c5 may be Black's best.

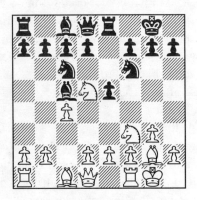

Critical is then 8 d3 ♘xd5 9 cxd5 ♘d4 10 ♘d2 d6 11 e3 ♘f5 12 ♘c4 a6 (G.Serper-V.Korchnoi, New York 1996, varied with 12...a5 13 ♗d2 a4 14 b4 ♗b6!? and now Korchnoi suggested 15 ♘xb6 cxb6 16 e4 ♘d4 17 ♗e3 ♗d7 18 ♖c1 ♖c8 19 ♖xc8 ♕xc8 20 ♗xd4 exd4 21 ♕d2, with an edge) 13 ♗d2 ♗d7 when White looks a little better due to his queenside pressure. An old classic, M.Botvinnik-H.Ree, Wijk aan Zee 1969, saw the direct 14 b4 (after 14 ♖c1, Black created sufficient diversionary kingside play in the game A.Minasian-V.Tkachiev, Fuegen 2006, with 14...♖c8 15 ♘a5 ♖b8 16 ♕c2!? h5! 17 b4 ♗b6 18 ♘c4 ♗a7) 14...♗a7 15 ♘a5 ♗c8 16 ♖c1

♘h6?! (16...g6, with Tkachiev's ...h5 in mind, is better) 17 ♖c3 f5 18 ♕c2 ♖e7 19 ♖c1 ♗b6 20 d4 ♘g4 21 dxe5 ♘xe5 22 ♘c4 ♘xc4 23 ♖xc4 ♗d7 24 a4 a5 25 bxa5 ♗c5 26 ♖xc5 dxc5 27 ♕xc5, and White won.

8 cxd5 ♘d4 9 ♘xd4 exd4

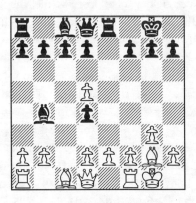

10 e3!

This is critical. White immediately strikes at d4, encouraging Black to clarify the central pawn structure in White's favour by exchanging on e3, after which recapturing with White's d-pawn leaves White with extra space, cramping control of d5 and attacking possibilities down the c-file.

10 b3 is also playable but allows Black to draw a little more breath and can lead to unclear complications, in particular after the gambit line 10...d6 11 ♗b2 ♗c5 12 e3 ♗f5.

10...c5?!

This well-intentioned move seeks to bolster Black's hold on d4 but is dealt a serious blow by Timman's fine play. Alternatively:

a) The view that 10...dxe3 11 dxe3 leads only to dreary defence was confirmed by Z.Ribli-U.Andersson, Reggio Emilia 1991, which continued 11...d6 12 &d2 &c5 13 b4 &b6 14 ♕c2 a5 15 ♖fc1 a4 16 a3 &g4 17 h3 &h5 18 &c3 ♖e7 19 ♕b2 f6 20 &d4 &xd4 21 ♕xd4 b6 22 ♖c3 &f7 23 ♖ac1 ♖a7 24 h4 &e8 25 &h3, with a clear advantage.

b) 10...d6!? 11 ♕c2 (White can also consider accepting the gambit: J.Sykora-J.Jirka, correspondence 1995, saw 11 exd4 &f5 12 d3 ♕f6?! — 12...♕d7 is better − 13 ♕a4 a5 14 a3 &xd3 15 axb4 &xf1 16 &xf1, winning) 11...&c5 12 b3 (12 e4, followed by d3 and f4, is another idea) 12...&g4 plays to establish this bishop on e2 and a pawn on d3.

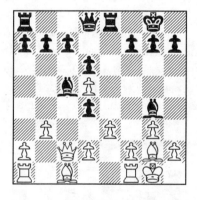

However, White found plenty of room to squeeze on the queenside and play round this pawn, eventually winning it in S.Ionov-S.Dvoirys, Moscow 1983, which continued 13 &b2 &e2 14 ♖fe1 d3 15 ♕c4 ♕g5 16 &d4 &b6 17 ♖ec1 ♖e7 18 a4 h5 19 a5 &xd4 20 ♕xd4 ♕f5 21 ♖a4 b5 22 ♖b4 a6 23 ♕f4 ♕d7 24 ♖e4 ♖xe4 25 ♕xe4 ♕d8 26 ♕d4 b4 27 &e4 ♖b8 28 &xd3, and White won.

c) Black's best move may be 10...&c5 which is still far from played

out. Then 11 ♕c2 d6 transposes into Ionov-Dvoirys. White can also press for an advantage with 11 b3:

c1) 11...b6!? 12 &b2 &a6 13 ♖e1 ♕f6 14 ♕c2 dxe3 15 dxe3 ♕g6 was W.Uhlmann-L.Portisch, Skopje 1972; now Uhlmann recommends 16 ♕c3.

c2) 11...d6 12 ♕c2 dxe3 (12...&g4 again leads to Ionov-Dvoirys) 13 fxe3 ♕g5 14 ♖f4 saw White able to work the half-open f-file and both long diagonals well in H.Tarnowiecki-E.Bang, correspondence 2002, which continued 14...&d7 15 &b2 c6?! 16 ♖af1 ♖e7 17 dxc6 bxc6 18 &e4 h6 19 &h7+ ♔f8 20 &f5 ♔g8 21 &xd7 ♖xd7 22 b4 &b6 23 ♕xc6, and White won.

Returning to the fateful move 10...c5:

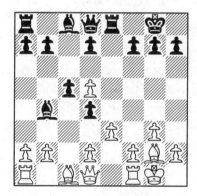

11 a3 &a5 12 exd4 cxd4 13 d6!

This powerful gambit severely disrupts Black's development and clearly decides the opening in White's favour. Black has to remove White's pawn from d6, but the time taken to win it will allow White to build up serious threats against Black's king.

13...♕f6

Timman considers that the possibly better 13...♖e6 14 b4 ♗b6 15 d3 ♖xd6 16 ♗f4 ♖e6 17 ♗d5 d6 is also not entirely satisfactory.

14 d3 ♕xd6 15 ♗f4

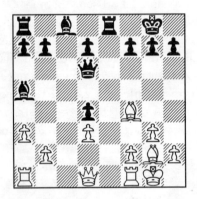

15...♕a6

Or 15...♕f6 16 ♕a4 ♗b6 17 ♖fe1 with a winning advantage (Timman).

16 b4 ♗d8 17 ♖e1 ♖f8 18 ♕h5 d6 19 ♗d5 ♗d7

With his queen cut off on the queenside, the rest is now simply pure agony for Black on the kingside. If 19...g6 then 20 ♗xf7+! ♖xf7 21 ♖e8+ ♖f8 22 ♕d5+ ♔g7 23 ♖xf8 ♔xf8 24 ♗h6+ with a crushing attack.

20 a4 ♖c8 21 ♗e4 g6 22 ♕f3 ♖c7 23 b5 ♕b6 24 ♗h6 a6 25 ♗d5 ♗f5 26 g4 ♗c8 27 ♖e2 axb5 1-0

Black doesn't wait for 28 ♖ae1, followed by the crushing ♖e8.

**Game 5
S.Mamedyarov-L.Drabke
European Ch., Antalya 2004**

---

1 c4 e5 2 ♘c3 ♘f6 3 ♘f3 ♘c6 4 g3 ♗b4

5 ♗g2 0-0 6 0-0 ♗xc3

Exchanging on c3 pre-empts ♘d5 possibilities and by doubling White's pawns is also highly thematic. It is often a prelude to very solid play by Black in the centre based around pawns on d6 and e5 without any double-edged ...e4-advance.

7 bxc3

White usually recaptures towards the centre. Without ...e4 having been played, the main alternative plan based on 7 dxc3 and the manoeuvre ♘e1-c2-e3 hasn't got the same bite. Black's game lacks weak points and he can complete his development easily. Indeed, White didn't achieve much in A.Chernin-V.Ivanchuk, Warsaw 2002, after 7...d6 8 ♗g5 (otherwise Black continues with 8...♗e6 and 9...♕d7, preparing ...♗h3) 8...h6 9 ♗xf6 ♕xf6 10 ♘e1 ♗e6 11 b3 ♕d8 12 ♘c2 ♕d7 13 ♘e3 ♗h3 14 ♗xh3 ♕xh3 15 ♘d5 ♕d7 16 e4 ♘e7 17 ♘xe7+ ♕xe7 18 ♕g4 a5 19 a4 b6, and Black defended.

7...d6

This unassuming move is a solid choice. Black can also opt for the more ambitious 7...♖e8 intending ...e4. Play then usually continues 8 d3 (8 ♕c2!? and 8 ♖b1!? are possible, but 8 d3 leads more directly to the c3, c4 and d3 pawn centre that is critical in this line) 8...e4 9 ♘d4 exd3 10 exd3 when Black has two main plans. He will play to fix White's slightly awkward clutch of central pawns by exchanging knights on d4, followed by ...d5, either immediately or after first playing ...h6:

a) 10...♘xd4 11 cxd4 d5 invites the sharp pinning line 12 ♗g5 (12 ♖b1 is a good alternative, probably best met by transposition with 12...h6 to variation 'b'). Outcomes then depend on how far White's dynamic advantages (pressure on d5, better development and queenside play) outweigh the relative weakness of his doubled d-pawns. White didn't, though, achieve much in H.Kallio-L.Fressinet, Plovdiv 2003, which continued 12...h6 (Hübner's 12...c6!? is also critical when I quite like 13 ♖b1, and if 13...dxc4 14 dxc4 h6 15 ♗e3 White has a bishop-pair edge) 13 ♗xf6 ♕xf6 14 cxd5 ♕xd4 15 ♕c2 ♕e5 16 ♖ab1 ♖b8 17 ♖fc1 ♖e7 18 ♕c3 (18

♕c5!?, and if 18...b6 19 ♕a3 a5 20 d4 might be better) 18...♕d6 19 ♕d4 b6 20 ♖c6 ♕d8 21 d6 cxd6 22 ♖xd6 ♖d7, with an eventual draw.

b) 10....♘xd4 11 cxd4 h6 is Black's most solid choice. But White can still probe with 12 ♗f4 d5 13 ♖b1! which is an important rook move, and can also be played on White's 12th move. White encourages Black to loosen his queenside pawns to create queenside chances before Black can consolidate by developing his bishop on e6 and queen on d7:

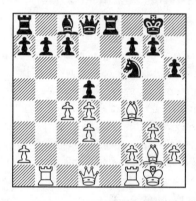

b1) 13...b6!? 14 ♗e5 ♗b7?! (Salov suggested 14...c6, and if 15 ♗xf6!? ♕xf6 16 cxd5 cxd5 17 ♗xd5 ♗h3 with counterplay, but 15 a4 and if 15...♗e6 16 a5 ♖c8 17 ♕a4 may improve) 15 ♕f3 ♘h7 16 h4 ♕e7!? (or 16...♘f8!? 17 cxd5 ♘g6 18 ♖fe1) 17 ♕g4! ♘f6 18 ♕f4 ♘h5 19 ♕f3, with a plus in J.Hodgson-V.Salov, Amsterdam 1996.

b2) A.Karpov-V.Anand, Frankfurt (rapid) 1997, continued with the more solid 13...c6 14 ♕d2 (14 a4!? b6 15 a5 or 15 c5, and if 15...♗g4 16 ♕b3, may again be more testing) 14...b6 15 a4 ♗f5 16 c5 ♘d7 17 ♖fc1 ♕f6 18 ♖b4 ♖e6 19

♗f1 ♖ae8 and in an unclear position, White now lost a pawn with 20 ♗c7?! (20 cxb6 axb6 21 ♗c7 is better) 20...bxc5 21 dxc5 ♘xc5, and if 22 ♖xc5 ♕e7 23 ♕c3 ♖e1, forcing 24 ♗e5 ♖xe5.

c) 7...♖e8 8 d3 e4 9 ♘d4 h6!? is a good idea but permits White greater choice, including the critical 10 dxe4!? ♘xe4 11 ♕c2 d5. L.Portisch-V.Salov, Tilburg 1994, continued 12 cxd5 ♕xd5 13 ♖d1 ♗f5 14 ♕b2 ♘xd4 15 cxd4 ♕d7 16 ♗f4 c6 17 a4 ♖ad8 18 a5 ♘f6 19 ♖a3 ♘d5 20 ♗c1 ♖e7 21 f3 ♘c7 22 e4 ♗e6 23 ♗e3 ♘b5 24 ♖ad3, with a pull.

d) 7...♖e8 8 d3 e4 9. ♘d4 ♘e5?! is a risky choice. Y.Yakovich-A.Deviatkin, Moscow 2004, went on 10 ♗g5 (Razuvaev's 10 dxe4 ♘xc4 11 ♕b3 ♘b6 12 f3 is promising too) 10...exd3 11 exd3 h6?! (11...d6 12 f4, and if 12...♘g6 13 ♕d2 h6 14 ♗xf6 ♕xf6 15 ♖ae1, may be better but still looks good for White) 12 ♗xf6 ♕xf6 13 ♖e1 ♖e7 14 ♕d2 d6 15 f4 ♘g6 16 ♖xe7 ♘xe7 17 ♖e1 ♗d7 18 ♗xb7, and White won.

Returning to 7...d6:

8 d3

setting up the critical possibility of e4, followed by an eventual f4, occupying the centre and creating the basis for a pawn-storm attack on the kingside.

8...h6

Black usually continues his policy of solid development and wait and see. He prevents ♗g5 and prepares to play ...♗e6 without needing to worry about the possible reply ♘g5. Black can play a wide range of other moves, although none are as strategically clear as the text:

a) 8...e4!? 9 ♘d4 exd3 10 exd3 ♘xd4 (or 10...♗d7 11 ♖b1 ♖b8 12 h3 ♘xd4 13 cxd4 b5 14 ♗d2 bxc4 15 dxc4 ♗f5 16 ♖b3 with an edge, S.Arkhipov-Z.Ilincic, Kecskemet 1990) 11 cxd4 saw White enjoy a pleasant pull in J.Watson-E.McCormick, St Paul 1982, which continued 11...c6 12 ♖b1 h6 13 ♖e1 (13 a4 d5 14 ♗f4 is also good) 13...d5 14 ♗a3 ♖e8 15 ♖xe8+ ♕xe8 16 ♕d2 b6 17 ♗d6 ♗e6 18 c5, and White later won.

b) Black can defend solid but somewhat grim positions after 8...♗d7 9 e4.

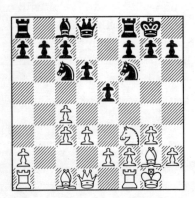

White invariably replies this way,

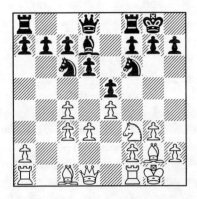

One good example continued with

9...♕c8?! (White was also better after 9...a6!? 10 a4 ♘a5 11 ♘h4 ♘e8 12 f4! exf4 13 ♗xf4 ♘c6 — or 13...g5 14 ♕h5! — 14 ♘f3 ♕c8 15 d4 ♗g4 16 ♕d3 ♘f6 17 ♘h4 in J.Smejkal-H.Hecht, Siegen Olympiad 1970) 10 ♖b1 b6 11 ♘h4 ♗h3 12 ♘f5 ♗xg2 13 ♔xg2 ♕e6 14 f4 ♖fe8 15 ♕f3 ♖ad8 16 ♖b2 ♘e7 17 ♘e3 c6 18 f5 ♕c8 19 g4 ♘d7 20 g5 f6 21 ♔h1 fxg5 22 ♖g2 ♖f8 23 ♘g4 h5 24 ♘h6+ ♔h7 25 ♕xh5 1-0, W.Uhlmann-D.Hiermann, Austrian League 2005.

c) White won a fine and instructive endgame in M.Botvinnik-K.Langeweg, Hamburg 1965, after 8...♖e8 9 e4 ♘e7 (D.Komljenovic-A.Baburin, Benasque 1998, varied with 9...♘d7!? 10 ♘h4 ♘f8 11 ♖b1 ♖b8 and now 12 d4!? is a worthy alternative to the game's 12 ♘f5) 10 ♘h4 ♘g6 (or 10...c6 11 ♖e1 ♘g6 12 ♘f5) 11 ♘f5 c6 12 ♖b1 (Uhlmann recommends 12 ♕f3!? ♗xf5 13 ♕xf5 ♕a5 14 ♗d2 ♕a4 15 ♖fc1 a6 16 h4) 12...d5 13 cxd5 cxd5 14 c4 dxe4 15 dxe4 ♗xf5 16 exf5 ♘e7 17 ♗xb7 ♖b8 18 ♕xd8 ♖exd8 19 ♗e3 ♖d7 20 ♗f3 ♖c8 21 g4...

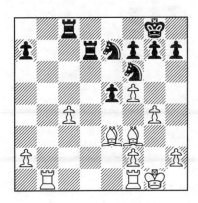

... 21...♖xc4 22 ♖b8+ ♖c8 23 ♖xc8+ ♘xc8 24 ♖c1 ♘d6 25 ♖c5 e4 26 ♗e2 h6

27 h3 ♘fe8 28 ♔g2 ♔f8 29 ♔g3 ♔e7 30 ♖a5 ♘c8 31 ♖e5+ ♔d8 32 ♗b5 ♖e7 33 ♖xe7 ♔xe7 34 ♗xe8 ♔xe8 35 ♔f4 ♔d7 36 ♗c5 1-0.

Going back to Black's main defence, 8...h6:

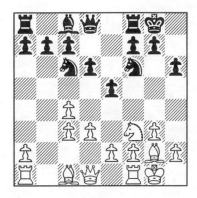

9 ♖b1

White activates his queen's rook before proceeding with his main plan based on e4. The immediate 9 e4 is also good, when Black must take care. Two horror stories illustrate how the defence should not be conducted:

a) Black went badly wrong in V.Jansa-A.Bisguier, Skopje 1972, which continued 9...♘e7!? 10 ♘h4 g5?! 11 ♘f3 ♘g6? 12 ♘xg5! hxg5 13 ♗xg5 ♔h7 (both 13...♔g7 and 13...c6 also fail to 14 f4; the latter prettily after 14...♕b6+ 15 c5! ♕xc5+ 16 d4 – Jansa) 14 f4 exf4 15 gxf4 ♖g8 16 ♕e1 ♕e7 17 f5 ♗d7 18 fxg6+ ♖xg6 19 ♕h4+ 1-0.

b) B.Jobava-B.Lindberg, Oropesa del Mar 2001, also saw a rout after 9...♘e7 10 ♘h4 a5?! 11 f4 exf4 12 gxf4 ♘g6 13 ♘xg6 fxg6 14 d4 ♗g4 15 ♕d3 c6 16 ♗a3 ♖e8 17 h3 ♗h5 18 ♖ae1 ♕d7 19 e5 dxe5 20 fxe5 ♘h7 21 d5 ♘f8 22 ♖xf8+

♖xf8 23 e6 ♕e8 24 ♗xf8 ♔xf8 25 d6 ♔g8 26 c5 g5 27 d7 1-0.

c) 9...♗e6 is better. White can press with 10 ♘h4, with f5 a possible outpost, and the way cleared for an eventual f4.

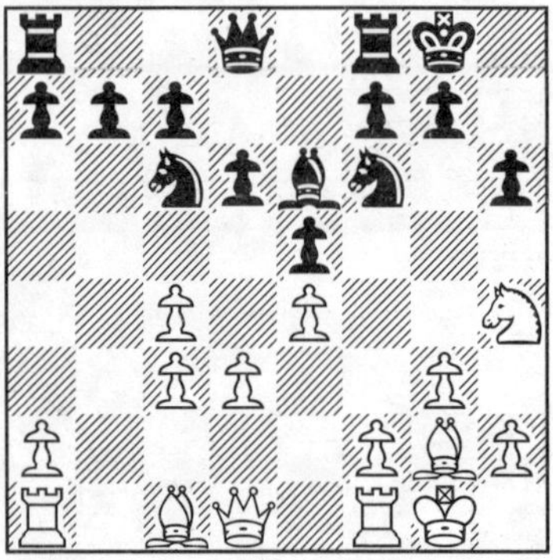

After 10...♖b8 11 ♖b1 a6 (11...♕d7 12 f4 ♗h3 13 ♗xh3 ♕xh3 14 ♘f5 is better for White) 12 a4 ♘h7 13 ♘f5 ♘e7 (13...♗xf5?! 14 exf5 only helps White) 14 ♘xe7+ (14 ♕f3!?) 14...♕xe7 15 a5 b5 16 axb6 cxb6 17 ♕a4 b5 18 ♕xa6 bxc4, White soon started to lose the thread in G.Serper-S.Zagrebelny, St Petersburg 1994, and perhaps here should prefer 19 ♖xb8!? ♖xb8 20 ♗a3 ♕d8 21 dxc4 ♖b6 22 ♕a4 (Serper).

9...♖b8

Black mostly plays this way. He can also consider the largely untested 9...e4 10 ♘d4 ♘e5!?. Critical may then be 11 dxe4 (more exotic was 11 f4!? exf3 12 ♘xf3 ♘xf3+ 13 ♗xf3 c6 14 e4 ♘h7 15 ♗g2 ♖b8 16 ♗f4 ♖a8 17 g4!?, with an edge in C.Braga-G.Gomez, Sao Paulo 2005) 11...♘xc4 12 ♕b3, and if 12...♘a5 (or 12...♘e5 13 f4 followed by 14 ♗a3) 13 ♕a4 c5 14 ♘f5, with good chances.

10 h3

White continues to make useful positional moves before committing himself to e4. This move allows White to prevent a possible exchange of bishops on h3 after ...♗e6 and ...♕d7. Shortly before this game, Mamedyarov won a tough battle after 10 e4 ♗e6 11 h3 (11 ♘h4 transposes into Serper-Zagrebelny, above) in S.Mamedyarov-M.Gagunashvili, Dubai 2004: 11...♘d7 12 ♘h4 ♘e7 (preventing ♘f5 and preparing ...f5) 13 ♕e2 (if 13 f4, then 13...exf4 14 gxf4 f5!) 13...f5 14 exf5 ♘xf5 15 ♘f3 (or 15 ♘xf5 ♗xf5 16 ♖xb7 ♖xb7 17 ♗xb7 ♗xh3) 15...♕f6 16 ♘d2 b6 17 ♘e4 ♕g6 18 ♔h2 ♖be8?! (18...♘f6 is better, but perhaps White can still play for a little with 19 ♗d2 and if 19...♘xe4 20 ♗xe4 ♕f7 21 ♖be1) 19 f4! exf4 20 ♗xf4 ♔h8 21 ♖be1 ♘f6 22 ♘xf6 ♖xf6 23 g4 ♘h4? 24 ♗c6 ♖ef8 25 ♗g3 ♖xf1 26 ♖xf1 ♖xf1 27 ♕xf1 ♕g5 28 ♕e1 1-0.

10...a6 11 a4 ♗e6 12 e4

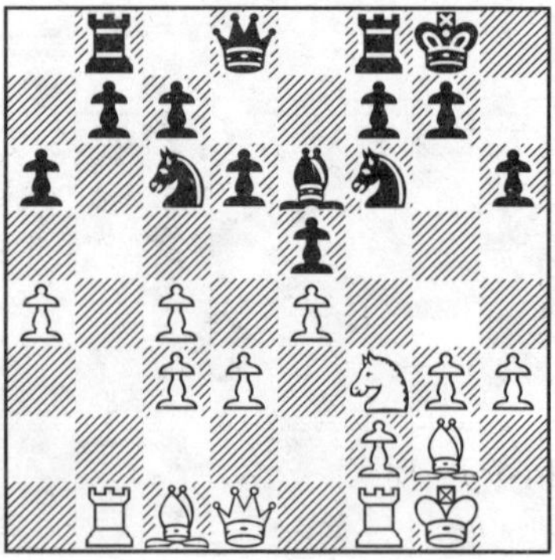

12...♘h7!?

12...♘d7 would repeat the Gagunashvili plan, with the sole slight difference in the placing of the a-pawns.

13 ♘h4 ♛d7 14 g4

Mamedyarov diverges from his ♔h2 against Gagunashvili, emphasizing his intent to control and occupy f5.

14...♘a5?!

Unfortunately Drabke sends his second knight quite definitely out of play to the queenside, where it plays little further part in the game. Gagunashvili-like, he should have routed this piece kingwards with 14...♘e7, and if 15 ♘f5 ♘g6. Perhaps White still stands a bit better after 16 f4, and if 16...exf4 17 ♗xf4 ♘xf4 18 ♖xf4 ♗xf5 19 ♖xf5, but in the game play turns definitely White's way.

15 ♗d2 c5 16 ♘f5 b6 17 f4 f6 18 h4

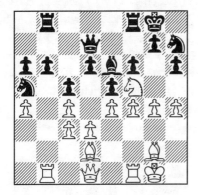

18...♖f7?

White is clearly making progress on the kingside but this move fatally blocks Black's bishop, enabling a quick conclusion. Black should at least have tried to get his knight on a5 back into play with 18...♘c6, although White's attack still looks ominous after, for example, 19 ♛f3, and if 19...exf4 20 ♗xf4 ♘e5 21 ♛g3 ♖fd8 22 ♖f2 ♛xa4 23 g5.

19 ♘xh6+ gxh6 20 f5 h5

Black's problem is not just that his bishop is lost, but that his h-pawn is also in trouble. The attempt to save it only leads to total collapse on the light squares.

21 g5 fxg5 22 hxg5 ♗xf5 23 exf5 ♖xf5 24 ♛xh5 ♖bf8 25 ♖xf5 ♖xf5 26 ♗h3 ♘f8

Unfortunately 26...♛f7 27 ♛xf7+ ♖xf7 28 ♗e6 doesn't work.

27 ♗xf5 ♛xf5 28 ♖f1 ♛d7 29 g6 ♛g7 30 ♖xf8+ 1-0

Just look at that knight on a5!

> ### Game 6
> ### J.Lautier-Bu Xiangzhi
> *Taiyuan 2004*

---

1 c4 e5 2 ♘c3 ♘f6 3 ♘f3 ♘c6 4 g3 ♗b4 5 ♘d5

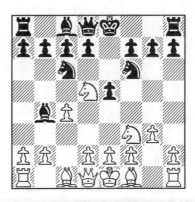

If White wants to avoid an exchange on c3 at any cost, he can certainly consider playing this very natural knight move at once. Joel Lautier has been one of its greatest champions in the last two decades.

5...♗c5

This simple retreat is Black's most popular option. He has three main alternatives:

a) After 5...a5 play usually transposes after 6 ♗g2 0-0 7 0-0 ♖e8 8 d3 to note 'c' to Black's 7th move in Game 4.

b) 5...♘xd5 is best played immediately if Black wishes to exchange knights. After 6 cxd5 6...♘d4 (the disastrous 6...e4? 7 dxc6 exf3 8 ♕b3! and 1-0 was T.Petrosian-H.Ree, Wijk aan Zee 1971) 7 ♘xd4 (White should avoid 7 ♘xe5? ♕e7 8 f4 when both 8...f6 9 e3 fxe5 10 exd4 exf4+ and 8...d6 9 ♘f3 ♘xf3+ 10 ♔f2 ♘d4 11 ♕a4+ c6 12 ♕xb4 ♘c2 are in Black's favour) 7...exd4 8 ♕c2 ♕e7 9 ♗g2, White can hope for an small advantage based on his extra space and chances to break on the queenside, but Black can put up stubborn resistance.

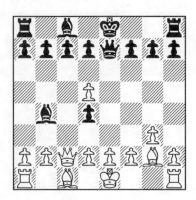

Practice has seen:

b1) B.Gelfand-V.Mirumian, Yerevan Olympiad 1996, continued 9...♗a5 10 0-0 ♗b6 (10...♕xe2? 11 b4! ♗b6 12 a4 a6 13 a5 ♗a7 14 ♕xc7 is good for White, and here 11...♗xb4? fails to 12 ♗a3!) 11 e3 d6 12 b3 0-0 13 ♗b2 dxe3 14 dxe3 ♗d7 (14...a5 15 a3 ♗d7 16 ♖fd1 ♖ac8 was M.Tal-S.Makarichev, Tbilisi 1978, when Gelfand points out that 17 ♖ac1 c5 18 ♗f1 is good for White) 15 ♖fd1 ♖fe8 16 a4 a5 17 ♗d4, with the better pawn structure, chances to play b4 and pressure down the queenside files.

b2) 9...♗c5 10 0-0 (10 b4 ♗xb4 11 ♕xc7 0-0 12 ♕c4 ♖e8 13 0-0 ♗c5 14 ♗b2 d6 15 e3 dxe3 16 fxe3 ♗d7 17 ♖f4 was also in White's favour in Cu.Hansen-H.Olafsson, Torshavn 1987) 10...0-0 11 e3 ♗b6 12 a4 dxe3 13 dxe3 a5 14 ♗d2 ♗c5 was V.Korchnoi-A.Karpov, World Championship (Game 27), Baguio City 1978, and now Filip recommended 15 ♖ab1 playing for b4.

b3) 9...c6?! 10 ♕d3 ♗c5 11 b4!? (11 0-0 0-0 12 b3 or 12 e3 may be even better) 11...♗xb4 12 ♕xd4 0-0 13 ♗b2 f6 14 ♗e4 b6 15 ♕d3 h6 16 a3 ♗a5 17 d6 ♕e6 18 ♗f3 ♗b7 19 h4 ♖ab8 20 g4 favoured White in M.Gurevich-A.Gipslis, Jurmala 1985.

b4) The rare 9...c5

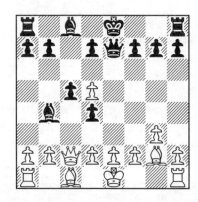

10 0-0 0-0 11 e3 d6!? (11...dxe3 straightens out Black's pawns but leaves White with a good pawn centre

and the better dark-squared bishop after either 12 dxe3 or 12 fxe3) 12 exd4 (White might also play 12 b3 ♗g4 13 ♗b2) 12...cxd4 13 ♕c4 ♗c5 14 b4 ♗b6 15 ♗b2 ♕f6 16 ♖fe1 looks good for White after something like 16...♗f5 17 ♗e4 ♖ac8 18 ♕d3 ♗xe4 19 ♖xe4 ♕f5 20 ♖xd4 ♕xd3 21 ♖xd3.

c) 5...e4 is Black's main alternative to our game move.

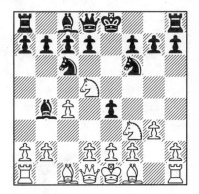

Now 6 ♘xb4 ♘xb4 7 ♘d4 0-0, with ...d5 to follow, achieves little. White must try 6 ♘h4 0-0 (note that White's knight on h4 cannot be trapped after 6...d6 7 ♗g2 g5?! 8 ♕a4!; V.Topalov-M.Adams, Las Palmas 1993, continued 8...♗d7 9 ♘xb4 ♘d4 10 ♕d1 gxh4 11 ♘c2! h3?! 12 ♗xe4! and White won, while 8...♗c5 9 d4! ♗xd4 10 ♗xg5 ♗xf2+ 11 ♔d1! ♗d4 12 ♖f1 also fails, as analysed by Danailov) 7 ♗g2 ♖e8 8 0-0 ♗c5 (White has a pull after 8...♗f8 9 d3 exd3 10 ♕xd3; for example, T.Petrosian-H.Liebert, Siegen Olympiad 1970 saw 10...♘e5 11 ♕c2 c6 12 ♘xf6+ ♕xf6 13 b3 d6 14 ♗b2, followed by ♖ad1, with good chances) 9 d3 exd3 10 ♕xd3 ♘e5.

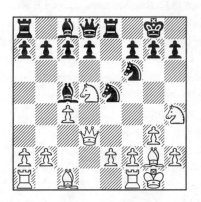

In this complex position, although White's knight looks potentially misplaced on h4, it can rejoin the struggle and White can certainly continue to fight for an edge with 11 ♕c3 or 11 ♕c2:

c1) Recently 11 ♕c3 has been giving White more purchase. C.Bauer-E.Najer, Fuegen 2006, continued 11...c6 (or 11...♘xd5 12 cxd5 d6 13 b4 – 13 b3, and if 13...a5 14 a3 followed by ♗b2, is also possible – 13...♗b6 and now White should consider 14 ♗b2, as well as the 14 ♘f3 a5 15 ♘xe5 axb4 16 ♕xb4 ♖xe5 17 e3 of E.Bareev-S.Rublevsky, Sochi 2005)12 ♗e3 cxd5 13 ♗xc5 d6 14 ♗d4 ♘e4 15 ♗xe4!? (15 ♕c1!? ♘xc4 16 b3 ♘e5 17 ♕b2 ♕e7 18 ♖ad1 ♗d7 19 ♖fe1 is a playable gambit) 15...dxe4 16 ♖ad1 ♗h3 17 ♖fe1 ♕c7 18 b3 h6 19 ♘g2 ♗xg2 20 ♔xg2 ♕c6 21 a4 a6 22 a5 ♖ac8 23 h3 ♖e6 24 ♕e3 ♘g6 25 ♗c3 ♕c5 26 ♕xc5 ♖xc5 27 ♖d4 ♘e7 28 ♖ed1 ♘f5 29 ♖d5 ♖xd5 30 cxd5 ♖g6 31 ♔h2 h5 32 e3 ♔f8 33 ♖c1 h4 34 g4 ♘e7 35 ♗d4 ♖g5 36 ♖c7 ♖xd5 37 ♖xb7 ♘c6 38 b4, and White won.

c2) However, Black's defences have

been standing up well after 11 ♕c2: for example, 11...c6 12 ♗e3 cxd5 13 ♗xc5 d6 14 ♗d4 dxc4 15 ♖ad1 d5 16 e4 ♗g4 17 f3 ♗d7 18 exd5 b5 gave Black good chances in J.Lautier-G.Kasparov, Moscow (rapid) 2002.

Returning to 5...♗c5:

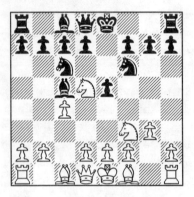

6 d3

Again transpositions abound and it is useful to think in terms of broad plans. Apart from the text, whose aim is to delay kingside development while undertaking some early queenside play, White can first complete his kingside development by playing ♗g2 and 0-0 and then choose either d3 or e3. Black, too, can at various times choose defences based on ...♘xd5. Lines in which this exchange occurs early will be considered in the note to Black's sixth move.

It will also become apparent that in some lines below, White's best may eventually be to retreat his knight from d5 to c3 to avoid exchanges. This leads to positions that usually arise from 4...♗c5 defences (see Game 7 of our next chapter) but with an extra move

for Black. As the positions arising are fairly closed, this is perhaps less of a 'victory' for Black than it might seem to be. At any rate, if such a retreat seems best in certain positions, White should play it. It will, however, pay to compare such positions both here and in Game 7 as there are similarities.

Those two alternative options to the text:

a) 6 ♗g2 0-0 7 0-0 d6 8 d3 is usually followed by moves such as e3 and a3 keeping several queenside and central options open. If Black isn't to exchange on d5, he must guard against ♗g5. Play usually continues 8...h6 9 e3, after which Black has mainly tried three moves:

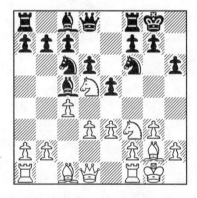

a1) 9...a6 10 a3 ♗a7 (10...♘xd5 11 cxd5 ♘e7 12 d4 exd4 13 ♘xd4 leads to a desirable pawn structure for White that we will meet frequently below, including an exemplary demonstration of White's chances in the main game) 11 ♘c3 (probably best, since although White has not played b4 by comparison to a key position that can arise from the 4...♗c5 defence, he still has good queenside prospects and Black hasn't yet fully equalized in the centre; instead 11 b4 ♘xd5 12 cxd5 ♘e7 13 ♘d2 ♗f5 14 ♘c4 ♕d7 15 ♗b2 was roughly equal in J.Lautier-V.Ivanchuk, Dortmund 1995) 11...♗f5 12 b4 ♕d7 13 ♖e1 (13 ♗b2 and if 13...♗h3 14 ♖c1 ♗xg2 15 ♔xg2 d5!? 16 c5 is also possible) 13...♗h3 14 ♗h1 ♖ae8 15 ♖a2 ♘g4 16 ♕b3 ♔h8 17 a4 ♘e7 18 a5 c6 19 b5, with a queenside edge in B.Jobava-Z.Gyimesi, Calvia Olympiad 2004.

a2) Black sometimes plays 9...a5!? but this weakens b5. R.Hübner-A.Karpov, Bad Kissingen 1980, continued 10 b3 (10 ♘c3 ♗a7 11 a3 transposes to the note to Black's 10th move in our main game) 10...♘xd5 (10...♗a7 11 ♘c3 ♗e6 12 ♗b2 ♕c8 13 a3 ♖e8 14 ♖c1 gave White a pull too in Cu.Hansen-C.Gabriel, German League 1999) 11 cxd5 ♘e7 12 d4 exd4 13 ♘xd4 ♕d7 14 ♗b2

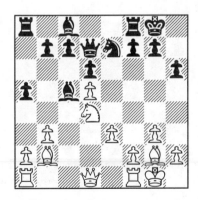

with the better central pawns and extra space.

a3) Black also failed to equalize after 9...♗g4!? 10 h3 ♗h5 11 ♗d2 a6 12 b4 ♗a7 13 ♘xf6+ ♕xf6 14 ♗c3 ♘d8 15 ♖c1

♕e7 16 ♕d2 c6 17 ♔h2 f5 18 ♘g1 ♘f7 19 ♖ce1 e4 20 f4 in M.Marin-S.Brynell, Gothenburg 2000.

b) 6 ♗g2 0-0 7 0-0 d6 8 e3 usually transposes into d3 set-ups after 8...a6 (8...♗g4!? 9 h3 ♗h5 10 d3 ♘xd5?! – 10...a5, 10...a6 and 10...♗b6 are all better – 11 cxd5 ♘e7 12 g4 ♗g6 13 d4 exd4 14 ♘xd4 ♕d7 15 e4 c6 16 dxc6 bxc6 17 ♗f4 ♖fd8 18 ♖c1 ♖ab8 19 ♘b3 ♗b6 20 ♕f3 ♕e6 21 h4 f6 22 ♖fd1 ♖bc8 23 h5 ♗f7 24 ♗h3 g5 25 ♗h2 c5 26 ♗f1, with a strong attack, was H.Stefansson-J.Hjartarson, Gardabaer 1996) 9 d3, although Black doesn't have to play 9...h6. The more ambitious 9 d4!? is tempting, but White's early attempt to establish a strong pawn centre also provides Black with targets: for example, 9...♗a7 10 ♘c3 (10 dxe5 ♘xe5 achieves nothing) 10...h6 11 h3 ♗f5 12 a3 ♘e4 13 ♘e2 ♗h7 14 b4 exd4 15 exd4 ♘e7 16 ♘f4 ♘f5 17 ♗b2 c6 18 ♖e1 ♖e8 19 ♖e2 ♘g5, with good chances, was P.Svidler-B.Gelfand, Monaco (rapid) 2006.

Returning to the immediate 6 d3:

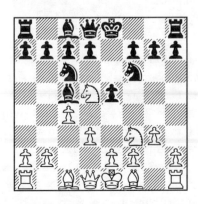

6...h6

White has an edge after 6...♘xd5 7 cxd5 ♘d4 8 ♘xd4 (8 ♗g2 and possibly 8 ♘d2 are also not bad, but not, of course, 8 ♘xe5? ♕e7 and if 9 f4 d6, forcing 10 e3, when only Black can claim any advantage) 8...♗xd4 (Black unsuccessfully tried 8...exd4 in A.Yusupov-T.Petrosian, Vrbas 1980, which continued 9 ♗g2 0-0 10 0-0 d6 11 ♗d2 a5 12 e4 dxe3 13 fxe3 ♕g5 14 d4 ♗b6 15 ♖f4 ♗d7 16 ♕b3 ♗f5 17 ♖af1 ♗g6 18 ♕c4 ♕e7 19 h4 h6 20 ♔h2 ♖ae8 21 ♕e2 ♕d8 22 ♗c3 f6 23 e4 ♗h7 24 ♕h5 ♕e7 25 ♗h3 ♔h8 26 e5, with a near winning attack) 9 ♗g2 0-0 10 0-0 d6 11 e3 ♗b6. Black's game then looks solid, but White can play for a queenside initiative. He has two possibilities:

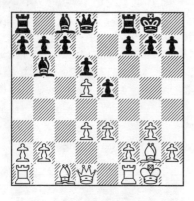

a) After 12 b4 ♗d7 (or 12...a5 13 bxa5 ♖xa5 14 ♗d2 ♖a3 15 ♗b4 ♖a6 16 a4 f5 17 a5 ♗a7 18 ♕h5 ♖f6 19 ♗d2 ♖f7 20 ♖fc1 f4 21 exf4 exf4 22 ♗xf4, with a plus in the game C.Blanco Gramajo-Z.Bernardino, correspondence 2002) 13 a4 a5 14 b5 f5 15 ♗d2 ♕f6 16 ♖c1 ♕g6 17 ♖c4, White controls f4, allowing time for manoeuvres, such as ♔h1 and f4, and has a pull. A.Karpov-V.Anand,

Frankfurt (rapid) 1997, continued 17...f4?! 18 exf4 ♕xd3 19 ♕c1 exf4 20 ♗xf4 ♕g6 21 ♗e3 ♖ac8 22 ♗xb6 cxb6 23 ♖xc8 ♗xc8 24 ♕c7 ♕g4 25 f4 g5 26 ♕xd6, and White won.

b) White developed queenside and eventually strong central pressure after 12 a4 in J.Sykora-W.Brandhorst, correspondence 2005, and following 12...a5 13 ♗d2 ♗d7 14 ♔h1 (14 b4 may also test Black, but not 14 ♗c3?!, as played in Cu.Hansen-V.Anand, Middelfart (rapid) 2003, which finished 14...f5 15 ♔h1 ♕e8 16 b3 ♖f6 17 f4 ♖h6 18 e4 ♕g6 19 fxe5 ♕xg3 0-1) 14...♕g5 15 ♕c2 ♕h5 16 b4 ♖fc8 17 b5 f6 18 ♖ac1 ♗g4 19 f3 ♗d7 20 ♕d1 ♕g6 21 ♖c3 ♗c5 22 f4 ♗b4 23 ♖b3 ♗g4 24 ♕c2 ♗c5 25 ♖e1 ♕h5 26 ♗c3 ♖e8 27 e4 ♗b6 28 ♕d2 exf4 29 gxf4 ♖e7 30 ♖b2 ♕h6 31 ♖f1 f5 32 ♕e1 ♖f8 33 ♕g3 ♗h5 34 ♖c2 ♗g4 35 e5, White won.

7 a3

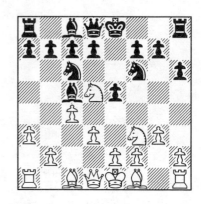

7...a5

The choice between ...a5 and ...a6 is often difficult for Black. The text move holds up White's queenside expansion plans, but weakens Black's queenside light squares. However, here 7...a6 doesn't seem to equalize. J.Lautier-P.Cramling, Yerevan Olympiad 1996, continued energetically 8 b4 ♗a7 9 ♗b2 d6 10 ♘xf6+ ♕xf6 11 b5 axb5 12 cxb5 ♘d8 13 ♗g2 ♘e6 14 e3 ♘c5?! 15 d4 e4 16 ♘e5 dxe5 17 dxc5 ♗xc5 18 ♕d5 ♕e7 19 ♕xe4 ♗d6 20 0-0 0-0 21 a4, with good chances.

8 ♗g2 0-0

Play transposes in the case of 8...d6 9 e3 0-0 10 0-0.

9 e3

According to Lautier, Black obtains roughly equal chances after 9 0-0 ♘xd5 10 cxd5 ♘d4 11 ♘xd4 exd4. But even here, 11 ♘d2 and if 11...d6 12 e3 ♘f5 13 ♘e4 ♗b6 14 ♗d2 ♘e7 15 ♘c3, may still allow White to play for a queenside edge.

9...d6 10 0-0

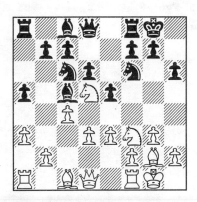

10...♘xd5!?

With d4 no longer available to Black's remaining knight and with d4 by White a positional threat, this move may be slightly suspect. White can, however, also play for a pull against other moves:

a) White's bishop-pair and extra space gave him a long-term initiative in V.Korchnoi-T.Petrosian, Ciocco 1977, after 10...♗a7 11 ♘c3 ♘h7 12 ♔h1 ♗g4 13 ♕c2 f5 14 ♘b5 ♕d7 15 ♘xa7 ♖xa7 16 b3 ♖aa8 17 ♘g1 ♖ae8 18 ♗d2 ♘f6 19 f3 ♗h5 20 b4 b6 21 ♗h3 ♗f7 22 ♘e2 axb4 23 axb4 ♘e7 24 b5 ♖d8 25 d4 (25 ♖a7 is also good), and White squeezed.

b) 10...♗g4 11 h3 ♗h5 12 ♘c3 is worth comparing with certain lines in Game 7. From this position, 12...♘h7 13 g4 ♗g6 14 d4 ♗a7 15 d5 ♘b8 16 e4 ♘d7 17 ♖e1 ♕e7 18 ♖a2 ♖fd8 19 b4 gave White a slight spatial plus in E.Agrest-S.Brynell, Munkebo 1998.

11 cxd5 ♘e7 12 d4 exd4 13 ♘xd4

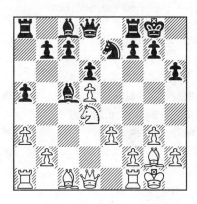

White has the better pawns and controls more space. Now he aims to build on these advantages by making further territorial gains in the centre and on the queenside.

13...♘g6

After 13...♘f5, Lautier intended 14 ♘e2 (14 ♘xf5 ♗xf5 15 e4 ♗d7 is colourless), and if 14...a4 15 e4 ♘e7 16 ♘d4 ♘g6 17 ♗e3.

14 b3 ♗d7

The mobility of White's pawns is White's main trump. After 14...♘e5 15 ♗b2, and if 15...♗g4 16 f3 ♗d7 17 h3 ♘g6 18 f4, he stands well.

15 h3 ♖e8 16 ♗b2 a4?!

This is a doubtful, anxious move that only creates a potential long-term target for White. Better was 16...♗b6.

17 b4 ♗b6 18 ♖c1 ♕e7 19 ♔h2 ♖ac8 20 ♖e1

White defends e3, raising the prospect of f4, followed eventually by a possible e4.

20...♘f8 21 ♖c4

White prepares to double rooks on the c-file and creates a further worry for Black, as a future b5 will attack Black's a-pawn. Lautier, however, suggests that the more direct 21 e4!? c5 22 dxc6 bxc6 23 ♕d2 may have been even stronger.

21...f5?!

Black gravely weakens e6. For good or ill, he had to try 21...c5.

22 ♕d3 ♕f7 23 ♖ec1

Now 24 b5, and if ...♖a8 25 ♖xc7, looms as a dangerous threat.

23...♘g6 24 ♘e6!

Black's game caves in.

24...♘e5

Or 24...♗b5 25 ♘xg7 ♘e5 26 ♗xe5 ♖xe5 27 ♘e6 ♖a8 28 ♕d1 ♗xc4 29 ♖xc4 c6 30 ♘f4 (Lautier), and White has more than ample compensation for the exchange.

25 ♗xe5 dxe5 26 ♘xc7

Winning a very big pawn and the game.

26...e4 27 ♕d1 ♖ed8 28 b5 ♗e8 29 d6!

Lautier concludes with a flourish. If 29...♗xb5? then 30 ♗f1! intends 30...♗d7 (or 30...♗c6 31 ♖xc6 bxc6 32 ♗c4) 31 ♘d5 and wins.

29...♔h7 30 ♗f1 ♗d7

Black also loses after 30...♗xc7 31 ♖xc7 ♖xc7 32 ♖xc7 ♕a2 33 ♕d4 ♕xf2+ 34 ♗g2 ♖d7 35 ♕d5.

31 ♕xa4 h5 32 ♕d1 h4 33 ♘d5 hxg3+ 34 fxg3 ♗a7 35 ♖c7 f4 36 exf4 ♗f2 37 ♗g2 ♕g6 38 ♘e7 ♕xg3+ 39 ♔h1 ♕h4 40 ♖xd7! 1-0

Black doesn't wait to be shown Lautier's elegant winning line 40...♖xc1 41 ♗xe4+ g6 42 ♘xg6+ ♔h6 43 ♖h7+ ♔xh7 44 ♘xh4+.

Summary

This chapter comprehensively covers the main lines of the reversed Sicilian after White's most promising move 4 g3 and Black's main reply, 4...♗b4. Games 1 and 2 show how to play Garry Kasparov's dynamic and very promising variation 5 ♗g2 0-0 6 0-0 e4 7 ♘g5 ♗xc3 8 bxc3 ♖e8 9 f3, while Game 3 shows that White's old and safe alternative 7 ♘c2 can also cause Black problems, albeit rather less critical ones. Games 4 and 5 show that White can also press against 6...♗xc3 and 6...♖e8, and Game 6 shows finally that White can avoid the main lines by playing 5 ♘d5 and still hope for a minimal edge.

1 c4 e5 2 ♘c3 ♘f6 3 ♘f3 ♘c6 4 g3 ♗b4 *(D)* **5 ♗g2**
     5 ♘d5 – *Game 6*
5...0-0 6 0-0 e4 *(D)*
     6...♖e8 – *Game 4*
     6...♗xc3 – *Game 5*
7 ♘g5
     7 ♘e1 – *Game 3*
7...♗xc3 8 bxc3 ♖e8 9 f3 *(D)*
     9...exf3 – *Game 1*
     9...e3 – *Game 2*

4...♗b4

6...e4

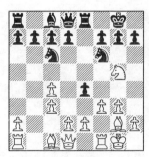

9 f3

Chapter Two

The Four Knights: 4 g3 without 4...♗b4

1 c4 e5 2 ♘c3 ♘f6 3 ♘f3 ♘c6 4 g3

The first three games in this chapter consider Black's three main developing alternatives to 4....♗b4, namely 4...♗c5, 4...♘d4 and 4...g6. These are all cases of straightforward and solid development. White's strategy remains much the same as against 4....♗b4: exert control on the long light-squared diagonal, with d5 as the pivotal square, and seek opportunities to expand from that sound base, generally in the centre and/or on the queenside. Game 7 considers **4....♗c5**, focusing principally on the variation 5 ♗g2 d6 6 0-0 0-0 7 d3 h6.

The diagram indicates the main strategic outlines. Black has a well-supported d6/e5 pawn centre, can develop easily and his dark-squared bishop exerts important pressure on the a7-g1 diagonal. White's game, on the other hand, possesses latent power, particularly on the queenside, where he can play for expansion with b4, and in the centre, where he can play for an

eventual break with d4, perhaps after e3. White can and will take the game to Black, but Black can resist fiercely.

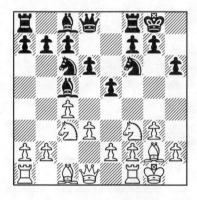

Game 8 considers **4....♘d4**. The idea behind this line is, at a cost in time, to ease Black's defensive challenge by a simplifying minor piece exchange. It focuses principally on the variation 5 ♗g2 ♘xf3+ 6 ♗xf3 ♗b4 7 ♕b3 ♗c5.

We can see that White's lead in development is tangible. Despite the knight exchange, Black still has work to do to equalize.

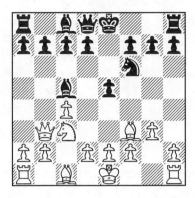

Note that Black played 6...♗b4, rather than the more natural 6...♗c5, to draw White's queen to b3 in the hope that this will be a poor square. On d1, White's queen might support a quick e3 and d4, while on b3 the queen obstructs the natural queenside expansion a3 and b4. On the other hand, White's queen can quickly get back into useful play, commonly via c2.

Game 9 considers **4...g6**. Black aims to transpose into certain lines of the King's Indian Defence, but White can prevent this. We will focus on the variation 5 ♗g2 ♗g7 6 d4 exd4 7 ♘xd4 0-0 8 0-0 ♖e8 9 ♘c2...

...which gives White a clear space advantage. Black has a slight lead in time and must try to use this to obtain compensating piece play. If White can establish an unopposed and well-supported c4/e4 pawn structure, he will have a long-term pull and a further range of expansionary options. From a relatively cramped, if solid base, Black has no easy task to frustrate White.

Games 10-12 consider the more important and common reversed Dragon. This arises after the moves **4...d5 5 cxd5 ♘xd5 6 ♗g2 ♘b6 7 0-0 ♗e7**.

The Sicilian Dragon is one of Black's fiercest variations against 1 e4 and it is a good line to play for an advantage as White with an extra tempo. Black, too, has good equalizing prospects, as long as he sticks to more solid paths. To attempt to play some of the sharper anti-Dragon variations, a tempo down, is rather risky.

Game 10 considers the complex of lines based on **8 ♖b1** when White is ready to play b4 before playing d3. This is a common theme across our coverage, reflecting a modern sense of urgency. White has a powerful light-squared bishop, a strong centre and flexible pawns. A b4-b5 flank attack mixes well with long h1-a8 diagonal pressure and longer-term potential to advance White's centre pawns. White has no obvious weaknesses and a very safe king.

Black also has a solid game and will find it easy to complete his development. Above all, he must seek to maintain a good share of the centre and control of d4. After an almost inevitable d3 by White, d4 becomes a pivotal strategic point. Both sides frequently wrestle for control of this square. White often strives to play d4, or simply to control that square, following an early e3.

Game 11 considers the complex of lines based on the variation **8 a3 0-0 9 b4 ♗e6 10 ♖b1 f6 11 d3.**

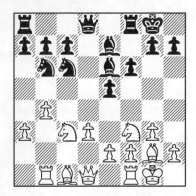

The lines based on .....♗e6 and ...f6 are considered by many to be Black's toughest response to White's opening. White has expanded on the queenside, but the fight for the centre clearly still has a long way to go. At present, Black

has d4 under control. Both sides need to formulate plans and this is a very tense battlefield in the modern game.

Finally, Game 12 considers the complex of lines based on the variation 8 a3 0-0 9 b4 ♖e8 10 d3 ♗f8 which is Black's second main defensive set-up. Again Black has d4 under control and the real battle clearly still lies far ahead.

Game 7
M.Marin-M.Grunberg
Romanian Ch., Baile Tusnad 2005

---

1 c4 e5 2 ♘c3 ♘f6 3 ♘f3 ♘c6 4 g3 ♗c5 5 ♗g2

White can also seek to refute Black's fourth move by playing the more incendiary 5 ♘xe5!?. The late world champion, Mikhail Botvinnik, once played this move, so it must be taken seriously. White is playing for an extra pawn in the centre. After 5...♗xf2+ 6 ♔xf2 ♘xe5 White has to concede some weaknesses in his game, but he also gains the bishop-pair.

Play usually continues 7 e4 leaving

Black with a major choice between the critical 7...c5 and the more restrained 7...d6!?:

a) 7...c5 sees Black battle for the d4-square. He seeks to keep the position closed and to find good play for his knights on the central dark squares. To hope for anything concrete, White must challenge Black's plans with 8 d4. After 8...cxd4 9 ♕xd4 0-0, White has extra space, the bishop-pair and radiates power down the d-file, but also has his own development and structural concerns, as well as an insecure king. Indeed, Black obtained adequate chances in V.Ivanchuk-V.Anand, Wijk aan Zee 1999, which continued 10 ♗f4 d6 (S.Joachim-V.Epishin, Bad Zwesten 2002, deviated with 10...♖e8 11 ♗g5 h6 12 ♗xf6 ♕xf6 13 ♗e2 b6 14 ♖hf1 ♕c6, with adequate play) 11 h3 ♗e6 12 ♗e2 ♕c8 13 ♖ac1 ♗xh3 14 ♘d5 ♕e6 15 ♘c7 ♕e7 16 ♘xa8 ♘c6 17 ♕e3 (Anand suggests 17 ♗xd6!? ♘xe4+ 18 ♔e1 ♘xd6 19 ♕h4 ♕xh4 20 gxh4, with a possible edge) 17...♘xe4+ 18 ♔f3 ♗f5 19 ♗d3 ♖e8 20 ♖he1 ♕d8 21 ♔g2 ♕xa8 22 ♕f3 ♘d4 23 ♕e3 ♘c6 24 ♕f3 ½-½.

b) 7...d6!? allows White more scope in the centre and Black may be taking a greater risk in this line, but he is not without long-term counterattacking prospects. The game D.Poldauf-J.Timman, Forchheim 2000, continued 8 d4 ♘g6 9 h3 0-0 10 ♗g2 ♖b8 11 ♖f1 ♗e6 12 b3 ♕c8 13 g4 h6 14 ♔g1 ♘h7 15 ♘e2 ♘g5 16 ♘g3 ♘h4 17 ♗b2 ♘xg2 18 ♔xg2 f6 19 ♖f4 ♗d7 20 ♕d3 b5!, with a rough balance.

Returning to the calmer 5 ♗g2:

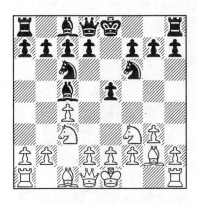

5...d6

Alternatively:

a) 5...e4?! has significant positional downsides. Black's e-pawn and f5-square are both weak after 6 ♘h4. S.Cvetkovic-A.Meszaros, Eger 1987, continued 6...♕e7 7 0-0 ♕e5 8 e3 ♕e6 9 d4 exd3 10 ♘d5 ♗d6 11 ♕xd3 ♘b4 12 ♘xb4 ♗xb4 13 ♘f5 0-0 14 a3 ♗e7 15 b4 d6 16 ♘xe7+ ♕xe7 17 ♗b2 ♖e8 18 ♖ac1 ♖b8 19 c5 ♖d8 20 cxd6 ♖xd6 21 ♕c2 c6 22 ♗d4, with a clear bishop-pair, middlegame plus.

b) 5...0-0 is better, but it gives White the extra option of playing 6 ♘xe5! under better circumstances than on his fifth move. Critical may then be the game J.Timman-E.Bareev, Wijk aan Zee 2002, which continued 6...♗xf2+ (6...♘xe5 7 d4 ♗d6 8 c5 is better for White) 7 ♔xf2 ♘xe5 8 b3 ♖e8 (J.Timman-I.Sokolov, Cannes (blitz) 2006, varied with 8...c5, but after 9 ♖f1 d6 10 ♔g1 ♖e8 11 ♗b2 ♗g4 12 h3 ♗h5 13 g4 ♗g6 14 d3 ♘c6 15 ♕d2 ♘d7 16 ♘d5 ♘de5 17 ♘f4 ♕h4 18 ♕e1 ♕xe1 19 ♖axe1, White kept the advantage; likewise, 8...d6 9 ♖f1 ♖b8 10 d4 ♘g6 11

♔g1 h6 12 e4 ♗g4 13 ♕d3 a6 14 a4 ♘h7 15 h3 ♗e6 16 ♗e3 ♕c8 17 ♔h2 ♘g5 18 h4 did in E.Ragozin-T.Polak, German League 2002) 9 ♖f1 d5!? 10 d4! ♘eg4+ 11 ♔g1

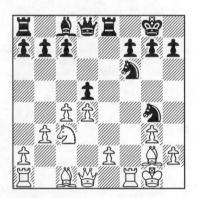

11...dxc4 12 bxc4 ♘e3!? 13 ♗xe3 ♖xe3 14 ♕d2 ♖e8!? (14...♕e8 15 ♖ae1 c6 16 ♖f3 ♖xf3 17 ♗xf3 might have minimized White's advantage according to Ftacnik), and now Ribli suggests 15 ♘d5! and if 15...♘xd5 16 ♗xd5 ♗e6 17 ♗xb7 ♖b8 18 ♗c6 with a clear advantage.

6 0-0

White can delay castling, but play usually only transposes after 6 d3; for example, 6...h6 7 a3 a6 8 b4 ♗a7 9 ♗b2 0-0 10 0-0 and we're back in our main game. One independent try is 6 e3!? 0-0 7 a3 (7 0-0 transposes to the notes to White's 7th move, below), and then 7...a6 8 d4 ♗a7 9 h3 exd4 10 exd4 ♖e8+ 11 ♗e3 is possible: for example, D.Gurevich-A.Shabalov, Denver 2003, continued 11...♘a5 12 b3 b5 13 0-0 bxc4 14 ♘d2 ♗e6 15 b4 ♘b3 16 ♘xb3 cxb3 17 d5 ♗xh3!? 18 ♗xh3 ♗xe3 19 fxe3 ♖xe3 20 ♕d4, with unclear play.

6...0-0

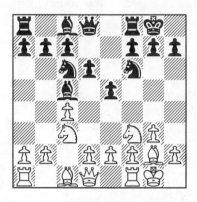

7 d3

Playing 7 e3 followed by d4 is a better plan now than on the last move, but the text move is more flexible and poses more of a threat. After 7 e3 a6 (7...♗b6 is also not bad) 8 d4 ♗a7, Black's bishop on a7 may seem rather out of the game, but White will not find it easy to make progress without reopening the a7-g1 diagonal. J.Timman-D.Sadvakasov, Hoogeveen 1999, continued 9 h3 h6 10 b3 ♖e8 11 ♗a3 (neither does 11 d5 ♘e7 12 a4 b5 bring any advantage) 11...exd4 12 ♘xd4 ♘xd4 13 exd4 ♖b8 14 ♕d3 ♗d7 15 ♖fe1 b5 16 ♗b2, and now Black can equalize with 16...bxc4 17 ♕xc4 c6 18 ♗xc6 ♖xe1+ 19 ♖xe1 ♗xh3.

7...h6

Black can delay this move as ♗g5 isn't yet a dangerous threat. A.Onischuk-M.Sadler, Elista Olympiad 1998, continued 7...a6!? 8 ♗g5 (probably premature) 8...h6 9 ♗h4 ♘d4! (completely neutralizing White's pin) 10 ♗xf6 ♕xf6 11 ♘e4 ♕e7 12 ♘xc5 dxc5 13 e3 ♘xf3+ 14 ♕xf3 ♖d8 15 ♖ad1 a5 16 a5 16 ♕h5 ♖a6 17 ♗e4 ♕g5 18 ♕e2 ♖ad6, with equality.

8 a3

Trying to exploit Black's last move by playing 8 ♘a4 achieves nothing. Black needn't retreat his dark-squared bishop, as an exchange on c5 gives him good central dark-square control: for example, G.Milos-V.Anand, Sao Paulo (rapid) 2004, continued 8...♖e8 9 ♘xc5!? dxc5 10 b3 ♕d6 11 ♗b2 ♗f5 12 ♕d2 ♖ad8 13 ♖ad1 b6 14 ♗c3 ♕e6 15 ♕b2 ♗h3 16 ♖fe1 ♗xg2 17 ♔xg2 a5 18 a3 ♘h5 19 e3 ♕d6 20 ♕e2 ♘f6, and Black stood well.

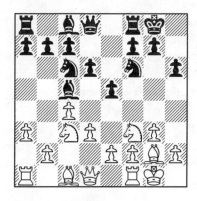

8...a6

Black can also play 8...a5!?, but weakening b5 and creating other queenside targets can tell against him. A.Delchev-S.Savchenko, Ohrid 2001, continued 9 e3 ♖e8 10 b3 ♗f5 11 h3 ♗b6 12 ♗b2 ♕d7 13 ♔h2 ♘e7 14 ♖e1 c6 15 e4 ♗h7 16 d4 exd4 17 ♘xd4 ♖ad8 18 ♘a4 ♗a7 19 ♕d2 d5!? (tactically doubtful, but otherwise White plays ♖ad1 with good chances) 20 exd5 cxd5 21 c5 ♘e4 22 ♕xa5 ♘c6 23 ♘xc6 bxc6 24 ♗d4 ♗b8 25 ♘c3 ♗c7 26 ♕a6, and White won.

9 b4

White usually follows this most natural move up with a queenside fianchetto. White adopted a different plan in L.Portisch-C.Garcia Palermo, Reggio Emilia 1992, which continued 9 e3!? ♗a7 10 b4 ♗e6 11 ♖e1 ♕d7 12 ♖b1 ♖ad8 13 ♕c2 ♘e7 14 a4 ♗h3 15 ♗h1 ♘g4 16 a5 f5 17 b5 axb5 18 ♘xb5 ♗b8 19 ♘c3 c6 20 ♗d2 ♖f7 21 ♖b3 f4 22 ♕b1 fxg3 23 fxg3 ♘c8 24 ♕d1 ♗a7 25 ♕e2 ♖df8 26 ♖eb1 ♔h8 27 ♖xb7 ♕xb7 28 ♖xb7 ♖xb7 29 ♗g2 ♗xg2 30 ♔xg2 ♖bf7 31 h3 ♖xf3 32 hxg4 ♖3f7 33 g5, with good chances.

9...♗a7 10 ♗b2

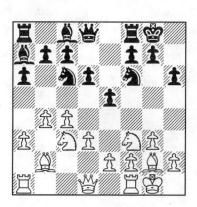

10...♗e6

Black intends ...♕d7, connecting his rooks with ...♗h3 in mind. He has also tried many other moves here:

a) 10...♗g4 attempts to pin, but Black can never give up the bishop-pair lightly. H.Stefansson-J.Gunnarsson, Hafnarborg 2003, continued 11 h3 (or 11 ♖c1!? ♕d7 12 e3 ♘e7 13 ♕c2 c6 14 c5! ♘g6 15 cxd6 ♕xd6 16 h3 ♗f5 17 e4 ♗e6 18 ♘a4 ♖ad8 19 ♖fd1 ♗c8 20 d4 exd4 21 ♘xd4 ♕c7 22 ♘c5, and White enjoyed a very active form of the reversed Dragon in M.Marin-E.Valeanu, Baile Tusnad 2005) 11...♗e6 12 ♖c1 ♕d7 13 ♔h2 ♖ab8 (White also had a pull after 13...♘e7 14 e3 ♘g6 15 ♘e2 c6 16 ♕c2 ♖ad8 17 e4 b5 18 cxb5 cxb5 19 ♕c6 in J.Lautier-V.Topalov, Monaco (blindfold) 1997) 14 e3 b5 15 ♘d2 ♘e7 16 e4 ♘e8 17 f4 exf4 18 gxf4 f5 19 ♘d5 bxc4 20 ♘xc4 fxe4 21 dxe4 ♘xd5 22 exd5 ♗f5 23 ♘a5 ♗b6 24 ♘c6 ♖a8 25 ♖e1 ♖f7 26 ♕d2 ♘f6 27 a4, and White stood well.

b) 10...♖e8 is a sound move, but allows White a useful tempo to press in the centre. V.Neverov-O.Korneev, Port Erin 2006, for example, continued 11 ♘d5 ♘xd5 12 cxd5 ♘e7 13 ♘d2 c6 14 dxc6 ♘xc6 15 ♖c1 ♗g4 16 h3

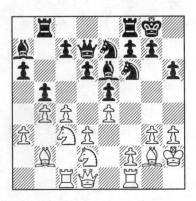

16...♗e6 17 e3 ♕d7 18 ♔h2 ♖ac8 19 ♘e4 f5 20 ♘c3 f4 21 exf4 exf4 22 ♘d5 fxg3+ 23 fxg3 ♘e5 24 ♖xc8 ♖xc8 25 ♗c1 ♖f8 26 ♖xf8+ ♔xf8 27 d4 ♘c6 28 ♗e3 ♗xd5 29 ♗xd5 ♕f5 30 ♗g2 ♕f6 31 ♕g4 ♕e7 32 ♗f2, with advantage.

c) 10...♗f5!? was famously played in M.Tal-L.Kavalek, Montreal 1979, which continued 11 ♘h4!? (11 ♖c1, and if

11...♕d7 12 ♘d5 ♘xd5 13 cxd5 ♘d4 14 ♘h4 ♗h7 15 e3 ♘f5 16 ♘f3 ♘e7 17 ♕b3, is possibly better) 11...♗d7 12 ♖c1 ♘e8 13 ♘d5 g5!? 14 ♘f3 f5 15 ♘d2 ♘d4 16 c5!? c6 17 ♘b6 ♗xb6 18 cxb6 ♕xb6 19 ♘c4 ♕a7 20 e3 ♘e6 21 d4 exd4 22 exd4 d5 23 ♘e5, with good play.

11 ♖c1

White also pressed successfully in M.Brodsky-B.Gelfand, Tallinn (rapid) 2005, after 11 ♘d2!? ♕d7 12 ♘d5 ♘h7 13 e3 ♖ab8 14 ♔h1 ♘e7 15 ♘xe7+ ♕xe7 16 d4 ♗f5 17 e4 ♗d7 18 d5 f5 19 exf5 ♗xf5 20 ♕e2 ♘f6 21 f4 e4 22 ♗xf6 ♕xf6 23 ♘xe4 ♕g6 24 ♖ae1, with an excellent game.

11...♕d7 12 e3

White anticipates an eventual ...d5, after which he might either play for an active form of the reversed Sicilian by exchanging pawns on d5 or aim to block Black's dark-squared bishop out of the game by playing c5. White can also again play 12 ♘d2, strengthening his grip on the central light squares, as Miles once did.

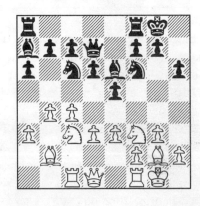

12...♖ac8 13 ♕a4

White has a little extra space, more

flexibility and menacing pawns. Yet another promising continuation is 13 ♖e1!?. V.Bologan-S.Volkov, Moscow 2005, continued 13...♖fe8 14 ♘d2 d5 15 cxd5 ♘xd5 16 ♘a4 ♗h3 17 ♘e4 ♗xg2 18 ♔xg2 b6 19 ♕b3 ♖e6 20 ♘d2 ♖ce8 21 ♘f3, with good play.

13...♗b6?!

This turns out badly. Perhaps better was 13...♘b8 when White might play for a slight endgame pull after 14 ♕xd7 ♘bxd7 15 a4 followed by a5, and he may also emerge with an edge after 14 b5, and if 14...♗b6 15 bxa6 ♕xa4 16 ♘xa4.

14 ♘d2 d5!? 15 c5!

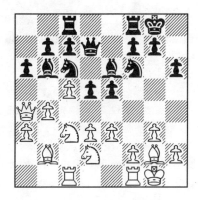

White incarcerates Black's bishop on a7. Black may have expected this and hoped to dig his bishop out of its queenside grave in due course, but it turns out to be hard to achieve this.

15...♗a7 16 ♘e2 ♗h3 17 ♕c2 ♖fe8 18 ♘f3 ♗xg2 19 ♔xg2 e4 20 dxe4 dxe4 21 ♘fd4 ♘e5 22 c6!

White splits Black's queenside pawns, creating a game-winning weakness. Although he unblocks squares on the a7-g1 diagonal, this only partially allows Black's bishop back into the game, as it will clearly be tied to passive defence of the rickety c7-pawn.

22...bxc6 23 ♘xc6 ♘xc6 24 ♕xc6 ♖e6 25 ♕xd7 ♘xd7 26 ♖fd1 ♖e7 27 ♘f4 ♗b6 28 ♘d5 ♖e6 29 ♘f4 ♖e7 30 ♘d5 ♖e6 31 ♘xc7

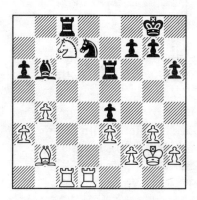

White wins a pawn, and with the more active remaining pieces, has a technically winning advantage.

31...♖xc7 32 ♖xc7 ♗xc7 33 ♖xd7 ♗e5 34 ♗xe5 ♖xe5 35 ♖a7 ♖e6 36 g4 ♖g6 37 ♔f1 ♖c6 38 h3 g6 39 ♔g2 ♔g7 40 h4 ♔f6 41 g5+ hxg5 42 hxg5+ ♔xg5 43 ♖xf7 a5 44 ♖b7 axb4 45 axb4 ♖c4 46 b5 ♖b4 47 b6 ♔g4 48 ♖b8 g5 49 b7 ♖b1 50 ♔h2 ♖b6 51 ♔g1 ♖b2 52 ♔f1 ♖b1+ 53 ♔e2 ♖b2+ 54 ♔d1 ♖b6 55 ♔d2 ♖d6+ 56 ♔c3 ♖d7 57 ♔c4 ♖f7 58 ♔d5 ♔f3 59 ♔e6 ♖xb7 60 ♖xb7 ♔xf2 61 ♔f5 1-0

Game 8
Cu.Hansen-J.Hector
Nordic Championship,
Aarhus 2003

---

1 c4 e5 2 ♘c3 ♘f6 3 ♘f3 ♘c6 4 g3 ♘d4!?

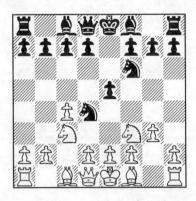

Black achieves a simplifying exchange of knights with this move at the cost of a slight loss of time.

5 ♗g2

This is White's usual choice. His best alternative is 5 e3 ♘xf3+ 6 ♕xf3 with the sensible, if modest plan of completing kingside development and playing d4. W.Uhlmann-H.Fronczek, Dresden 2000, for example, continued 6...♗c5 7 ♗g2 0-0 8 0-0 c6 9 ♕d1 d6 10 d4 ♗b4!? 11 ♗d2 exd4 12 exd4 h6 13 ♖e1 ♗xc3 14 ♗xc3 d5 15 cxd5 ♘xd5 16 ♕b3, with a pull. However, White must avoid 5 ♘xe5?! ♕e7 6 f4 d6 7 ♘d3 ♗f5 when Black stands well.

5...♘xf3+ 6 ♗xf3 ♗b4

Black provokes 7 ♕b3, so that White's queen no longer supports an e3 and d4 advance and also obstructs White's b-pawn. White has a clearer pull after the immediate 6...♗c5 7 0-0 (White was less successful with the extremely ambitious 7 d3 h6 8 a3 0-0 9 e3!? c6 10 b4 ♗e7 11 d4!? in J.Lautier-E.Sutovsky, Gothenburg 2005, but after 11...exd4 12 ♕xd4 d5, 13 cxd5!? ♘xd5 14 ♘xd5 cxd5 15 ♕xd5 ♗f6 16 ♖a2 ♗e6

17 ♕xd8 ♖fxd8 18 ♖c2 ♖ac8 19 ♖xc8 ♖xc8 20 0-0 needs further testing according to Ribli) 7...0-0 8 d3 (possible too is 8 e3 intending d4):

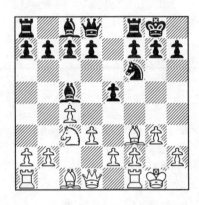

a) J.Smejkal-L.Portisch, Milan 1975, continued 8...h6 9 ♗g2 c6 10 ♗d2 d6 11 ♘a4 ♗d4 12 e3 ♗b6 13 ♘xb6 axb6 14 ♗c3 ♖e8 15 d4 e4 16 d5 ♕e7 17 a4 c5 18 b4 ♗f5 19 bxc5 bxc5 20 ♕b3 ♖ad8 21 ♖fb1 ♖d7 22 ♕b2 ♘g4 23 ♖a3 ♘e5 24 ♗xe5 ♕xe5 25 ♕xe5 ♖xe5 26 ♖ab3 ♖ee7 27 a5, with an endgame edge.

b) 8...c6 9 ♗g5 h6 10 ♗xf6 ♕xf6 11 ♘e4 ♕e7 12 ♘xc5 ♕xc5 13 ♕d2. 13...a5 14 a3 a4 15 ♖ac1 f5 16 ♖fd1 ♕e7 17 c5!, also brought the Czech grandmaster success in the later game J.Smejkal-D.Campora, Vrsac 1981.

7 ♕b3

This move is a serious test. If Black now exchanges on c3, White gets the bishop-pair. However, retreating the bishop costs Black a tempo and White retains his slight lead in time and a certain initiative. White can also play 7 0-0, 7 ♕c2 and 7 d4!?, of which the last has hardly been tested, but is well motivated.

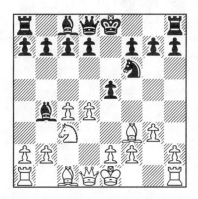

G.Kamsky-D.Campora, Buenos Aires 1993, continued 7...e4 8 ♗g2 0-0 9 0-0 ♗xc3 10 bxc3 ♖e8?! (10...h6 may be critical, although 11 f3 still seems challenging) 11 ♗g5 (S.Conquest-R.Smith, Hamilton 1999, was also very promising after 11 ♕c2 h6 12 f3 exf3 13 ♖xf3 d6 14 ♗xh6! gxh6 15 ♖af1 ♘e4 16 ♖xf7) 11...h6 12 ♗xf6 ♕xf6 13 f3 exf3?! (13...e3 14 f4 d6 15 ♖b1 may minimize White's advantage) 14 ♗xf3 ♕g5 15 ♗d5 ♖e7 16 ♕d3 c6 17 ♖f5 ♕g4 18 ♗f3 ♕g6 19 ♗h5 ♕h7 20 ♖e5 ♕xd3 21 exd3 ♖e6 22 ♖b1 g6 23 ♖xe6 dxe6 24 ♗f3 ♔f8 25 c5 a5 26 c4, with good winning prospects.

7...♗c5

Black rarely exchanges on c3, while both 7...a5 and 7...♗a5 also have drawbacks. The former saw White exploit Black's weak queenside squares and the continuing awkwardness of the b4-bishop in R.Vaganian-M.Tseitlin, Telavi 1982, which continued 8 d3 0-0 9 0-0 ♖e8 10 ♘a4 ♗f8 11 ♗g5 h6 12 ♗xf6 ♕xf6 13 c5! ♖b8 14 ♖fc1 c6 15 ♕c3, and the latter permits 8 ♕a3 c6 9 0-0 ♗b6 10 d3 ♕e7 11 b4 d6 12 ♗g5 ♗h3 13 ♖fc1 0-0?! 14 b5 ♖ac8 15 bxc6 bxc6 16 ♘e4,

which gave White some advantage in J.Smejkal-C.Garcia Palermo, German League 1989.

8 0-0

There is also 8 d3:

a) After 8...h6 White can consider the rather more speculative bayonet attacking idea 9 h4!? c6 (White's last was more accurate than 9 g4 because 9...♘h7?! now runs into 10 ♘e4! ♗e7 11 ♕b5 c5 12 ♗e3 a6 13 ♕a4 ♕c7 14 ♘c3 ♕d8 15 b4, as it did in J.Piket-B.Avrukh, Amsterdam 2001) 10 g4 and now Black must defend with care:

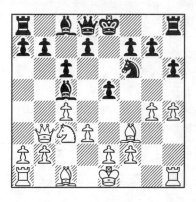

a1) Critical may be 10...♗e7, after which S.Mikhailuk-G.Sagalchik, Seattle 2002, continued 11 g5 hxg5 12 ♗xg5 (perhaps 12 hxg5!? ♖xh1+ 13 ♗xh1, intending 13...♘h7 14 g6 fxg6 15 ♗e4 ♘f8 16 ♗e3 d6 17 0-0-0) 12...d6 13 0-0-0 ♕c7 14 ♖dg1 ♗e6 15 ♗e3 ♗f8 16 h5 d5 17 ♗g5 dxc4 18 dxc4 ♘d7 19 ♗e3 f5 20 h6!? gxh6 21 ♗h5+ ♔d8 22 f3, with unclear complications.

a2) 10...d5!? 11 g5 hxg5 12 hxg5 ♖xh1+ 13 ♗xh1 ♘g4 14 cxd5 ♗xf2+ 15 ♔d1 ♗b6 16 ♔c2 ♗d7 17 dxc6 bxc6 18 ♗d2 ♗e3 19 ♖f1 ♕e7 20 ♘e4 ♗e6 21

♕a4 ♔f8 22 ♗f3 ♗xd2 23 ♖h1! ♘h6 24 ♔xd2 ♘g8 25 ♕xc6 saw White emerging from the complications with the upper hand in B.Gulko-J.Hector, Copenhagen 2000.

a3) According to Gulko, White also stands well after 10...d6 with either 11 ♖g1 or 11 g5 hxg5 12 hxg5 ♖xh1+ 13 ♗xh1 ♘g4 14 ♘e4 ♗b6 15 ♕a3 ♗c7 16 ♗d2.

However, Black doesn't have to meet 8 d3 with 8...h6. Instead:

b) 8...c6 9 g4 is possible, although here the bayonet attack has less bite: 9...d6 10 g5 ♘d7 11 ♘e4!? (White might settle for a nominal space advantage after 11 h4 ♕b6 12 ♕xb6 ♗xb6) 11...0-0 12 ♖g1 ♗b6 13 ♗e3 ♗xe3 14 fxe3 f5 15 gxf6 ♘xf6 16 0-0-0 ♔h8 17 d4 ♕e7 18 ♕c3 ♘xe4 19 ♗xe4 ♗f5, and Black drew in L.Aronian-B.Gelfand, Saint Vincent 2005.

c) 8...0-0 with a further divide:

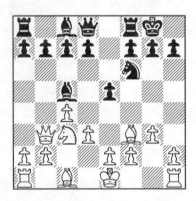

c1) The bayonet idea is now completely toothless due to 9 g4 d5! and if 10 g5 dxc4 11 ♕xc4 ♘d7 12 ♘e4 ♗e7 13 ♗e3 ♘b6 14 ♕b5 ♘d5, with equality.

c2) 9 0-0 transposes to the notes to Black's 8th move, below.

c3) 9 ♗g5!? c6 10 0-0 h6!? (Black preferred 10...♗e7 in E.Tomashevsky-P.Svidler, Moscow 2005, when Ribli's 11 ♕c2, and if 11...h6 12 ♗xf6 ♗xf6 13 b4, might be better than the game's 11 ♖fd1) 11 ♗xf6 ♕xf6 12 ♘e4 ♕e7 13 ♘xc5 ♕xc5 14 ♕c3 a5 15 a3 a4 16 ♖fc1 ♕e7 17 c5! d5 18 cxd6 ♕xd6 19 ♕b4! ♕c7 (or 19...♕xb4!? 20 axb4 ♗e6 21 ♖c5 f6, and if 22 b5 ♖a5 23 b4 ♖xb5 24 ♖xa4) 20 ♖c5 ♗e6 21 ♖ac1 ♖fd8 22 ♖b5 ♖d7 23 h4 ♗b3 24 ♖b6 ♖f8 25 ♕c5, with the better game for White in J.Timman-J.Hector, Malmö 2005.

Returning to 8 0-0:

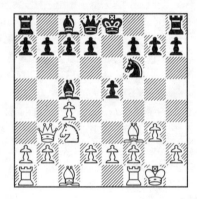

8...c6!?

Black needn't yet commit himself to this move. He can first play 8...0-0, and only after 9 d3, 9...c6, which avoids White's plan to play d4 in one move after e3 and ♖d1 in our main game. Black can also continue to delay a decision in the centre by playing 9...h6, which is more common. White can press with 10 ♗d2, 10 ♗g2 or 10 e3, while Black usually replies with ...c6, ...♖e8, ...♗f8 or ...♗b6, followed by

...d6. White will then move his queen and advance his queenside pawns. If White gets in c5 before Black advances his d-pawn, he has the option to exchange pawns on d6, with active forms of the reversed Sicilian. Thus we have:

a) Cu.Hansen-L.Christiansen, Munich 1992, continued 10 ♝d2 ♜e8 (10...c6 11 ♝g2 ♜e8 12 ♜ad1 b6!? 13 ♛a4 ♝b7 14 b4 ♝f8 15 b5 ♛c8 16 ♛b3 ♛c7 17 a4 gave White a space advantage in Y.Yakovich-A.Zatonskih, Isle of Man 2005) 11 ♜ac1 ♜b8!? (11...c6, with ...♝b6 or ...♝f8, followed by ...d6 in mind, is better) 12 ♛a4 a6 13 b4

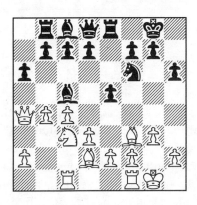

13...♝f8 14 b5 ♝c5 15 bxa6 bxa6 16 ♜b1 ♜b6, and now 17 ♛a5, and if 17...d6 18 ♞a4 ♜xb1 19 ♜xb1, gives White queenside pressure.

b) Hansen later preferred 10 ♝g2 and 10...♜e8 11 h3 c6 12 ♔h2 ♛b6?! (Black should again prefer either 12...♝f8 or 12...♝b6) 13 ♞a4! ♛a5 14 ♞xc5 ♛xc5 gave him an edge in Cu.Hansen-H.Westerinen, Reykjavik 1998.

c) L.Van Wely-J.Piket, Merrillville 1997, saw 10 e3 a6!? (10...♜e8, and if 11

♜d1 ♝f8, or 10...c6 11 ♜d1 ♝b6, intending 12 d4 exd4 13 exd4 d6 14 ♞a4!? ♝c7 15 d5 cxd5 16 cxd5 a6, may be tougher) 11 ♜d1 ♝a7 12 d4 ♛e7 13 dxe5 ♛xe5 14 ♞d5 ♞xd5 15 cxd5 d6 16 ♝d2 ♝c5 17 ♝c3 ♛f5 18 ♝g2 a5 19 ♝d4 b6 20 ♛c3, with good chances.

White also has two independent options after 8...0-0. One is 9 ♞a4 ♝e7 10 ♜d1, intending d4, but White's knight on a4 will lose time returning to the centre, giving Black good equalizing chances. The more direct 9 ♜d1!? might be better.

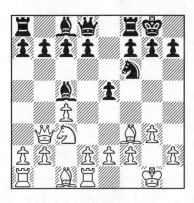

M.Marin-F.Cuijpers, Sitges 1999, continued 9...♛e7 (the later M.Marin-S.Conquest, Barcelona 2006, varied with 9...♜e8!? 10 d3 h6 11 e3 ♝f8 12 ♛c2 ♛e7 13 b4 c6 14 b5!?, reaching a tense and roughly balanced position) 10 d3 c6 (or 10...h6 11 ♞a4) 11 ♝g5 h6 12 ♝xf6 ♛xf6 13 ♞e4 ♛e7 14 ♞xc5 ♛xc5 15 ♛c3 ♛e7 16 c5! ♜d8 17 ♜d2 d5 18 cxd6 ♛xd6 19 ♜ad1 ♝e6 20 d4 exd4 21 ♜xd4 ♛e7 22 a3 ♛f6, and now Marin gives 23 h4! and if 23...♜xd4 24 ♜xd4 ♜d8 25 ♜xd8+ ♛xd8 26 ♛e5! with good chances.

Returning to the more ambitious 8...c6:

9 e3

Rather than play 9 d3, White seeks to exploit Black's 8th move by playing aggressively for d4 without loss of tempo.

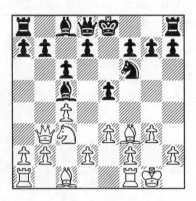

9...d6

In E.Bareev-P.Svidler, Monaco (blindfold) 2005, Black preferred the remarkably ambitious 9...0-0!? 10 ♖d1 d5?!, but after 11 cxd5 cxd5 White missed the cold-blooded 12 d4! which appears to refute Black's play after 12...e4 (or 12...exd4 13 exd4 ♗b6 14 ♗g5) 13 dxc5 exf3 14 ♘xd5 ♗e6 15 ♘xf6+ ♕xf6 16 ♕xb7 ♕f5 17 ♖d4 ♖ad8 18 ♗d2 (Vlassov).

10 ♖d1 ♕e7

White is also better after 10...♕b6!? 11 ♕c2, threatening ♘a4, followed by d4.

11 d4 ♗b6 12 ♕c2 0-0

White has a good centre and his extra space gives him an edge. Black might try to obtain counterattacking chances without castling by playing 12...h5, but this doesn't look convinc-ing. White seems to strike faster in the centre and on the other wing after 13 b4, and if 13...h4 then 14 c5 ♗c7 15 cxd6 ♗xd6 16 b5 ♗d7 17 bxc6 bxc6 18 ♖b1.

13 d5

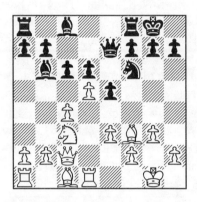

13...♗g4!?

Hector's position is reasonably solid, but he lacks counterplay. Exchanging his better bishop may not help in that respect, but it is better than shutting in his dark-squared bishop behind an otherwise desirable Benoni centre with 13...c5?!. Perhaps Black might try 13...♗d7, keeping three minor pieces on the board, but White still seems a little better after 14 b3 ♖ae8 15 ♗b2 (or 15 ♗a3) 15...e4 16 ♗g2.

14 ♗xg4 ♘xg4 15 h3!

Although playing this move involves a slight weakening in White's kingside pawns, it more crucially prevents any Black counterplay based on ...f5. Black must retreat his knight to f6 as 15...♘h6?! 16 e4! reveals an attack on h6 and is highly effective.

15...♘f6 16 b3 ♗c5

Black cannot improve his defensive chances by playing 16...e4!? 17 ♗b2 as the potential vulnerability of his d- and e-pawns is then clearly more significant than White's slightly weakened light squares.

17 ♔g2 cxd5?!

But this is a serious misjudgement. Black should have tried 17...a6. By exchanging on d5, Black loses control of key central light squares and reduces his potential counterattacking strike force. Hector will now be able to advance his f-pawn, but this achieves very little and Hansen's obvious structural advantages tell heavily against Black.

18 ♘xd5 ♘xd5 19 ♖xd5

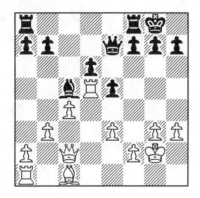

19...f5 20 ♗d2

White will play his queen's rook to d1 and force through b4, with a clear advantage.

20...a5 21 ♖d1 ♖f6 22 a3! ♖af8

Black can no longer prevent b4. After 22...♗xa3? 23 ♕a2 ♗c5 24 b4, and if 24...♗a7 (or 24...♗b6 25 c5) 25 ♖xa5, White wins.

23 b4 axb4 24 axb4 ♗b6 25 c5 ♗c7

25...dxc5 26 bxc5 ♗c7 27 ♗c3 is also clearly better for White.

26 ♗c3 ♖h6 27 cxd6 ♗xd6 28 ♕d3 ♖ff6 29 f4!

While White dominates the centre, Black flails at the side of the board. This devastating, blockading thrust both stops Black's attack and wins material.

29...♖fg6 30 ♕xf5 ♕h4 31 ♗e1!

This final defensive move completely secures the kingside. White can now launch his own decisive attack.

31...exf4 32 exf4 ♕xf4 33 ♕xf4 ♗xf4 34 ♖d8+ ♔f7 35 ♖1d7+ ♔e6 36 ♖xb7 ♗d6 37 ♗f2 ♖h5 38 ♖e8+ ♔f6 39 ♗d4+ 1-0

> ### Game 9
> ### Cu.Hansen-H.Kallio
> *Nordic Championship, Aarhus 2003*

1 c4 e5 2 ♘c3 ♘f6 3 ♘f3 ♘c6 4 g3 g6

This line is solid, but fairly uncommon. Black hopes to transpose to certain variations of the King's Indian Defence with d4 (or d3), but White can avoid this.

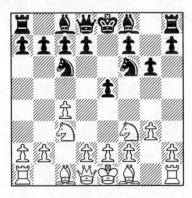

5 &g2

White can also play 5 d4 exd4 6 &xd4 &g7 7 &g2, which transposes. Instead 7 &xc6 used to be thought a little better for White, with the seemingly 'natural' recapture 7...bxc6 transposing to a line that more often arises after a different move order which we will consider in Game 14 (see the note there to Black's 7th move). However, the line 7...dxc6! 8 ♕xd8+ &xd8 has recently proved to be a persistent equalizer. For his doubled pawns, Black has very lively piece play: for example, 9 e4 &g4 10 &e2 &xe2 11 &xe2 ♖e8 12 f3 &d7 13 &g5+ &c8 14 ♖ac1 a5 was fine for Black in B.Gulko-V.Kramnik, Novgorod 1995.

5...&g7 6 d4

If White wants to play this move, which avoids transposition to a line of the King's Indian Defence after 6 0-0 0-0 7 d4 d6, he should play it now. Instead 6 ♖b1!? is an interesting sideline, planning to play b4 after either 6...0-0 or 6...d6, followed by transposition to d3 lines, whereas after 6...a5, White reverts to 7 d4 and if 7...d6 8 dxe5 &xe5

9 &xe5 dxe5 10 ♕xd8+ &xd8 11 &e3! he can exploit some surprise dark-square weaknesses.

6...exd4 7 &xd4 0-0 8 0-0

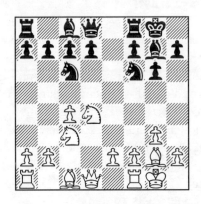

8...♖e8

Black has traded central space for piece activity and must use his pieces well if he is to have any hope of preventing White from consolidating his grip on the centre and using this as a platform to gain more space. Black's rook occupies its natural square on e8, exerting uncomfortable pressure on e4. Other moves have less bite:

a) After 8...&xd4 9 ♕xd4 d6, Black has achieved a simplifying knight exchange but brings White's queen into the game. J.Sunye Neto-C.Martinez, Bogota 1992, continued 10 ♕h4 (Dorfman's 10 ♕d3 ♖e8 11 &g5 is also quite reasonable) 10...&g4 11 ♕xd8 ♖xd8 12 &g5 f6 13 &f4 &e5 14 ♖fd1 &e6 15 b3 ♖ab8 16 &b5 ♖d7 17 &d5 &f7 18 &d4 &xd5 19 cxd5 ♖e8 20 ♖ac1 ♖ee7 21 ♖c2 f5 22 &g5 &f6 23 h4 &g4 24 &e6, with a definite plus.

b) 8...&g4 9 &c2 (9 &xc6!? dxc6 is still solid for Black, but 9 e3 is better)

9...d6 10 ♗d2 a5 11 ♖b1 f5 12 h3 ♘f6 13 ♔h2 ♗e6 14 ♘e3 ♕d7 15 ♘ed5 ♖ae8 16 b3 ♘b4 17 ♘xf6+ ♗xf6 18 e3 ♗g7 19 a3 ♘c6 20 ♘d5, with an edge, was M.Petursson-E.Gausel, Gausdal 1996.

9 ♘c2

White avoids exchanges and plans to move his knight to e3, keeping a clamp on d5. This is more promising than 9 ♘xc6 as White will again find it hard to make real progress in the queenless middlegame after 9...dxc6 10 ♕xd8 ♖xd8.

A better alternative is 9 e3 and then:

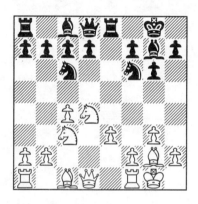

a) 9...♘xd4!? 10 exd4 d6 11 ♗e3 c6 12 h3 ♕b6 13 ♕d2 ♕a6 14 b3 ♗d7 15 ♖fe1 ♖ad8 16 ♗f4 gave White the better chances in V.Iordachescu-N.Kurenkov, Dieren 2005.

b) 9...♘e5?! 10 b3 d6 11 h3 h5 12 ♗b2 c6 13 ♕c2 a5 14 ♖ad1 ♕c7 15 ♗a3, with a plus, was M.Stangl-E.Bacrot, Balatonbereny 1996.

c) White's edge, however, was kept to an absolute minimum in the later V.Filippov-E.Bacrot, Moscow 2004, after 9...♖b8 10 ♘de2 d6 11 b3 ♗f5 12 ♗b2 ♘e4.

9...d6 10 ♘e3

This is currently considered White's best. Instead B.Gelfand-E.Bacrot, 1st matchgame, Albert 2002, saw 10 b3 ♗f5 11 ♗b2 ♘e4 12 ♗xe4 ♗xe4 13 ♘e3 ♘d4 14 ♘xe4 ♖xe4 15 ♕d3 ♕e8 16 ♖ad1 c6 17 ♖d2, and now Gelfand suggests that 17...♕e7! followed by ...♖e8 equalizes. Practice has shown that Black also enjoys sufficient counterplay after 10 e4 ♘e5 11 b3 c6 12 ♗a3 d5!.

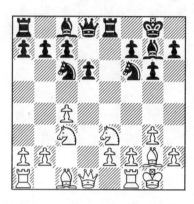

10...♘e5

Black has a sound position, but is a little cramped and it isn't easy to organize a freeing pawn break based on one or other of ...b5, ...d5 or (after e4) ...f5. Thus V.Tichy-S.Kupka, Czech League 1998, saw White retain an edge after 10...a6 11 ♘ed5 h6 12 ♖b1 ♖b8 13 a4 ♘e5 14 b3 ♗e6 15 e4. However, Black fared a little better in D.Johansen-B.Watson, Auckland 2004, in which 10...♘g4!? 11 ♘ed5 ♘ce5 12 h3 ♘h6 13 ♘e4 ♘d7 14 ♗g5 f6 15 ♗d2 ♘f7 16 ♗c3 f5 17 ♗xg7 ♔xg7 18 ♘ec3 c6 19 ♘e3 ♕f6 20 ♕d2 a5 21 ♖ad1 restricted White to at most a minimal edge.

11 b3 ♘fg4 12 ♘xg4 ♗xg4 13 ♗b2

Black has achieved a simplifying minor piece exchange, but faced with two raking bishops and White's continuing control of the central light squares, he still remains short of equality.

13...♕d7 14 ♕d2 ♗h3 15 ♖ad1 a5 16 ♘d5 ♗xg2 17 ♔xg2

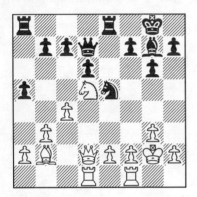

Black has eased his game further by exchanging the light-squared bishops, but White's control of the central light squares guarantees him a continuing advantage.

17...♕c6 18 e4 a4 19 ♗c3

White prevents Black's rook making use of a2 as an entry square and prepares to put further pressure on the long dark-square diagonal with ♕b2. Ribli considers that White might also maintain the pressure after 19 f4, and if 19...♘d7 then 20 ♗xg7 ♔xg7 21 ♕d4+ f6 22 b4.

19...b6 20 ♕b2 f6

Black would not have wished to make this weakening move, but 21 f4 was a threat that had to be parried.

21 ♖fe1 ♖a7 22 ♗d4 ♕a8 23 ♕c3 ♘d7

24 ♕c2 axb3 25 axb3 ♕b7

Black has some potential play down the a-file, but it doesn't diminish White's rather more promising prospects across the rest of the board. Black doesn't achieve much either after 25...♖a2 26 ♕d3, which raises the further uncomfortable possibility of playing ♕f3 with kingside pressure.

26 ♕b2 ♕a8 27 b4

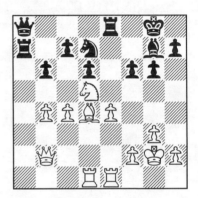

27...c6?!

Increasingly anxious about his lack of activity and the prospect of further space-gaining play by White (b4-b5 by White is an immediate threat), Black gambits a rather doubtful pawn to break the bind. It would probably have been better to sit tight, and wait for White to force matters, in the hope of more tangible counterplay later.

28 ♘xb6 ♘xb6 29 ♗xb6 f5 30 ♕d2 ♖b7 31 ♗a5 fxe4 32 ♕xd6 ♖f7 33 ♕d8!

White has successfully consolidated his extra pawn and now elegantly forces a transition into a clearly better endgame

33...♕xd8 34 ♖xd8 ♖xd8 35 ♗xd8 ♖b7 36 ♖xe4 ♖xb4 37 ♗e7 ♖a4 38 ♗c5 ♖a5

39 ♗e3 ♔f7 40 h4 h6 41 ♔f3 ♖a2 42 c5 ♖c2?!

Now White's rook takes advantage of the a-file to make a decisive penetration to the 7th and 8th ranks. Perhaps 42...♖a8 puts up the most resistance.

43 ♖a4 ♔e6 44 ♖a8 ♗f6 45 ♖c8 ♔d7 46 ♖g8 1-0

Game 10
M.Kobalia-A.Karpatchev
*Russian Championship,
Elista 2001*

---

1 c4 e5 2 ♘c3 ♘f6 3 ♘f3 ♘c6 4 g3 d5 5 cxd5 ♘xd5 6 ♗g2

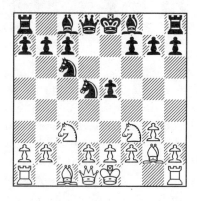

6...♘b6

Delaying ...♘b6 only encourages White to play for an advantageous d4-break in the centre. If instead Black plays ...♘xc3, White recaptures with his b-pawn obtaining an extra centre pawn. Thus White should be happy to see:

a) 6...♗e6 7 0-0 ♗e7 8 d4! gives White an edge and now:

a1) 8...exd4 9 ♘xd4

9...♘xc3 (note that 9...♘xd4?! 10 ♕xd4 ♘xc3 11 ♕xc3 loses material after either 11...♗f6 12 ♕b4 ♖b8 13 ♗xb7 or 11...0-0 12 ♗xb7 ♖b8 13 ♗f3 ♖b5 14 ♕c6 ♕b8 15 b3, with advantage in M.Marin-J.Skjoldborg, Stockholm 2001) 10 bxc3 ♘xd4 11 cxd4 c6 12 ♖b1 ♕d7 13 ♕c2 0-0 14 ♗f4 ♖ac8 15 ♖fc1 ♗a3 16 ♖d1 ♕e7 17 ♗e4 h6 18 ♖d3 b5 19 ♖c3 ♗c4 20 ♗h7+ ♔h8 21 ♖e3 ♗e6 22 ♗f5, and White stood well in the game L.Christiansen-E.Handoko, Surakarta 1982.

a2) 8...♘xc3 9 bxc3 e4 10 ♘d2 f5 11 e3 (White gained an endgame pull after 11 ♖b1 ♖b8 12 ♕a4 0-0 13 f3 exf3 14 ♗xf3 ♗d5 15 ♗xd5+ ♕xd5 16 ♖b5 ♕d7 17 ♕b3+ ♔h8 18 ♕d5 ♕xd5 19 ♖xd5 g6 20 e4 in L.Psakhis-A.Scetinin, Leeuwarden 1993) 11...0-0 12 c4 ♘b4 13 ♖b1 b6 14 ♗b2 a5 15 ♗a1 ♘xa2 16 f3 exf3 17 ♕xf3 ♗b4 18 ♖f2 ♕e7 19 ♕d1 ♘c3 20 ♗xc3 ♗xc3 21 ♗xa8 ♖xa8 22 ♘f3 was G. Kasparov-V.Korchnoi, Paris (rapid) 1990, and while Black drew, I suspect that Korchnoi would not have risked playing this line against Kasparov at classical time rates!

b) 6...♗e7?! is tactically suspect. J.Pribyl-Z.Rousar, Chrudim 2004, continued 7 ♘xe5! ♘xc3 8 ♗xc6+ bxc6 9 dxc3 ♛xd1+ 10 ♔xd1 ♗b7 11 ♗e3 c5 12 ♖e1 f6 13 ♘f3 ♔f7 14 ♘d2, and White won.

c) 6...♗c5!? is more interesting, but the attempt to play an aggressive anti-Dragon system a tempo down is risky: for example, 7 0-0 ♗e6 8 ♘xe5 (8 d3 ♘xc3 9 bxc3 ♗e7 10 ♖b1 is also good for White) 8...♗xf2+ 9 ♖xf2 ♘xe5 10 d4 ♘g4 11 ♖f3 0-0 12 e4 ♘xc3 13 bxc3 c6 14 ♛f1 h6 15 e5 ♘d5 16 ♖f4 ♗xg2 17 ♛xg2, gave White a strong attack in G.Serper-S.Turmo, Sioux Falls 1998.

d) 6...♘xc3 is better, leading after 7 bxc3 e4 8 ♘g1 f5 to another aggressive reversed anti-Dragon system.

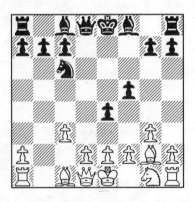

White has three good responses, including the 9 ♘h3 ♗d6 10 0-0 ♗e6 11 d3 of D.Hoppenstein-B.Hanison, correspondence 2004, Tal's simple 9 d3 exd3 10 exd3 ♗e6 11 ♘f3 ♗e7 12 0-0, and 9 f3!? exf3 (B.Larsen-J.Timman, Bled 1979 varied with 9...e3, but 10 dxe3 ♛xd1+ 11 ♔xd1 ♗e6 12 ♘h3 0-0-0+ 13 ♔c2 ♗c4 14 ♘f4 g6 15 ♘d3 ♗g7 16 e4 fxe4 17 fxe4 ♘e5 18 ♘xe5 ♗xe5 19 ♗f3, maintained a slight advantage) 10 ♘xf3 ♗d6 11 d4 0-0 12 0-0 ♔h8 13 c4 (13 ♗g5!? ♛e8 14 ♛d3 h6 15 ♗f4 ♗d7 16 ♖ae1 is also possible) 13...♗d7 14 ♔h1, with good attacking prospects in C.McNab-R.Vujatovic, Edinburgh 2003.

Returning to the prudent 6...♘b6:

7 0-0

White can also hyper-accelerate a3 or ♖b1 by playing them on this move. This probably has no more than transpositional effect, except in the rarely played line 7 ♖b1 g6!? when N.Miezis-T.Bromann, Copenhagen 2004, continued 8 d3 ♗g7 9 ♗g5 ♘e7 10 ♛c1 h6 11 ♗d2 c6 12 b4 ♗e6 13 0-0 f5 14 a4 g5 15 b5 c5 16 ♘e1 ♖b8 17 a5 ♘d7 18 b6 axb6 19 axb6 ♘xb6 20 ♘b5 ♘bc8 21 ♛xc5, with a pull.

7...♗e7

Against 7...g6!? White replies 8 b3, and if 8...♗g7 9 ♗a3 looks interesting, while 8 d3 is, of course, also good. So too was 8 a4 a5 9 d3 ♗g7 10 ♗g5 ♘e7 (or 10...f6 11 ♗e3 0-0 12 d4 exd4 13 ♘xd4 ♘xd4 14 ♗xd4, with an edge in L.Psakhis-E.Ermenkov, Groningen

1990) 11 ♕c1 h6 12 ♗d2 c6 13 e4!? ♘d7 14 ♗e3 ♘f8 15 ♖d1 ♘e6 16 ♘e2 ♘d4 17 ♘exd4 exd4 18 ♗d2 ♗e6 19 b4!? axb4 20 ♗xb4 ♗b3 21 ♖e1 ♖xa4 22 ♖xa4 ♗xa4 23 ♕a3, with good play in A.Kharlov-A.Morozevich, Elista 1995.

8 ♖b1

Increasingly White delays d3 as long as possible, hoping to extract as much advantage as possible from early play on the queenside. Games 11 and 12 examine White's most popular way to do this, by playing 8 a3, with the idea of an immediate b4. White also plays 8 ♖b1 with b4 in mind due to a tactical justification.

8...g5!?

This aggressive response is playable but clearly burns a few positional boats. If Black achieves nothing concrete on the kingside – and it's clearly not at all easy to get at White's king – he could suffer badly for the gaping gaps he has created close to his own king. Black usually prefers caution with 8...0-0. Many players are now content to steer for transposition into solid lines considered in Game 11 after

8...0-0 9 b4 a6 10 a3, but there are also plenty of independent options after 8 ♖b1:

a) 8...0-0 9 b4 and now:

a1) White's last is tactically justified by the line 9...♘xb4?! 10 ♘xe5 c6 11 a3 ♘4d5 12 ♘xd5, establishing a healthy pawn centre. G.Kasparov-J.Timman, Wijk aan Zee 2001, continued 12...cxd5 13 a4 ♗f6 14 d4 ♗f5 15 ♖b5 a6 16 ♖b2 ♖c8, and now Kasparov recommends 17 g4! ♗e4 (or 17...♗xe5?! 18 dxe5 ♗xg4? 19 ♕d4) 18 f3 ♗g6 19 ♘xg6 hxg6 20 e3 ♖e8 21 f4 ♘c4 22 ♖b3, with good chances.

a2) Black should also avoid 9...♗xb4?! 10 ♘xe5 ♘xe5 11 ♖xb4 which gives White a good centre and the bishop-pair.

a3) Black usually plays 9...a6...

...after which 10 a4!? (rather than transpose with 10 a3 to our next game – to note 'c1' to Black's 9th move after 10...♗e6 11 d3 f5 or to note 'b' to Black's 11th following 10...f6 11 d3 ♗e6 – with White perhaps able to claim a minor gain as reaching the positions with a3 and b4 this way cuts out lines based on ...a7-a5 in one move) 10...♘xb4 (10...♗f5 11 b5 axb5 12 axb5 ♘d4 13 d3 is another possibility) 11 ♘xe5 a5 allows Black to secure his knight firmly on b4, with equal chances. M.Kobalia-S.Tiviakov, Linares 1998, continued 12 d4 c6 13 f4!? c5! with good play for Black.

b) Black's most radical reply is the ambitious 8...♗e6 9 b4 e4!? (9...♘xb4?! 10 ♘xe5 ♘xa2 11 ♗xb7 ♘xc3 12 dxc3 ♕xd1 13 ♖xd1 ♖d8 14 ♗c6+ ♔f8 15 ♗a3 ♗d6 16 ♗f3 is better for White — Romanishin) 10 ♘xe4 ♗xa2.

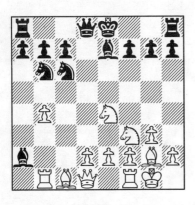

L.Aronian-A.Naiditsch, Mainz (rapid) 2005, continued in some style with 11 ♖a1 ♘xb4 12 ♗b2 f5!? (or 12...♗d5!? 13 ♘d4 0-0 14 ♘f5, with good attacking prospects) 13 ♗xg7 fxe4 14 ♗xh8 exf3 15 ♗xf3 ♗d5 16 e4 ♗f7 17 d4 c6 18 ♗h5 ♕d6 19 ♖a5 ♗xh5 20 ♕xh5+ ♕g6 21 ♕h3 ♘c4 22 ♖f5 a5 23 d5 a4 24 ♗c3 a3 25 ♖h5 a2 26 ♖xh7 ♘c2 27 ♖g7 ♕d6 28 dxc6 bxc6 29 ♕h5+ ♔d7, and now 30 e5! wins, as pointed out in *Schach Magazin 64*.

c) 8...f6 is playable, but Black must be prepared for the double-edged 9 d4!? (White side-stepped the challenge with 9 a3 ♗e6 10 b4 0-0 11 d3 in L.Aronian-A.Khalifman, Sochi 2005, transposing into Game 11; instead M.Kobalia-E.Solozhenkin, St Petersburg 1998, saw 9 b4!? ♘xb4 10 d4 ♗f5 11 ♖b2 ♘c6 12 ♘h4 ♗d7 13 dxe5 fxe5 14 ♘f3 0-0 15 ♘d5, and now Kobalia recommended 15...♗e6, with good chances for Black), after which 9...exd4 10 ♘b5

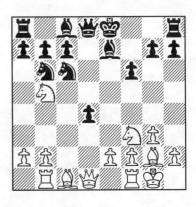

10...♗f5 11 ♗f4 ♖c8 12 ♖c1 d3 13 exd3 ♘d5!? 14 ♘fd4 ♘xf4 15 ♘xf5 ♘xg2 16 ♖xc6 bxc6 17 ♘xa7 ♕d5 18 ♘xc8 ♕xf5 19 ♘xe7 ♔xe7 20 ♔xg2 ♕d5+ 21 ♔g1 ♕xa2 22 ♖e1+ ♔d8 23 ♕g4 ♖g8 24 ♕e4 ♕d5 25 ♕xh7 saw White win in A.Khalifman-S.Tiviakov, Linares 1995, although Khalifman was later prepared to defend this line for Black.

d) 8...a5 prevents b4, but it weakens b5 and the defence of Black's knight on b6. Its robustness may depend on an evaluation of Kiril Georgiev's recommendation 9 d3 0-0 (or 9...♗e6 10 ♗e3 ♘d5 11 ♘xd5 ♗xd5 12 ♕a4 0-0 and now 13 a3 f6 14 ♖bc1 ♖f7 15 ♕b5 a4! was balanced in V.Zvjaginsev-

A.Kharlov, Krasnoyarsk 2003, but 13 ♖bc1!?, and if 13...f6 14 ♖fd1, may be better) 10 ♗e3 ♗e6 11 ♗xb6 cxb6 12 ♕a4! (L.Aronian-V.Topalov, Wijk aan Zee 2007, and A.Kosten-S.Haslinger, British League 2006, continued respectively 12 e3 and 12 ♘d2 but after 12...b5 in both cases, Black equalized).

White now rapidly mobilized his central pawns in G.Kasparov-N.Faulks, London simul 2003, which continued 12...f6 13 ♖fd1 ♕e8 14 e3 ♕f7 15 d4 exd4 16 exd4 ♘b4 17 d5 ♗f5 18 d6 ♗xd6 19 ♖xd6 ♗xb1 20 ♘xb1 and White won.

Returning to the ambitious 8...g5!?:

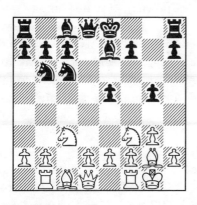

9 d3

Now 9 b4!? g4! 10 ♘e1 ♘xb4 is an unclear gambit. A.Khalifman-C.Lutz, FIDE World Championship, New Delhi 2000, continued 11 ♘c2 ♘c6 (White gained an attack after 11...♘xc2 12 ♕xc2 0-0 13 a4 c6 14 d3 ♘d7 15 ♗h6 ♖e8 16 f4 in A.Kosten-M.Godard, French League 2001) 12 ♗xc6+ bxc6 13 d4 f6 14 dxe5!? ♕xd1 15 ♖xd1 fxe5 16 ♗a3 a5 17 ♗xe7 ♔xe7 18 ♘e1 ♗a6 19 ♘d3 ♗xd3 20 exd3 ♖hd8 21 ♘e4 ♘d5 22 ♖bc1, with compensation.

9...h5

Black aims to establish a knight on d4. Alternatively:

a) 9...g4 10 ♘e1 h5 11 ♘c2 drives White's knight to an excellent square for the counterattack. J.Hodgson-E.Bareev, Belgrade 1993, continued 11...h4 12 b4 hxg3 13 fxg3 ♘xb4? 14 ♘xb4 ♕d4+ 15 e3 ♕xc3 16 ♘d5 ♘xd5 17 ♗xd5 ♗e6...

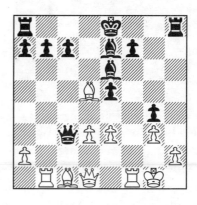

...and now Bareev considers that 18 ♕a4+ would have virtually refuted Black's ambitious play.

b) 9...♗e6 10 ♗e3 g4 11 ♘d2 is also less convincing than the text move, as

Black's pawn on b7 is undefended and b4 looms.

10 ♗e3

Stronger than 10 a3 h4 11 b4 hxg3 12 hxg3, as in G.Serper-V.Korchnoi, Groningen 1993, and now Korchnoi gives 12...♕d6! with good play for Black.

10...g4

Korchnoi's notes also mention 10...f5 11 d4 e4 (or 11...f4 12 d5 fxe3 13 dxc6 exf2+ 14 ♔h1) 12 ♘e5 ♘xe5 13 dxe5 ♕xd1 14 ♖fxd1 c6, and White stands better.

11 ♘d2 ♘d4 12 ♘c4!

White improves over the 12 ♖c1?! h4 13 ♘c4 ♘xc4 14 dxc4 c6 15 ♕d3 f5! of N.Miezis-I.Smirin, New York 1998.

12...♘xc4 13 dxc4 c6

It's hard to say whether Black's extended kingside pawns are a source of strength or weakness. At present Black's knight on d4 holds his position together, but White can hope to undermine it and develop his own counterplay on the queenside.

14 b4 ♗f5 15 ♖b2 ♘c2?!

This is an important moment. Ribli suggests that Black's knight should not

lightly give up its strong post on d4 and his preferred 15...h4!? looks better.

16 ♕xd8+

This exchange is good enough, but Ribli's even more active suggestion 16 ♗c5!?, and if 16...♕xd1 (or 16...♗xc5 17 bxc5) 17 ♖xd1, may give White a substantive pull.

16...♖xd8 17 ♗xa7 ♘xb4

Black didn't have an easy choice between this and 17...♘a3 18 ♗b6 ♖a8 19 e4 ♘xc4 20 ♖e2 ♘xb6 21 exf5. White has good prospects in both cases.

18 a3 ♖a8 19 axb4 ♖xa7 20 b5 ♗d7 21 bxc6 bxc6 22 ♖b8+ ♗d8 23 ♘e4

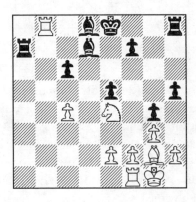

White's active pieces and slightly better pawns provide ample compensation for Black's bishop-pair. Given the simplified nature of the position, the game seems on its way to a draw, but it's Black who needs to take just a little more care, mainly because of his rather uncomfortable king position.

23...♔e7 24 ♘c5 ♖h6 25 ♗e4 ♗c7 26 ♘xd7 ♔xd7 27 ♖g8 ♔d6 28 ♖d1+ ♔c5 29 ♖c8 ♗b6 30 ♖b1 ♗c7 31 ♖d1 ♔xc4?!

Black's errant king estranged from

his weakened kingside pawns continues to cause some anxiety on Karpatchev's part. Having opposite-coloured bishops on the board is a mixed blessing as Black's h- and g-pawns are uncomfortably situated on vulnerable light squares. Here 31...♗b6 hoping to repeat the position might have been best.

32 ♖d7 ♗b6 33 ♖xa7 ♗xa7 34 ♗xc6 ♖f6 35 e3 ♔d3 36 ♗d5

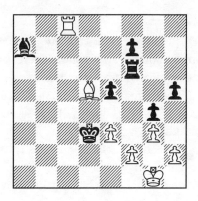

36...h4?

This rush of blood to the head loses. Black can probably still draw with 36...♗b6 and if 37 ♖f8 (or 37 ♖h8 ♔e2 38 ♗c4+ ♔e1 39 ♖xh5 ♖xf2 40 ♖xe5 ♖f3) 37...♖d6 38 ♗xf7 ♖f6 39 ♖b8 ♖xf7 40 ♖xb6 ♔e4 41 ♔g2 ♔f5.

37 gxh4 ♖h6 38 ♗xf7 ♖xh4 39 ♗e6 ♔e4 40 ♖c4+ ♔d3 41 ♖a4

Not, of course, 41 ♖xg4? ♖xg4+ 42 ♗xg4 ♗xe3! 43 fxe3 ♔xe3 44 h4 ♔f4, and draws. White must take Black's g-pawn with his bishop.

41...♗c5 42 ♗xg4 ♗xe3 43 fxe3 ♔xe3 44 ♔g2 e4 45 ♔g3 ♖h8 46 h4 ♖h7 47 h5 ♖h8 48 ♖a1 ♖f8 49 ♔h4 ♖g8 50 h6 ♔f4 51 ♖f1+ 1-0

---

1 c4 e5 2 ♘c3 ♘f6 3 ♘f3 ♘c6 4 g3 d5 5 cxd5 ♘xd5 6 ♗g2 ♘b6 7 0-0 ♗e7 8 a3

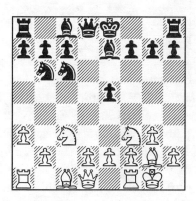

8...0-0

Black gains no advantage from delaying castling:

a) 8...♗e6 9 b4 a5 (White has a minimal edge after 9...♘d4!? 10 ♖b1 ♘xf3+ 11 ♗xf3 c6 12 b5 ♖c8 13 bxc6 bxc6 14 d3 0-0 15 ♗b2, P.Dittmar-O.Romanishin, Saint Vincent 2004) 10 b5 ♘d4 11 ♖b1 a4?! (better is 11...♘xf3+, although 12 ♗xf3 ♘d5 13 ♗b2 0-0 14 a4 f6 15 d4! ♘xc3 16 ♗xc3 exd4 17 ♕xd4 ♕xd4 18 ♗xd4 ♖ad8 19 e3, maintained a pull in N.McDonald-O.Jakobsen, Budapest 2003) 12 ♘xe5 f6 (12...♗b3?! allowing 13 ♖xb3 is just bad) 13 ♘d3 ♖a7 14 ♘f4 ♗f7 15 e3 ♘b3 16 d4, with an extra pawn was Y.Yakovich-J.Hector, Koge 1997.

b) White is also comfortably placed after 8...a5 9 d3 ♗e6 10 ♗e3 ♘d5 11 ♘xd5 ♗xd5 12 ♕a4.

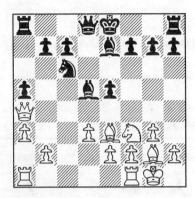

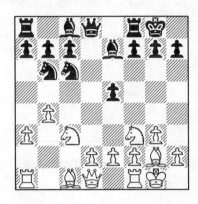

H.Gretarsson-B.Thorfinnsson, Reykjavik 2005, continued 12...0-0 13 ♖ac1 ♖e8 14 ♕b5 ♗f8 15 ♘g5 ♗xg2 16 ♔xg2 ♖b8 17 ♕c4 ♕f6 18 f4 h6 19 ♘e4 ♕e6 20 ♕xe6 ♖xe6 21 f5 ♖ee8 22 f6 g6 23 ♖c4, with a bind.

c) After 8...f5 9 d3 ♗f6, White's most ambitious reply is 10 e4!?. K.Georgiev-V.Korchnoi, Sarajevo 1998, continued 10...0-0 11 b4 a6 (or 11...♔h8 12 ♗b2 ♗e6 13 exf5 ♗xf5 14 ♘e4, with an edge in F.Olafsson-J.Donner, Bled 1961) 12 ♗e3 (12 ♗b2!? is also possible) 12...♘d4 13 ♖c1 ♔h8 14 ♘e2 fxe4 15 dxe4 ♗g4!? 16 ♗xd4 exd4 17 e5 ♗xf3 18 ♗xf3 ♗g5 19 ♗xb7 d3 20 ♘f4 ♗xf4 21 gxf4 ♖b8 22 ♗xa6 ♖xf4 23 ♕xd3 ♕g5+ 24 ♔h1 ♕xe5 25 ♖c5, and White won.

d) 8...g5?! leads after 9 b4 g4 10 ♘e1 h5 (or 10...f5) to unclear and double-edged play. However, C.Matamoros Franco-B.Thorfinnsson, Reykjavik 2006, saw the much stronger 9 d4! exd4 10 ♘b5 ♗f6!? 11 ♗xg5! ♗xg5 12 ♘xg5 ♗g4 13 ♕d2! 0-0 14 ♕f4 ♗xe2 15 ♖fe1 ♗h5 16 ♗xc6 bxc6 17 ♘xd4 c5 18 ♘f5, and White won.

9 b4

9...♗e6

This move, followed by ...f6, is popular, sound and solid. There are also the following possibilities:

a) Black's main alternative is 9...♖e8, preparing ...♗f8, which will be seen in Game 12.

b) 9...f6 10 d3 ♗e6 transposes to the main game after 11 ♖b1 or to variation 'c' of the notes to White's 10th move, below.

c) The ultra-defensive 9...a6 strictly isn't necessary and is rare. After 10 d3 ♗e6, White has several good options:

c1) White can play 11 ♖b1, transposing into lines that can also arise after 8 ♖b1. I.Rausis-M.Nielsen, Dianalund 2005, continued 11...f5 (the more solid 11...f6 is note 'b' to Black's 11th move, below) 12 ♘a4 (also promising is 12 ♗b2, after which 12...♗f6 13 ♘d2 ♕e7 14 ♘b3 ♖ad8 15 ♘c5 ♗c8 16 e4, gave White an edge in N.Miezis-I.Starostits, Riga 2006) 12...♘xa4 13 ♕xa4 ♗d5 14 ♗b2 ♗f6 15 ♕c2 ♔h8 16 ♖bc1 ♖c8 17 ♖fd1 ♕e8 18 ♕c5 ♖d8 19 e4 ♗b3 20 ♖d2 ♗e6 21 ♘xe5 ♘xe5 22 ♗xe5 ♗xe5 23 ♕xe5, and White won.

c2) 11 ♗b2 f5 12 ♖c1 (12 ♘a4!?, and if 12...♘xa4 13 ♕xa4 ♗f6 14 b5 axb5 15 ♕xb5, also looks better for White) 12...♗f6 13 ♘d2 ♕e8 14 ♘b3 ♖d8 15 ♘c5 ♗c8 was D.Rogozenko-D.Tjiam, Dutch League 2000, and now 16 ♖e1 may be best.

10 ♖b1

By covering b3, White makes b5 a real threat, attacking e5 and restricting Black's options. The older move 10 d3 (although this used to be played mostly on move 8) isn't forcing, but it remains a sound developing move and a serious test. After 10 d3, both players can choose from a wide variety of possible plans:

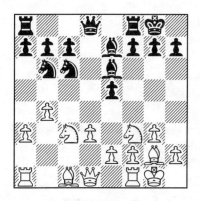

a) One of Black's best tries is the energetic 10...a5 11 b5 ♘d4, which loosens up White's queenside and develops Black's knight on its strongest square. It may simply transpose to variation 'a' in the note to Black's 11th move in the main game after 12 ♖b1. However, the game D.Navara-G.Timoscenko, Czech League 2004, continued 12 ♘d2!? (note too the fiendish trap 12 ♗b2 f6 13 ♘d2, when Black is lost after both 13...♘d5?

14 ♗xd5 ♗xd5 15 e3 and 13...♗d5? 14 ♘xd5 ♘xd5 15 e3 ♘e6 16 ♕b3) 12...c6 13 bxc6 ♘xc6 14 ♖b1 a4 (or 14...♖c8 15 ♗b2) 15 ♗xc6 bxc6 16 ♕c2 ♕c7 17 ♗b2 ♖fc8 18 ♘ce4 c5!? 19 ♗xe5 ♕xe5 20 ♖xb6 c4 21 dxc4 ♗xa3 22 ♖fb1 ♗f5 23 ♖6b5, and White won.

b) Black can also play 10...♘d4. The game M.Gurevich-R.Swinkels, Gibraltar 2007, continued 11 ♗b2 (11 ♖b1 and 11 ♘d2 are also possible) 11...♘xf3+ 12 ♗xf3 c6 13 ♕c2 f6 14 ♘e4 ♕e8 15 ♘c5 ♗xc5 16 bxc5 ♘d5 17 d4 exd4 18 ♗xd4 ♕f7 19 ♖ab1 ♖fd8 20 e3, with a slight pull.

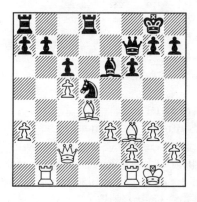

c) After 10...f6 White can transpose into the main game with 11 ♖b1. Instead W.Uhlmann-W.Rosen, Dresden 2003, continued 11 ♗e3 ♘d4!? (11...a5 12 b5 ♘d4 might be better) 12 ♗xd4 exd4 13 ♘b5 c5 14 bxc5 ♗xc5 15 ♖c1 a6 16 ♖xc5 axb5 17 ♖xb5 ♖xa3 18 ♖b4, and White won.

d) 10...f5!? 11 ♗b2 (11 ♗e3 is also good, but not 11 b5 ♘d4 12 ♘xe5? ♗f6 13 f4 ♘b3) 11...♗f6 12 ♘d2 ♘d5!? 13 ♘a4 b6 (N.Spiridonov-M.Drtina, Trnava 1987, had previously gone

13...♗f7!? 14 ♘c5 b6 15 ♘cb3 ♘d4, and now 16 e3 ♘xb3 17 ♘xb3 looks a shade better for White) 14 ♖c1 ♕d7 15 ♘c3 ♖ad8 16 ♘xd5 ♗xd5 17 ♗xd5+ ♕xd5 18 ♕b3 e4 19 ♗xf6 ♖xf6 20 dxe4 fxe4 21 ♕xd5+ ♖xd5 22 ♘xe4, and White won in T.Tao-S.Solomon, Melbourne 1993.

Returning to the modern continuation 10 ♖b1:

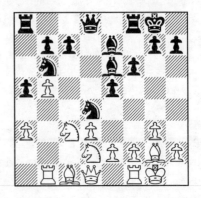

10...f6 11 d3

Natural development is best. White can seek unusual positions with 11 ♘e4!?, but this move has largely fallen into disuse because Black is equal after 11...♗a2 12 ♖b2 ♗d5.

11...♘d4

Occupying d4 is one of Black's main ideas in this system. Black won't give ground in the centre without a fight. The same idea is also critical after first disturbing the queenside. Thus we also have:

a) 11...a5 12 b5 ♘d4 should be met by 13 ♘d2, avoiding exchanges and intending to reactivate White's knight after evicting Black's knight from its strong central outpost by playing e3. Black now has the following options:

a1) The main focus recently has been on the line 13...♕c8 14 e3 ♘f5, after which White has three main choices: 15 ♕e2, 15 ♕c2 and 15 a4!?. In each case, White generally seeks to play f4, opening up play in the centre and down the half-open f-file. If White can then mobilize his centre pawns, he can hope to advance them gradually and develop a spatial advantage:

a11) After 15 ♕e2 ♘d6 (E.Bareev-Y.Yakovich, Kazan 2005, had previously gone 15...a4 16 ♗b2 ♘d6 17 f4 exf4!? 18 ♖xf4 c6 19 bxc6 bxc6 20 ♘f3 c5 21 ♘d2 ♖a7 22 ♗a1 ♕a6 23 e4, with a rough balance, but 16 ♘c4 may better, as indicated by John Watson) 16 a4!? ♗g4! 17 f3 ♗e6 18 f4 ♘f7, Black can occupy b4 with reasonable chances. E.Bareev-A.Shirov, Poikovsky 2006, continued 19 ♘b3 ♗b4 20 ♕c2 ♗h3 21 ♘e4 ♗xg2 22 ♔xg2 f5 23 ♘f2 ♕e6 24 e4 ♘xa4 25 ♘xa5 ♗xa5 26 ♕xa4 ♗b6 27 ♕b3 ♕xb3 28 ♖xb3, with an eventual draw.

a12) Following 15 ♕c2 ♖d8 16 ♖d1 (L.Van Wely-S.Tiviakov, Hilversum 2006, varied with 16 ♗b2 ♘h6 17 ♖fd1

♘f7 18 ♖bc1 ♗f8, and now 19 a4, and if 19...♗b4 20 ♘ce4, may improve for White), White pursued a policy of queenside and central development in M.Marin-D.Komljenovic, Benasque 2005...

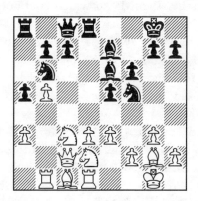

...which continued 16...♔h8 17 a4 ♘d5 18 ♘xd5 ♗xd5 19 ♗xd5 ♖xd5 20 ♗b2 ♗b4 21 ♘f3, with a slight pull.

a13) 15 a4!?, though a useful move, may reveal White's hand a bit early. Black targeted b4 and achieved a roughly balanced, if slightly unclear position after 15...♖d8 16 ♕c2 ♖b8 17 ♖d1 c6 18 bxc6 bxc6 in K.Georgiev-M.Gurevich, French League 2001.

a2) 13...c6?! 14 e3 ♘xb5 15 ♘xb5 cxb5 16 ♖xb5 ♘d5 17 ♗b2 ♖b8 18 d4 exd4 19 ♗xd4 b6 20 ♕h5 with a clear advantage, M.Marin-D.Smerdon, Turin Olympiad 2006.

a3) White also achieved a pull in C.Bauer-A.Karpatchev, Metz 2006, after 13...♗d5 14 ♘de4 a4 (promising too was 14...♗f7 15 e3 ♘e6 16 f4 f5 17 ♘f2 exf4 18 gxf4 ♖b8 19 ♔h1 c5 20 bxc6 bxc6 21 ♕c2, in L.Aronian-A.Khalifman, Sochi 2005) 15 ♘xd5

♘xd5 16 e3 f5 17 exd4 fxe4 18 ♕g4 exd4 19 ♗b2 ♘c3 20 ♗xe4 ♘xe4 21 ♕xe4 b6 22 ♖bc1 ♗c5 23 ♖c4.

b) 11...a6 is a less active approach and allows White to hope for a pull. N.Miezis-M.Nezar, Montpellier 2003, continued 12 ♘e4 ♗a2 13 ♖b2 ♗d5 14 ♘c5 ♖b8 15 e4 ♗f7 16 ♗e3

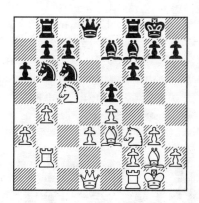

16...♗d6 (or 16...♘d7 17 ♘b3 ♗d6 18 ♕c2 ♕e7 19 ♘c5 ♗xc5 20 bxc5 ♘a7 21 ♖fb1 ♘b5 22 ♖a1 ♗h5 23 ♘h4 ♘d4 24 ♗xd4 exd4 25 ♖c1 ♘e5 26 f4, with good chances in N.Miezis-V.Tukmakov, Geneva 2002) 17 ♕c2 ♕e8 18 ♖c1 ♘d8 19 ♘h4 ♘c8 20 ♘f5 ♘e7 21 ♕d2 ♗e6 22 ♘h4 ♗c8 23 d4 b6 24 ♘d3 a5 25 dxe5 fxe5 26 bxa5, and White won.

c) 11...♕d7 12 ♘e4 ♘d5 13 ♕c2 a6 (worse is 13...b6?! 14 ♗b2 ♖ac8 15 ♖bc1 ♘d4 16 ♗xd4 exd4 17 ♕c6 ♕xc6 18 ♖xc6 ♗d7 19 ♘xd4 ♗xc6 20 ♘xc6 ♖ce8 21 ♖c1 f5 22 ♘d2 ♘f6 23 ♘xa7, and White won in A.Karpov-J.Hjartarson, Seattle 1989) 14 ♗b2 ♖fd8 15 ♖fc1 ♗f8 16 ♘fd2 ♕f7 was Y.Yakovich-A.Gabrielian, Voronezh 2006, and now 17 ♘c5, and if 17...♗c8 18 ♘db3, gives White a pull.

d) 11...♕e8 12 ♘d2 (12 ♗e3 and 12 ♘e4 are also good) 12...♕f7 13 ♘b3 ♖ab8 14 ♕c2 ♖fd8 15 ♗xc6 bxc6 16 ♘a5 ♕e8 17 ♗d2 f5 18 ♖fc1 ♖d6 19 b5, with good chances was another thematic encounter in V.Ivanchuk-J.Timman, Tilburg 1990.

e) 11...♘d5!? 12 ♕c2 (12 ♘e4 and 12 ♗b2 are also good) 12...♘xc3 13 ♕xc3 ♕d7 14 ♗e3 ♗d5 15 ♖fc1 ♗d6 16 ♗c5 ♖fc8 17 ♘d2 ♗xg2 18 ♔xg2 ♘e7 19 ♘e4 ♔h8 20 d4 b6 21 ♖d1 saw White advancing in the centre with advantage in Z.Azmaiparashvili-L.B.Hansen, Amsterdam 1989.

Returning to 11...♘d4:

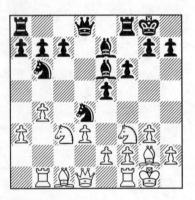

12 ♘d2!

As in the same position with pawns on a5 and b5, White does best to avoid an immediate knight exchange: for example, M.Suba-E.Bareev, Chalkidiki 2002, saw 12 ♗b2 ♘xf3+ 13 ♗xf3 c6 14 ♗a1 ♖f7 15 a4 a5 16 bxa5 ♖xa5, with balanced chances.

12...c6

Black usually plays either this move or 12...♘d5. Against both White can play for a modest pull, based on his slightly better pawns, extra centre pawn and queenside space. After 12...♘d5 13 ♗b2 (13 ♘de4, and if 13...f5 14 ♘xd5 ♗xd5 15 ♘c3 ♗xg2 16 ♔xg2, is also possible), White developed an initiative in Z.Azmaiparashvili-K.Aseev, Lvov 1990, which continued 13...♘xc3 (or 13...c6 14 ♘xd5 ♗xd5 15 ♗xd5+ ♕xd5 16 ♗xd4 ♕xd4 17 ♕b3+ ♔h8 18 ♖fc1 ♖fd8 19 a4 ♕d5 20 b5, with a slight advantage in K.Lerner-K.Aseev, St Petersburg 1993) 14 ♗xc3 c6 15 ♗xd4 ♕xd4 16 ♘b3 ♕d7 17 ♘c5 ♗xc5 18 bxc5 ♗d5 19 ♕c2 ♖f7 20 ♖b4 ♖d8 21 ♖fb1 ♗xg2 22 ♔xg2 ♕d5+ 23 ♔g1 ♖dd7 24 ♖1b3 ♖fe7 25 ♖c3 g6 26 ♕c1 ♕f7 27 e4 ♕e8 28 ♖cb3 ♕d8 29 ♕b1 ♕a5 30 ♕c2 ♕d8 31 ♖a4 a6 32 ♕b1, and White won.

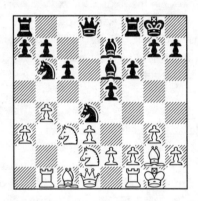

13 ♘de4

White increases his control of c5 and retains the option of e3. White also made progress after the immediate 13 e3!? in D.Contin-R.Zelcic, Saint Vincent 2004, which continued 13...♘b5 (or 13...♘f5 14 ♘b3 ♘d5 15 ♕c2 ♘xc3 16 ♕xc3 ♔h8 17 ♗b2 ♕d7 18 ♖fd1 ♖fd8 19 ♘c5, with a plus in B.Damljanovic-

P.Popovic, Novi Sad 2002) 14 ♕c2 ♘xc3 15 ♕xc3 ♗d5 16 e4 ♗a2 17 ♖a1 ♗e6 18 ♘b3 ♕c8 19 a4 ♚h8 20 ♘c5, with definite pressure.

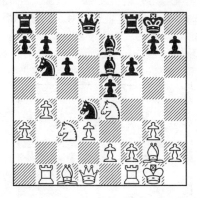

13...♘d5

Black recentralizes, prepares to exchange his offside knight, and defuses any immediate threat of ♘c5. He has also occasionally tried other moves:

a) 13...♖f7 14 e3 (14 ♘c5 ♗xc5 15 bxc5 ♘d5 achieves little) 14...♘b5!? 15 ♘xb5 (quieter play is also possible: B.Zueger-O.Cvitan, Turin Olympiad 2006, continued 15 ♗b2 ♘xc3 16 ♗xc3 ♕d7, and now 17 ♕c2 ♘d5 18 ♗a1 looks slightly better for White) 15...cxb5 16 ♗b2 ♘a4 17 ♗a1 ♖c8 (the sharper 17...f5!? 18 ♘c5 ♘xc5 19 bxc5 ♕d7?! 20 ♗xe5 saw White win in Y.Yakovich-A.Demianjuk, Salekhard 2006) 18 d4, with an edge was E.Bareev-R.Ponomariov, Moscow (rapid) 2002.

b) 13...♗g4!? 14 ♗e3 (White might also try 14 h3 ♗h5 – or 14...♗e6 15 e3 – 15 g4 ♗f7 16 e3) 14...♘d7 15 ♕d2 ♚h8 16 h3 ♗h5 17 f4 f5 18 ♘g5 h6 19 ♘f3 ♘xf3+ 20 ♗xf3 ♕e8 21 ♗g2 exf4 22 ♗xf4 ♗f6 23 e4 fxe4 24 ♘xe4 ♗e5 25

♖be1, with an edge, K.Georgiev-A.Kharlov, Niksic 1996.

14 ♗b2 ♗f7!?

Black plays a waiting game, but White's reply secures good chances. So too did 14...b6 15 e3 ♘f5 16 ♕f3 ♕d7 17 ♖bc1 ♘h6 18 ♕e2 ♖ad8 19 ♖fd1, with the better game in A.Granero Roca-X.Pinero Fernandez, Vila Real 2001.

15 ♘xd5 ♗xd5

White stands well after 15...cxd5 16 ♗xd4, and if 16...exd4 (or 16...dxe4 17 ♗c5 exd3 18 ♕xd3) 17 ♘c5 ♗xc5 18 bxc5 ♕c7 19 ♕a4 ♕xc5 20 ♖fc1 ♕e7 21 ♕xd4 ♕xe2 22 ♗xd5, with some advantage.

16 ♗xd4 exd4 17 ♕c2 ♖e8 18 ♘d2 ♗f8 19 ♖fe1 ♚h8 20 ♗xd5 ♕xd5 21 ♕c4

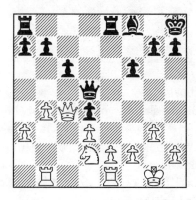

21...♕d7!?

Perhaps Black should have taken his chances in an endgame, but such positions are very pleasant to play for White with or without queens on the board. Black's game is almost wholly defensive and White enjoys a valuable long-term structural advantage. White also has the better minor piece and can play for a queenside minority attack.

22 ♘f3 ♖ad8 23 ♔g2 g6 24 ♖bc1 f5 25 ♕b3 ♗g7 26 ♖c5 ♗f6 27 b5

White's minority attack and pressure down the c-file counts – classical English Opening strategy. Black must open the c-file, allowing White's rook active play, or else permit White to exchange pawns on c6, leaving Black with a vulnerable c-pawn.

27...♕e7 28 ♖ec1 cxb5 29 ♕xb5 ♖d7 30 a4 ♔g7 31 ♖1c2

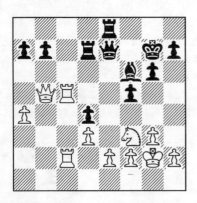

31...b6?!

Black should probably not have moved this pawn, which allows White's rooks to exploit the resulting weakness of c6.

32 ♖c6 ♖ed8 33 ♕c4 ♖d6 34 ♖c7 ♖8d7 35 ♖c8 ♖d5 36 ♕c6 g5

Perhaps Black should have tried to organize an earlier kingside diversion. It now looks too late to stem White's attack.

37 ♕a8 g4 38 ♘d2 ♖e5?

Under pressure, Black blunders, allowing White to triple his major pieces on the 8th rank with a mating attack. Black could still have played 38...♕f7, after which there is no quick knockout

blow because tripling major pieces on the 8th rank with 39 ♖b8!? ♖e5 40 ♖cc8? (40 ♔f1, and if 40...♕d5 41 ♕xd5 ♖exd5 42 ♘c4 ♖c5 43 ♖b2, followed by ♖a8 and ♖b5, keeps an endgame plus) fails to 40...♖xe2 41 ♖g8+ ♔h6 42 ♖bf8 ♕e6.

39 ♖g8+ ♔h6 40 ♖cc8

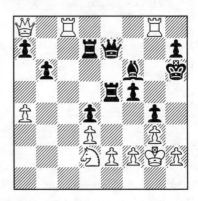

40...♖e6

Black has no defence. If 40...♖xe2 41 ♖ge8 wins, as does 40...♕e6 41 ♖c6 ♕d5+ (41...♖d6? 42 ♕f8+) 42 ♘e4! fxe4 (alternatively, 42...♔h5 43 ♖xf6 fxe4 – 43...♕xa8? 44 ♖g5 mate – 44 ♕f8, transposes, and 42...♖f7 43 ♖xf6+ ♖xf6 44 ♕xd5 loses a piece) 43 ♕f8+ ♔h5 44 ♖xf6 e3+ (or 44...exd3+ 45 ♔g1) 45 f3 gxf3+ 46 exf3 ♕a2+ 47 ♔h3, and White mates.

41 ♘c4 ♗g7 42 ♖ge8 1-0

Game 12
Z.Sturua-Xu Jun
Istanbul Olympiad 2000

---

1 c4 e5 2 ♘c3 ♘f6 3 ♘f3 ♘c6 4 g3 d5 5 cxd5 ♘xd5 6 ♗g2 ♘b6 7 0-0 ♗e7 8 a3

0-0 9 b4 ♖e8

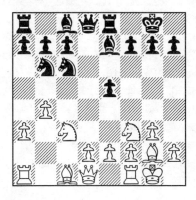

10 d3

With this move order, White can also play the sharp but unclear 10 b5!?. After 10...♘d4 11 ♘xe5 ♗f6 12 f4 ♗xe5 13 fxe5 ♖xe5, White has two gambit possibilities. If Black is prepared to return the pawn for positional stabilization and development, he is probably fine in both lines but holding on to the gambit is fraught with risk:

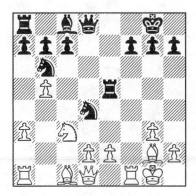

a) 14 e3 ♘xb5 15 ♗b2 ♘xc3 16 ♗xc3 ♖e7?! (16...♖f5 17 ♖xf5 ♗xf5 18 ♗xb7 ♖b8 19 ♕f3 ♗g6 followed by ...♘c4-d6 looks safer) 17 ♕h5 h6 18 ♖f4 c6 19 ♖af1 ♗e6 20 ♖h4 f5?! 21 ♗xg7 ♖xg7 22

♕xh6 ♕e7 23 e4 1-0 was the crushing course of A.Minasian-L.Aronian, Yerevan 2000.

b) 14 ♖f4!? ♘xb5?! (14...♘e6, intending 15 ♖h4 a6 16 d4 g5, looks solid) 15 ♗b2 ♘d6 16 ♘e4 ♖e7?! (16...♖f5!?) 17 ♕c2 f5 18 ♘xd6 cxd6 19 e4! fxe4 20 ♗xe4 h6 21 ♗h7+ ♔h8 22 ♕g6 ♘d5 23 ♕xh6 ♖e5 24 ♕h4 ♗d7 25 ♖f8+ 1-0 was A.Moskalenko-Y.Drozdovskij, online blitz 2004.

10...♗f8 11 ♗b2

White sometimes plays 11 ♗e3, but b2 is a more logical square for White's bishop in this line, as after 11 ♗e3 ♘d4, or first 11...a5 12 b5 ♘d4, White lacks the possibility of e3 to evict Black's knight from its powerful d4 outpost. Control of this square is the main point of this variation for Black. More interesting is 11 ♖b1, which both retains e3 options and covers b3 in anticipation of ...♘d4 and an eventual ...♗e6.

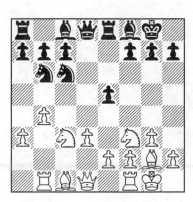

This line can also arise from an 8 ♖b1 move order. Black has then tried:

a) 11...♘d4 12 ♘e4 is a good try for an edge (12 ♘d2 c6 has a very solid reputation). White developed a persistent initiative in Z.Azmaiparashvili-J.Waitzkin, Philadelphia 1994, which continued 12...a5!? (if 12...c6 then 13 ♗b2, putting pressure on d4, may be best) 13 ♗d2 axb4 14 axb4 ♘b5!? 15 ♖a1 c6 16 ♘c5 ♖xa1 17 ♕xa1 ♕c7 18 ♖c1 f6 19 ♕a2+ ♕f7 20 ♕xf7+ ♔xf7 21 e4 ♖d8 22 ♗e3 ♘a8 23 ♗f1 ♘ac7 24 ♘d2 ♘d4 25 f4 exf4!? 26 gxf4 ♘ce6 27 ♔f2 b6? 28 ♘xe6 ♗xe6 29 f5 ♗c8 30 ♘c4 b5 31 ♘b6, and White won.

b) 11...♗g4!? 12 h3 ♗h5 13 ♖e1 doesn't solve Black's development problems completely either. Black then got the tactics wrong in O.Cvitan-N.Fercec, Pula 2004, after 13...a5?! 14 b5 ♘d4 15 ♘xd4 exd4 16 ♘e4 ♘d5 17 ♕b3 ♔h8 18 ♗b2 f5 19 ♘d2 ♘c3 20 ♗xc3 a4 21 ♕c2 dxc3 22 ♕xc3 ♗xe2 23 ♗xb7 ♖b8 24 ♗c6, and White won.

c) M.Sher-A.Baburin, Farum 1993, saw 11...a5 12 b5 ♘d4 13 ♘d2 a4 14 e3 ♘e6 15 ♘f3 ♘c5 16 d4 exd4 17 ♘xd4 g6

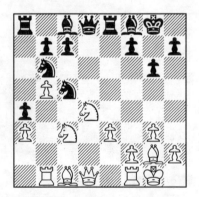

18 ♕c2 ♗g7 (K.Georgiev-B.Gelfand, Manila 1990, also gave White a pull after 18...♕e7 19 ♘ce2 ♗e6 20 ♘xe6 ♕xe6 21 ♗b2 ♕b3 22 ♖fc1 ♖ad8!? 23 ♘d4 ♕xc2 24 ♖xc2, but the murkier

22...♘d3!?, and then, for example, 23 ♘d4 ♕xc2 24 ♖xc2 ♘xb2 25 ♖bxb2 ♗xa3 26 ♖a2 ♗d6 27 ♗xb7 ♖ab8 28 ♗c6 ♖e7 29 ♗f3 ♖d7 30 ♘c6 ♖e8 31 ♖d2, while probably still better for White, needs a further test) 19 ♘ce2 ♘e6 20 ♗b2 ♘xd4 21 ♘xd4 ♕e7 22 ♖fe1 ♖b8 23 ♖bc1 ♗e5 24 ♕c3 f6 25 f4 ♗d6 26 e4, with a clear advantage.

However, White's most dynamic alternative may actually be the pretty rare 11 ♘e4!?.

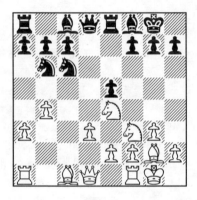

E.Bareev-R.Ruck, Gothenburg 2005, continued 11...♗g4 (11...♘d4 12 ♗b2 c6 13 ♘fd2, preparing e3, also looks better for White) 12 h3 ♗f5 13 ♘c5 ♗xc5 14 bxc5 ♘d7 15 ♗e3 ♘f8 16 ♕b3 ♖b8 17 ♕c3!? ♕d7!? (17...♘e6! equalizes, so perhaps 17 ♕b2, intending 17...♘e6 18 ♘h4, was more accurate) 18 ♔h2 ♗e6 19 ♘xe5 ♘xe5 20 ♕xe5 ♗xh3 21 ♗xh3 ♕xh3+ 22 ♔xh3 ♖xe5 23 ♖fc1, with a good endgame.

Returning to 11 ♗b2:

11...a5

Alternatively:

a) Black simply lost a pawn in M.Suba-S.Lupu, Manresa 1994, after

11...♘d4?! 12 ♘xd4 exd4 13 ♘b5 ♗d7 14 ♘xd4 ♘a4 15 ♕d2 ♘xb2 16 ♕xb2 g6 17 ♘f3 ♗g7 18 d4, and White won.

b) 11...♗g4 12 ♘e4 a5 13 ♘c5 ♗xc5 14 bxc5 ♘d7 15 ♖c1 ♕e7 16 ♕a4 ♗h5 17 ♖fe1 ♖ab8 18 ♕b5 ♗g4 19 ♘d2 ♗e6 was M.Marin-J.Lopez Martinez, Andorra 2004, and now 20 ♖c2 would have been strong, as pointed out by Lopez Martinez.

12 b5 ♘d4

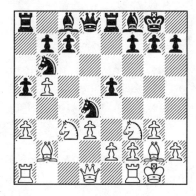

13 e3!?

White evicts Black's strong knight at the cost of a simplifying minor piece exchange. The older, more established move is 13 ♘d2. This has a good reputation against 13...a4 (after 14 e3 ♘e6 15 ♘f3, White is poised to play d4 and Black still has to sort out his minor piece development; for example, 15...f6!? 16 ♕c2 ♗d7 was M.Narciso Dublan-M.Perez Candelario, Spanish Team Championship 2004, and now 17 ♖fd1, with ♖ac1 to follow, would have been better for White), but Black has recently been defending robustly with the more solid 13...c6. Play usually continues 14 bxc6 ♘xc6 15 ♘b5 a4 16 ♖b1,

reaching a tense position where Black's stretched queenside pawns are compensated by his central pressure, particularly his grip on d4.

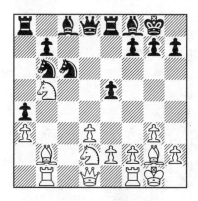

Robert Hübner has been involved in key developments for both sides:

a) 16...♗g4 17 ♖e1 ♕d7 18 ♗a1 ♗e6 19 ♕c2 ♖ec8 20 ♕b2 f6 21 d4!? was R.Hübner-R.Ruck, Leipzig 2002, which Hübner considered could be well met by 21...♖d8 22 dxe5 ♕xd2 23 ♘c7 ♕xb2 24 ♗xb2, and now either 24...♗b3 or 24...♔f7.

b) A year later, T.Markowski-R.Hübner, German League 2003, saw 16...♗e6 17 ♗a1 (M.Petursson-J.Fernandez Garcia, Novi Sad Olympiad 1990, had previously gone 17 e3!? ♗a2 18 ♖c1 ♗d5 19 ♘f3 e4 20 ♘fd4, and now Petursson suggested that 20...exd3 21 ♗xd5 ♘xd5 22 ♕xd3 was better for White) 17...♕d7 18 ♕c2 ♖ec8 19 ♕b2 f6 20 d4 ♖d8 21 ♖fd1 ♘a5 22 dxe5 ♘bc4 23 ♕d4 ♘xe5, and Black had slightly the better of an eventual draw.

13...♘xf3+ 14 ♗xf3 a4 15 ♕c2

White plans to put pressure on c7 and to continue to tie Black down to the defence of his b-pawn. Black can either go active now by developing his queen's bishop or stay on the defensive.

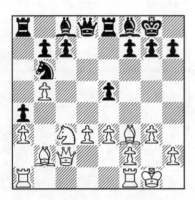

15...♗f5

Black goes active. He did too in K.Spraggett-B.Hartman, Canada 1992, which continued 15...♗h3!? 16 ♖fc1 (16 ♗xb7!? ♗xf1 17 ♖xf1 ♖a7 18 ♗c6 is a playable exchange sacrifice) 16...♖a7 17 ♘e4 ♖a5 18 ♘c3 ♖a7, and the game was drawn, but perhaps 17 ♘d1!?, and if 17...♕f6 (or 17...♗d6 18 d4) 18 ♗e4 ♗d6 19 f4, is an improvement.

White also seems a little better after 15...♖a7 16 ♖fc1, intending 16...♗d6 (or 16...♖e6 17 ♘e4) 17 ♘d5 ♘xd5 18 ♗xd5 ♗e6 19 ♕c4, but perhaps Black should play 15...♖a5!?, and if 16 ♖fc1 then 16...♖e6 or 16...♗d6.

16 ♖fd1 ♖a7

Black's rook can't now play to the more active square a5 because his b7-pawn would hang.

17 ♗e4 ♗e6?

Xu may have underestimated the force of White's aggressive reply. Sturua suggests that Black's best might

have been 17...♗xe4 18 dxe4 ♕f6 19 ♘d5, with an edge.

18 d4!

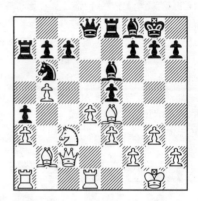

So much often turns in such positions on whether White can get in this move under favourable circumstances. Here the break comes as a promising sacrifice.

18...♗b3 19 ♗xh7+ ♔h8 20 ♕f5 g6?!

Sturua considers that Black had to play 20...♕f6 21 ♕xf6 gxf6 22 ♗d3 ♗xd1 23 ♖xd1, and although White has ample compensation for the exchange, he clearly still has a lot to do to win the point.

21 ♕h3 ♕c8

Black is mated after 21...♗xd1? 22 ♗xg6+ ♔g7 23 ♕h7+ ♔f6 24 ♘e4+ ♔e6 25 ♕xf7 mate. White wins too after 21...♗e6 22 g4 ♔g7 (or 22...♗xg4 23 ♕xg4 ♗xh7 24 dxe5 ♕c8 25 ♕h4+ ♗h6 26 ♘e4) 23 ♘e4 ♗e7 24 dxe5 ♕c8 25 ♘f6 ♖h8 26 ♕h4 ♗xg4 27 e6, as shown by Sturua.

22 g4 ♔g7 23 ♘e4 ♘c4

Or 23...♗xd1? 24 ♖xd1 ♘c4 25 dxe5 ♘xb2 (if 25...♗xa3 then 26 ♗d4) 26 ♗g8! and wins.

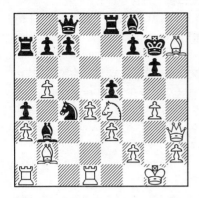

24 ♗c3?!

White wins this game brilliantly, but apparently he missed the most precise and prettiest way to win at this point. Ftacnik gives 24 ♗g8!!, intending 24...♔xg8 25 ♘f6+ ♔g7 26 dxe5 ♘xe5 (or 26...♖xe5 27 f4 ♗d6 28 fxe5 ♘xe5 29 ♖f1, winning) 27 f4 ♗d6 (or 27...♔xf6 28 ♗xe5+ ♖xe5 29 g5+) 28 ♘xe8+ ♕xe8 29 b6 ♖a6 30 fxe5 ♗xa3 31 ♖xa3 ♗xd1 32 e6+ f6 33 g5, and wins!

24...♘d6!?

Some commentators give 24...♗xd1 25 ♖xd1 ♗xa3 26 dxe5 ♗b2 as a possible saving line, but Sturua offers 27 ♖d7! ♕xd7 (or 27...♗xc3 28 g5) 28 e6+ ♗xc3 29 exd7 ♖h8 30 ♘xc3 ♖aa8 31 g5 ♖xh7 32 ♕f3, and wins. He also mentions the decisive 24...♗d6 25 ♕h4 ♗xd1 26 ♖xd1 ♖h8 27 ♕f6+ ♔xh7 28 ♘g5+ ♔h6 29 ♘xf7+ ♔h7 30 ♘g5+ ♔h6 31 ♘e6.

25 ♘f6!

Sturua has a choice of stunning con-

clusions. Ftacnik gives 25 ♗g8! and if 25...♘xe4 26 ♕h7+ ♔f6 27 dxe5+ ♔e7 28 ♗b4+ ♘d6 29 ♖d4, and wins.

25...♘xb5

All manner of king-hunts abound in this game. Another entertaining Sturua line runs 25...♗xd1 26 ♖xd1 ♘xb5 27 dxe5 ♘xc3 28 ♗g8 ♖xe5 29 ♕h7+ ♔xf6 30 ♕xf7+ ♔g5 31 ♕f4+ ♔h4 32 ♕g3+ ♔g5 33 ♕xe5+ ♔h4 34 ♕h8+ ♔g5 35 f4+ ♔xg4 36 ♔g2, and Black will be mated.

25...♔xf6 26 dxe5+ ♖xe5 27 f4 also wins, albeit more mundanely.

26 ♗b2

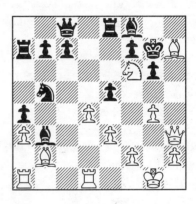

26...♔xf6

Or 26...♗xd1 27 dxe5 ♗xa3 28 ♖xd1 ♗xb2 29 ♗g8 ♗xe5 30 ♕h7+ ♔xf6 31 ♕xf7+ ♔g5 32 f4+ ♗xf4 33 ♕xf4+ ♔h4 34 ♕h6+ ♔xg4 35 ♕xg6+ ♔f3 36 ♕g3+ ♔e4 37 ♗d5+ ♔f5 38 ♖f1 mate (Sturua).

27 dxe5+ ♔e6 28 g5+ ♔e7 29 e6 fxe6 30 ♗f6+ 1-0

If 30....♔f7 31 ♗g8+ ♔xg8 32 ♕h8+ ♔f7 33 ♕h7+ and it's mate next move.

Summary

This chapter comprehensively concludes coverage of the main lines of the English Four Knights after 4 g3, including the reversed Dragon. Probably Black's best alternative to his two main moves, 4...♗b4 and 4...d5, is 4...♗c5, which is based on solid, straightforward development. White can nevertheless still press, building on his extra space and continuing grip on the long light-square diagonal.

After 4 g3 d5 5 cxd5 ♘xd5 6 ♗g2 ♘b6 7 0-0 ♗e7, White has two principal systems in 8 ♖b1 and 8 a3. These are genuine, reversed 'Open' Sicilians and three points should be stressed:

i. White's extra tempo requires Black to play the slower, more positional anti-Dragon lines;

ii. White's extra central pawn, and opportunities to gain ground quickly on the queenside with b4, tend to assume a more immediate positional importance in these lines than they do a tempo down with Black in the real Dragon.

iii. White should also always bear in mind that his advantages, as in most Sicilians, are mostly structural and tell often in the long term, in a wide range of possible endgames.

1 c4 e5 2 ♘c3 ♘f6 3 ♘f3 ♘c6 4 g3 *(D)* **4...d5**

        4...♗c5 – *Game 7*

        4...♘d4 – *Game 8*

        4...g6 – *Game 9*

5 cxd5 ♘xd5 6 ♗g2 *(D)* **6...♘b6 7 0-0 ♗e7 8 a3**

        8 ♖b1 – *Game 10*

8...0-0 9 b4 *(D)*

        9...♗e6 – *Game 11*

        9...♖e8 – *Game 12*

4 g3

6 ♗g2

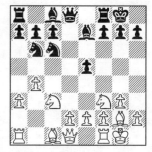

9 b4

Chapter Three

Black's Alternative Set-Ups after 1...e5

1 c4 e5 2 ♘c3

The six games in this chapter consider a range of defences in which Black combines 1...e5 with ...d6, ...g6 and ...f5 ideas or plays 2...♝b4. White can apply a number of different strategies against these systems, but with the exception of 2...♝b4, which is a special case, we shall be considering lines for White based on 4th move breaks with d4. White aims thereby to induce an exchange of pawns on d4, thus allowing him to establish a spatial edge in the centre, or in the event of ...e4, leading to positions where White can seek to undermine Black's e-pawn based on an eventual f3-break.

Game 13 chiefly focuses on **2...♘f6 3 ♘f3 d6** (there's also a discussion of the gambit 3...e4) 4 d4 e4 5 ♘g5 ♝f5 6 g4! *(see following diagram)*.

In this line White plays to win Black's e-pawn at the cost of his g-pawn, establishing an extra pawn in the centre. White can hope to make

something of this positional advantage, though Black can battle to create as much tactical confusion as possible.

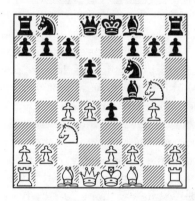

Game 14 considers three fairly rare follow-ups to **2...♘c6 3 ♘f3**: 3...♝b4, 3...♝c5 and **3...g6**. The last is the most important of these – after 4 d4 exd4 5 ♘xd4 ♝g7 6 ♘xc6 bxc6 7 g3 White has a spatial edge and certain structural advantages, and he can hope to expand gradually in the centre and on the kingside. Black's game plan is again essentially tactical, because against best play, he doesn't find it easy to counter-attack successfully with either of his natural potential pawn levers ...d5 and ...f5.

More aggressive is **2...♞c6 3 ♞f3 f5**, after which **4 d4 e4 5 ♞g5** is the subject of Game 15.

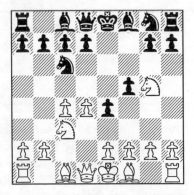

This is one of Black's toughest defences because he has spatial compensation for his slightly looser pawn structure. White generally struggles to undermine Black's hold on e4, by playing for f3 breaks, and he frequently combines this plan with other ideas, such as the unbalancing thrust d4-d5 and the space-gaining pawn advance b4-b5. White can hope to slowly conquer squares and territory in complex games involving long-term manoeuvres.

A major alternative is **5 ♗g5** to which I've decided to devote Game 16. White seeks to exchange the dark-squared bishops before moving his knight. Play isn't quite as rich as after 5 ♞g5, but careful treatment is still required by Black and White has chances of a modest pull.

A related variation is the **2...d6 3 ♞f3 f5 4 d4 e4 5 ♞g5** of Game 17.

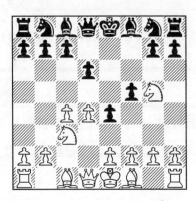

Many of the main ideas for both sides are similar to Game 15 and it is very hard to judge whether having a pawn on d6, rather than a knight on c6, makes much difference. It does, however, seem to be the case that 5 ♗g5 is a little less effective against a 2...d6 move order. Black can also try to reach the same set-up with 2...f5, but that is a less precise move order due to 3 d4, as we'll see in the notes to Game 17.

Finally, Game 18 considers the variation **2...♗b4**.

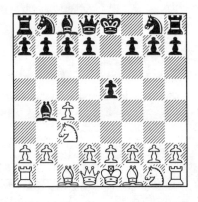

This is a relatively new and flexible

idea that has only really been developed and played a lot since the 1980s. Both sides face many novel problems. Should White allow Black to exchange his bishop for White's knight creating doubled c-pawns? Our coverage focuses mainly on White's most promising reply 3 ②d5, which emphatically answers no!

> ## Game 13
> ## A.Moiseenko-O.Romanishin
> *Ukrainian Team Ch. 2005*

1 c4 e5 2 ②c3 ②f6 3 ②f3 d6

It's well worth knowing that Bellon's sharp gambit, 3...e4!? 4 ②g5 b5, has largely been defused by 5 d3!:

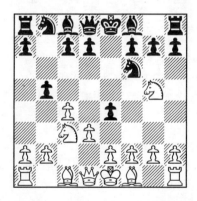

a) Black insisted on a pure gambit course with 5...⍚b4 in P.Van der Sterren-J.Bellon Lopez, Wijk aan Zee 1977, but after 6 ⍚d2 exd3 7 ②xb5 ⍚xd2+ 8 ⍙xd2 0-0 9 e3 ②c6 10 ⍚xd3 ②e5, and now 11 0-0, White is better.

b) Black also seems worse after 5...bxc4 6 dxe4 ⍚b7?! (L.Psakhis-D.Sermek, Groningen 1995, was also

unconvincing after 6...h6?! 7 ②xf7! ⍙xf7 8 e5 c6 9 exf6 ⍙xf6 10 e4 d5 11 exd5 ⍚c5 12 ⍚e3 ⍥e8, and now Psakhis recommends 13 ⍙h5+ ⍙f8 14 ⍚xc4; Black might be able to struggle a bit after 6...②c6!? 7 e3, but practice tells in White's favour and, for example, 7...h6 8 ②f3 ⍚b4 9 ⍚xc4 ②xe4 10 ⍚xf7+ ⍙f8 11 0-0 ②xc3 12 bxc3 ⍚a6 13 cxb4 ⍚xf1 14 ⍚b3 ⍙f6 15 ⍙d5 was promising in A.Maksimenko-V.Okhotnik, Falconara Marittima 2005) 7 e5 h6 8 ②xf7! ⍙xf7. 9 exf6 d5 10 e4 ⍚b4 11 fxg7 ⍥e8 12 ⍙h5+ ⍙g8 was L.Psakhis-Z.Basagic, Ohrid 2001, and now Psakhis gives 13 f3, with a clear advantage.

c) 5...exd3 6 cxb5 h6 7 ②f3 dxe2 8 ⍚xe2 keeps the material balance and is probably best.

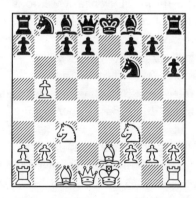

However, White has a pleasant lead in development and his knight can generally make good use of the d4-square, freeing his bishops for action and making it hard for Black to advance his central pawns without creating targets. A.Kosten-Z.Salem, Cairo 2003, continued 8...a6 9 0-0 ⍚e7 10 ②d4 0-0 11 ⍚f3 d5, and now Kosten gives 12

♗f4, with an edge.

Returning to 3...d6:

4 d4

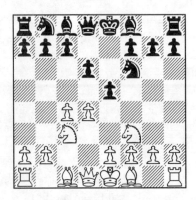

4...e4!?

Instead of this interesting, if slightly risky move, Black can, of course, attempt to transpose into Old Indian or King's Indian Defence variations by playing 4...exd4, 4...⚊bd7 or even 4...⚊c6.

5 ⚊g5

This is White's most active choice, but the retreat 5 ⚊d2, which also keeps e4 under threat, is another testing approach:

a) 5...♕e7 6 ⚊b3! is an important resource, intending ♗g5, followed by e3, reaching comfortable closed positions, in which White can target e4 and has queenside pressure. White was better in S.Rezan-D.Sutkovic, Omis 2005, after 6...c6 (or 6...h6 7 g3, intending 7...a5 8 ♗g2 ♗f5 9 d5, as analysed by Raetsky and Chetverik) 7 ♗g5 ♗f5 8 e3 ⚊bd7 9 ♗e2 ♕d8 10 ⚊d2 ♗e7 11 g4 ♗g6 12 ♗xf6 ⚊xf6 13 g5 ⚊d7 14 ⚊dxe4 ♕a5 15 ⚊g3.

b) White can also hope for a pull af-

ter 5...♗f5 6 ♕b3!, after which 6...⚊c6 (or 6...♕c8 7 e3 c6 8 h3 h5 9 ♗e2 ♗e7 10 a3 ⚊a6 11 f3 exf3 12 ⚊xf3 ⚊c7 13 0-0 ♜b8 14 ♗d2 ⚊e4 15 ♗e1, with advantage in J.Plaskett-A.Dunnington, Hastings 1988) 7 e3 ♜b8 8 g3 d5?! (8...h5 9 h3 is better) 9 cxd5 ⚊b4 10 ♗c4 ♗d6 11 a3 ⚊a6 12 ♕a4+ ♚f8 13 b4 was promising in A.Aleksandrov-V.Varavin, St Petersburg 2000.

5...♗f5

An important alternative is 5...♕e7 when 6 ♕c2 may suffice for a pull, but 6 f3!, undermining e4, is strong. Black was crushed in A.Moiseenko-J.Lopez Martinez, Gothenburg 2005, after 6...exf3 7 gxf3 g6 8 e4 ♗g7 9 ⚊h3 ♗xh3!? (9...0-0 10 ♗g5 c6 11 ♕d2 is better, but still good for White) 10 ♗xh3 ⚊xe4?! 11 ⚊xe4 ♕h4+ 12 ⚊f2 ♗xd4 13 0-0 ♗xf2+ 14 ♚g2 ♗d4 15 ♜e1+ ♚d8 16 ♜e4 ♕f2+ 17 ♚h1 ♗f6 18 ♗e3 ♕xb2 19 ♜b1 ♕c3 20 ♕d5 ⚊c6 21 c5 ♗e7 22 cxd6 1-0.

6 g4!

Play revolves around e4. White can also consider Gulko's 6 f3!? exf3 7 gxf3 and then:

a) White's potentially mobile central pawn mass is a serious long-term threat after 7...h6 8 ♘h3 d5 (or 8...♘h5 9 ♘f2 ♕h4 10 e4 ♗d7 11 ♗e3 ♗e7 12 f4 c6 13 ♕f3 f5 14 ♗e2 g6 15 e5, with a plus in B.Gulko-P.Garbett, Kona 1998) 9 cxd5 c6 10 e4 ♗xh3 11 ♗xh3 ♘xd5 12 0-0 ♘b6 13 ♗e3 ♕h4 14 ♗g2 ♘c4 15 ♗f2 ♕h5 16 ♕e2 ♘b6 17 ♖ad1 ♗e7 18 d5 0-0 19 d6 ♗h4 20 ♗xh4 ♕xh4 21 f4 ♘8d7 22 e5, and White won in B.Gulko-M.Ivanov, Las Palmas 1996.

b) 7...c5 8 dxc5! h6 9 ♘h3 ♕d7 10 ♘f4 dxc5 11 e4 ♕xd1+ 12 ♘xd1 ♗e6 13 ♘d5 ♗d6 14 ♘1c3 is clearly better for White, as analysed by Raetsky and Chetverik.

6...♘xg4

Black can't hold e4 and does best to seek as much imbalance as he can to compensate for White's coming pawn centre. Alternatively:

a) The meek 6...♗g6 saw Black crushed in J.Bellon Lopez-J.Hodgson, Dos Hermanas 1992, after 7 ♗g2 ♕e7 (probably best is 7...c6 8 ♘gxe4 ♗xe4 9 ♘xe4 ♘xg4 10 ♕b3, minimizing White's edge) 8 h4 h5 9 gxh5 ♖xh5 10

♘h3! ♖xh4 11 ♗g5 ♖g4 12 ♘d5 ♕d7 13 ♗xf6 ♖g2 14 ♘e3 ♖g4 15 ♘xg4 ♕xg4 16 ♕b3 gxf6 17 ♕xb7 ♗h5 18 ♘f4 ♕xf4 19 ♕xa8 1-0.

b) White can also press after 6...♗xg4 7 ♗g2 when 7...♗e7 8 ♘gxe4 ♘xe4 9 ♘xe4 is critical.

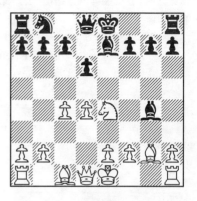

J.Piket-J.Van der Wiel, Dutch League 1995, continued 9...♘c6 (or 9...0-0 10 ♘g3 ♖e8?! 11 ♗xb7 ♘d7 12 ♗xa8 ♕xa8 13 f3 ♗h4 14 ♔f2 ♗h3 15 ♕d3, which wasn't wholly convincing for Black in J.Oms Pallise-E.Fernandez Romero, Seville 2004) 10 ♘g3 ♗f6 11 ♗e3 0-0 12 ♕d2 ♖b8 13 h3 ♗d7 14 ♘h5! ♗h4 15 ♖g1 g6 16 0-0-0 ♔h8 (or 16...♖e8 17 ♗d5 ♗xh3 18 ♖h1 ♗g4 19 ♘f4 – Piket) 17 ♘f4 ♘e7 18 ♗e4 ♘f5 19 ♗xf5 ♗xf5 20 d5 ♗f6 21 ♗d4 ♗e5 22 e4! ♗d7 23 ♗xe5+ dxe5 24 ♘d3 ♕e7 25 h4 f6 26 b3 ♖be8 27 ♔b2 f5 28 f4! fxe4 29 ♘xe5 ♕g7 30 h5, and White won.

7 ♘gxe4 ♗e7

Romanishin had previously preferred 7...c6 in D.Komarov-O.Romanishin, Saint Vincent 2000. However, White was able to mobilize his central pawns and establish a dangerous attack after 8 h3 ♘f6 9 ♘xf6+ ♕xf6 10 e4 ♗g6!? 11 h4 h6 12 ♗e3 ♕d8 13 h5 ♗h7 14 ♕f3 ♘d7 15 0-0-0 ♕a5 16 ♖g1 f6 17 ♗h3 0-0-0 18 c5! ♔b8 19 cxd6 ♘b6 20 ♗f4 ♘c4, and now 21 d7+ ♔a8 22 d5 would possibly win.

Black does not solve his problems with 7...♗xe4 8 ♘xe4 d5, after which 9 cxd5 f5 (or 9...♕xd5 10 ♗g2 ♕a5+ 11 ♗d2 ♕a6 12 ♕b3 ♘c6 13 ♘g5 0-0-0 14 ♘xf7, and White won in R.Knaak-G.Lorenz, Plauen 1980) 10 e3 ♗b4+ 11 ♗d2 ♗xd2+ 12 ♘xd2 ♕xd5 13 ♖g1 g6 14 ♗g2 ♕b5 15 ♕b3 ♕xb3 16 ♘xb3 ♘c6 17 ♖c1 won at least a pawn in M.Tal-P.Dekan, Prague radio simul 1960.

8 ♗g2

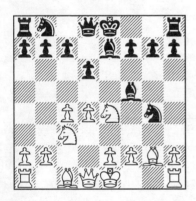

8...♗h4!?

Romanishin's play doesn't clearly improve on his game against Komarov. White's strong central pawns remain a significant positional asset and piece play alone can't stop them. White now amusingly demonstrates that point by driving all but one of Black's pieces back to his first rank. White also squeezes Black's pieces after 8...♘c6 9 h3, and if 9...♘f6 10 ♘g3 ♗g6 11 e4.

9 h3 ♘f6 10 ♘xf6+ ♕xf6 11 ♘d5 ♕d8 12 ♕b3 ♗c8 13 ♕e3+ ♔f8

White is better, but Black can still struggle. Moiseenko has a lead in development, but Romanishin has simplified and gained some manoeuvring space by exchanging knights and has no chronic weak points. White's dangerous centre pawns moreover remain on their starting squares. His pieces look good but his pawns still have much to achieve in the game.

14 ♗d2 ♘c6 15 0-0-0 a5 16 ♖hg1 h6 17 ♗e4 ♘b4 18 ♔b1

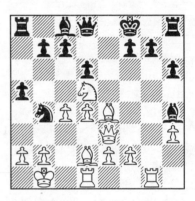

White coaxes Black to exchange on d5, so that he can open the c-file and shift his queen to c3, both putting pressure on c7 and enabling him to clear space to push his e-pawn.

18...♘xd5 19 cxd5 ♕f6 20 ♕c3 ♗f5!?

Black's defence isn't easy. Can he grab White's f-pawn? Probably not, though it's not entirely clear. After 20...♕xf2, the sacrificial flurry 21 ♖df1?! ♕xe2 22 ♖xf7+ ♔xf7 23 ♕xc7+ ♗e7 24 ♖xg7+ ♔xg7 25 ♕xe7+ ♔g8 26 ♕e8+ seems only to result in perpetual check. However, the more sober 21 ♗f3, and if

21...♗f6 22 ♗e3 ♕h4 23 ♕xc7, holding on to White's pawns and embarrassing Black's queen, looks better for White.

21 ♗xf5 ♕xf5+ 22 ♔a1

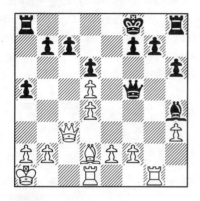

22...♖c8

Now 22...♕xf2 23 ♕xc7 looks very good for White.

23 ♖g4 ♗g5

With Black's c-pawn protected, 23...♕xf2 might be a better bet here, but after 24 ♗f4 threatening ♗xd6+, or perhaps 24 e4, White appears to have more than enough compensation.

24 ♗xg5 hxg5 25 e4 ♕xf2 26 ♖xg5 ♕h4 27 ♖dg1 ♕xh3 28 ♖5g3 ♕h1 29 ♖xg7 ♕xe4 30 ♕g3 ♖e8?

After a terrific struggle, Black overlooks a simple mate. He could still have wriggled with 30...♕f5 when White seems close to a win, such as after 31 ♖g5 ♕h7 32 a3, but he's not there yet.

31 ♖xf7+! 1-0

Game 14
L.Bruzon-Y.Quezada
Santa Clara 2002

1 c4 e5 2 ♘c3 ♘c6 3 ♘f3

3...g6

Black can also prioritize the development of his dark-squared bishop with one of the following:

a) White can't refute the unusual 3...♗b4, but he can hope for an edge after 4 ♘d5:

a1) 4...♗c5 5 e3 has ideas including d4, and a3 with b4. B.Gulko-Z.Hracek, Yerevan Olympiad 1996, continued 5...e4 6 d4 ♗e7 7 ♘d2 f5 8 g4! ♘b4 9 gxf5 ♘xd5 10 ♕h5+! ♔f8 11 cxd5 ♘f6 12 ♕h4 c6 13 ♘xe4 ♘xd5 14 ♕g4 ♘b4 15 ♖g1 ♖g8 16 ♔d1 d5 17 ♘g5 ♗xg5 18

♕xg5 ♕xg5 19 ♖xg5 h6 20 ♖g3 ♗xf5 21 ♗d2, with good chances.

a2) White obtains the bishop-pair after 4...e4 5 ♘d4 ♘xd4 6 ♘xb4. Z.Izoria-V.Gaprindashvili, Izmir 2002, continued 6...♘c6 (Black preferred 6...♘f6 7 e3 ♘c6 in A.Poluljahov-K.Landa, Cappelle la Grande 1999, when 8 ♘xc6 dxc6 9 d4 ♗g4 10 ♕b3 sufficed for an edge, but 8 ♘d5! and if 8...♘xd5 9 cxd5 ♘e5 10 ♕c2 f5 11 f4! exf3 12 ♕xf5 f2+ 13 ♕xf2, looks even better) 7 ♘d5 ♘e5 8 ♕c2 f5 9 d4 (9 f4!? exf3 10 ♕xf5 f2+ 11 ♕xf2 may be even stronger) 9...♘g6 10 g4 c6 11 gxf5 ♘6e7 12 f6 gxf6 13 ♘xe7 ♕xe7 14 c5, with an edge.

a3) White has a favourable form of a reversed Sicilian after 4...a5 5 a3 ♗c5 6 e3.

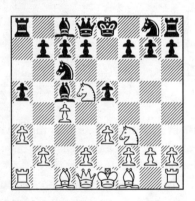

The move ...a5 adds little to the central battle and White quickly developed a lively kingside attack in Y.Seirawan-I.Ivanov, Los Angeles 1991, after 6...♘f6 7 d4 exd4 8 exd4 ♗e7 9 ♗d3 d6 10 0-0 0-0 11 h3 ♘xd5 12 cxd5 ♘b8 13 ♕c2 h6 14 ♗f4 ♘d7 15 ♕d2 ♖e8 16 ♗xh6 gxh6 17 ♕xh6 ♘f8 18 ♖ae1,

and White won.

b) White also has a pleasant game after 3...♗c5!? 4 e3. D.Komljenovic-P.Camacho Calle, Seville 2001, continued 4...♘f6 5 a3 d6 6 d4 ♗b6 7 b4 a5 8 b5 exd4 9 exd4 ♘b8 10 ♗d3 0-0 11 0-0 ♗g4 12 ♗e3 ♘bd7 13 ♘e4, with a pleasant advantage.

Returning to 3...g6:

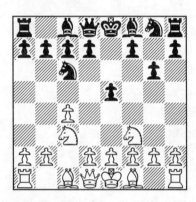

4 d4 exd4 5 ♘xd4 ♗g7 6 ♘xc6 bxc6

White is a little better after 6...dxc6 7 ♕xd8+ ♔xd8 8 ♗g5+ because of the Black king's awkward position. J.Oms Pallise-P.Martinez Rodriguez, Catalunya 1997, for example, continued 8...f6 9 0-0-0+ ♗d7 10 ♗h4 ♔c8 11 e3 ♘h6 12 ♘e4 g5 13 ♗g3 ♘f5 14 ♘c5 ♘xg3 15 hxg3 ♗f5 16 ♗d3 ♗xd3 17 ♖xd3 ♗f8 18 ♘e4 ♗g7 19 ♖hd1 b5 20 ♖d7, and White won.

7 g3 ♘e7

Black's knight can also play to f6, leading to different but not dissimilar middlegames. White has more space and controls the long light-squared diagonal, while Black has three pawn islands to White's two and it isn't yet clear how Black might eventually mobilize his centre pawns. Black's game may be somewhat structurally suspect, but his pieces, particularly his rooks and bishops, can rapidly become active if White puts a foot or two wrong as he seeks to press forward. After 7...♘f6 8 ♗g2 0-0 9 0-0, Black has three main choices:

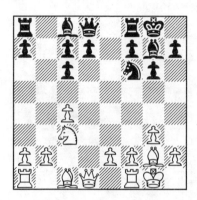

a) Following 9...♖b8 10 ♕a4, White attacks a7, with the better chances. L.Psakhis-M.Bartel, Moscow 2002, continued 10...a6 11 ♕a5 ♗b7 12 ♗f4!? d6 13 c5! ♘h5 14 ♗e3 d5 15 ♖ad1 f5 16 ♗d4 ♗xd4 17 ♖xd4 f4 18 ♖b4 ♗a8 19 ♖xb8 ♕xb8 20 b3 ♗b7 21 ♕b4 ♕a8 22 ♕d4 ♕e8 23 ♖e1 ♘g7 24 e4, with an edge. White's c5 and central dark-square blockading plan is an important and often successful strategic motif. However, he can often also succeed with a straightforward e4 and f4 pawn advance: for example, A.Kosten-J.Fernandez Fernandez, La Pobla de Lillet 2005, deviated with 11 ♕c2 and after 11...c5 12 b3 d6 13 ♗b2 ♗e6 14 ♖ad1 ♕c8 15 e4 ♗h3 16 f4 ♗xg2 17 ♕xg2 ♕e6 18 f5 ♕e8 19 ♖de1 ♕d7 20 g4, White was favourably pressing forwards.

b) 9...♖e8 10 ♕a4 (the calm 10 ♗f4 ♖b8 11 ♖b1 ♘g4 12 ♕d2 ♗a6?! 13 h3 ♘f6 14 b3 is also possible, as in A.Onischuk-V.Akopian, Elista Olympiad 1998) 10...a5 11 ♖d1 ♕e7 12 ♗f4 ♖a7 13 ♗e3 ♖a8 14 c5!...

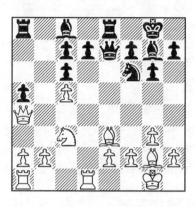

...saw Psakhis again applying the c5-plan in L.Psakhis-J.Ivanov, Andorra 1997, which continued 14...♗a6 15 ♖d2 ♖eb8 16 ♖ad1 ♗c8 17 a3 ♕e6, and now Psakhis gives 18 h3! with good chances.

c) 9...♗b7 again sees Black experience problems against a c5 and central blockading strategy combined with kingside play: for example, J.Nogueiras-H.Pecorelli Garcia, Holguin 1991, continued 10 ♕c2 d6 11 ♖d1 ♘d7 12 b3 ♕e7 13 ♗b2 ♖ae8 14 e3 ♗a8 15 ♖ac1 f5 16 ♗a3 ♕f7 17 c5 d5 18 ♘e2 ♘e5 19 h3 g5 20 ♖d4 ♗b7 21 ♖a4 ♗c8 22 ♖f1 ♘g6 23 ♗c1 a6 24 f4, with a plus.

Returning to 7...♘e7:

8 ♗g2 d6

Playing this move is the main point of developing Black's knight to e7 rather than f6: Black's queen's bishop now has development opportunities on the c8-h3 diagonal. However, the fundamentals of the position hardly change as White still has more space, powerful light-square control and the better pawn structure.

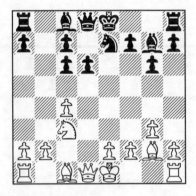

9 0-0 0-0 10 ♕c2

White also has good chances after the more frequently played 10 ♗g5, preparing ♕d2 to take control of the c1-h6 diagonal, or if Black plays ...f6, securing at least temporary closure of the long a1-h8 diagonal and reducing Black's potential dark-square counterplay. White still has to work hard to obtain any tangible advantage, but his game has definite promise. One example continued 10...♖b8 11 ♕c2 (the more straightforward 11 ♕d2 c5 12 ♖ad1 ♗e6 13 b3 f6 14 ♗f4 ♕c8 15 h4 ♘f5 16 ♘d5 is also promising, as in V.Gavrikov-O.Sutter, Zurich 1992) 11...f6 12 ♗e3 c5 13 ♖ad1 ♗d7 14 ♕d2 ♗e6 15 b3 a6 16 f4 ♕c8 17 ♖fe1 ♔h8 18 ♗f2 f5 19 e4, and after obtaining a classical central break, White turned his attention to the kingside in A.Potapov-L.Kernazhitsky, Cappelle la Grande 2003..

10...♗f5!?

In view of White's promising 13th move, this is provocative, but playing quietly doesn't necessarily assure full equality either. After 10...♗e6 White clearly pressed in W.Schmidt-T.Markowski, Warsaw 1995, with 11 b3 ♕d7 12 ♗b2 ♗h3 13 ♘e4 ♗xg2 14 ♔xg2 ♕e6 15 ♗xg7 ♔xg7 16 ♕c3+ f6 17 ♘g5 ♕f5 18 f4 ♕d7 19 e4, and Wolf's 11 c5!? d5 12 e3 a5 13 ♘e2 is another reasonable option.

11 e4 ♗e6

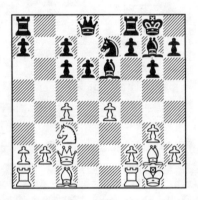

12 c5!

This is certainly critical. White prevents ...c5, followed by possible occupation of d4 by a black minor piece, with near equality. However even then Black may not achieve full equality and White skilfully managed to attack around a black knight on d4 in C.McNab-M.Thiruchelvam, London 2001, after 12 b3 c5 13 ♗b2 ♖b8 14 ♘d5 ♘c6 15 ♗xg7 ♔xg7 16 ♕c3+ ♘d4 17 ♖ae1 ♗xd5 18 cxd5 ♕c8 19 f4 f6 20 ♖f2 ♕a6 21 h4 ♕a3 22 g4 a5 23 g5 a4 24 gxf6+ ♖xf6 25 e5 dxe5 26 ♕a5 ♖bb6 27 d6 ♖fxd6 28 fxe5 ♖e6 29 ♗d5 ♖e7 30 ♕a8 ♘f5 31 ♖xf5 1-0.

12...d5!?

Black plays for high stakes. The chances are that he will emerge from the complications begun by this move with some fairly significant long-term pawn weakness with inadequate counterplay. Nor do Black's tripled pawns inspire confidence after 12...dxc5?! 13 ♘a4, but 12...♕b8!? may be a better idea. White had at best only a very slight pull in M.Illescas Cordoba-M.Godena, Lisbon 1993, after 13 cxd6 cxd6 14 ♗f4 ♖d8 15 ♖ad1 (15 ♖ac1!? ♕b4 16 ♖fd1 might be a slight improvement − Ribli) 15...♕b4 16 ♗d2 ♕c4 17 b3 ♕c5 18 ♖c1 ♖ac8 19 ♘e2 ♕xc2 20 ♖xc2 c5, and Black held.

13 ♖d1

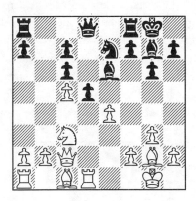

13...♗g4

Black improves on Z.Arsovic-B.Certic, Belgrade 1994, which had gone 13...f5?! 14 e5! ♕d7 15 f4 g5 16 ♗e3 ♘g6 17 ♕f2 gxf4 18 gxf4 ♖ab8 19 b3 ♔h8 20 ♘e2 ♖g8 21 ♔h1 ♗f8 22 ♗d4, with a clear advantage.

14 ♖d3 ♕c8 15 ♗g5 dxe4

Black clarifies the situation in the centre, leaving White dominant there,

with a definite advantage. But it's doubtful whether Black has anything better: for example, after 15...♖e8 White's simplest course is to maintain the pressure in the centre with 16 ♕d2.

16 ♗xe4 f6 17 ♗f4 ♖b8 18 ♖e1 ♗f5!?

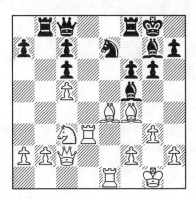

19 ♕a4?!

White misses 19 ♗xf5! ♘xf5 20 ♕a4 ♖xb2 21 ♕xc6, after which he will win Black's second c-pawn for virtually nothing.

19...♖xb2 20 ♗xf5 ♕xf5! 21 ♕c4+ ♘d5 22 ♘xd5 cxd5 23 ♖xd5 ♕c2 24 ♕d4!?

White decides to try to win in a favourable middlegame. He could also play for an endgame win with 24 ♕xc2 ♖xc2 25 ♖e7 ♖c8 26 ♖dd7 ♗f8 27 ♖xh7, although Black can still fight with 27...♖xc5, and if 28 ♗xc7 g5, preventing the consolidating ♗f4-e3.

24...f5 25 ♗e5 ♖b1 26 ♖xb1 ♕xb1+ 27 ♔g2 ♗xe5 28 ♖xe5 ♕xa2

Black could also have tried to defend with 28...♕b7+!? 29 ♔h3 c6.

29 ♖e7 ♖f7 30 ♖e8+ ♖f8 31 ♖xf8+ ♔xf8 32 ♕d8+ ♔g7 33 ♕xc7+ ♔f6!? 34 ♕d8+ ♔f7 35 ♕d7+ ♔f6 36 ♕d4+ ♔e6 37 c6 ♕c2

Black has defended well since White's wobble on move 19 and seems to have saved the half point. White's c-pawn can't progress to the queening square without the help of White's queen, which will in turn allow Black's queen to reach e4 and give perpetual check.

38 ♕d7+ ♔f6 39 ♕d6+ ♔f7 40 c7 ♕e4+ 41 f3

Or 41 ♔f1 ♕b1+ 42 ♔e2 ♕c2+ and draws.

41...♕e2+ 42 ♔h3 ♕xf3??

Quite possibly a tragic time trouble blunder. Having done all the hard work, Black now needed only to play 42...g5!, threatening ...♕f1 mate, and White can't win.

43 ♕d7+ ♔f6 44 ♕d4+ 1-0

Game 15
M.Marin-M.Manolache
Romanian Team Ch. 2000

---

1 c4 e5 2 ♘c3 ♘c6 3 ♘f3 f5 4 d4 e4 5 ♘g5

With this bold move, White pro-vokes Black's h- and g- pawns to advance in the hope that they become targets. White's knight can expect to find a purposeful future after a retreat to h3, either on f4, or on f2, after playing f3. And, as we shall see in the main game, if Black allows himself to be fully provoked by playing ...h6 and ...g5, White's knight finds a future full of promise via h3 on g1!

An important alternative is 5 ♗g5, the subject of our next illustrative game. White can also consider the unusual 5 ♘e5!? which leads after 5...♘xe5 (or 5...♘ge7 6 ♘xc6 ♘xc6 7 ♗f4 g5?! 8 ♗d2 ♗g7 9 h4 gxh4 10 e3 ♕g5 11 ♘d5 ♔d8 12 ♕c2 b6 13 0-0-0 ♘e7 14 f4, with good prospects in the game L.Christiansen-S.Maus, German League 1990; but here 7...d6 8 e3, and if 8...♗e7 9 h4 0-0 10 h5, leaves White with a minimal edge) 6 dxe5 to tactical, even trappy complications, in which White has done quite well in albeit very limited practice:

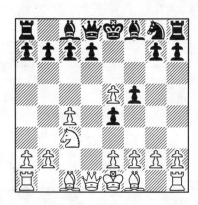

a) 6...♘e7 7 ♗g5 h6?! (7...c6 8 ♕d2 ♕c7 can be met by 9 ♗f4 or Ribli's 9 ♕f4, with an edge) 8 ♗h4 c6 (8...g5!? 9

e3 ♗g7 10 ♕h5+ ♔f8 11 ♗g3 also favours White) 9 e3 ♕a5 10 ♗g3 g6 11
♗e2 h5 was L.Christiansen-W.Browne,
Las Vegas 1989, and now 12 h4 ♗g7 13
♕d6 ♖h6 14 0-0 g5 15 ♕d4
(Christiansen) would have consolidated White's dark-square advantage.

b) 6...♗b4 7 ♕b3 ♕e7 8 ♗f4 ♘h6 9
♗xh6 gxh6 10 0-0-0 ♗c5 11 ♘d5 ♕xe5
12 f4 exf3 13 exf3 0-0 14 f4 ♕d6 15 g3
♖b8 16 ♗g2 c6 17 ♕c3 b5 18 b4 bxc4 19
bxc5 and White won, M.Narciso Dub-
lan-D.Recuero Guerra, Pamplona 2005.

c) After 6...d6, Ribli gives 7 exd6
♗xd6 8 ♘b5 ♗b4+ 9 ♗d2 ♕xd2+ 10
♕xd2 ♗xd2+ 11 ♔xd2, with an edge.

d) 6...c6!? 7 ♗f4, and if 7...g5 8 ♗g3
f4 9 e3 fxg3 10 ♕h5+ ♔e7 11 ♕xg5+ ♔e8
12 ♕h5+ ♔e7 13 hxg3, also looks good.

e) White also got something from
this line in the game M.Narciso Dub-
lan-V.Moskalenko, Solsones 2004, after
6...♘e7 7 g4!? fxg4 8 ♕d4 ♘c6 9 ♕xe4
♗b4 10 ♕xg4 0-0 11 ♕g3 d6 12 ♖g1 ♖f7
13 ♗g5.

Returning to 5 ♘g5:

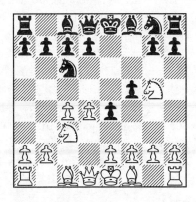

5...♘f6

Play transposes in the case of 5...h6

6 ♘h3 g5 7 ♘h3 ♘f6 8 e3. Black sometimes also plays 5...♗b4!?, which may
simply transpose into lines below, such
as 6 ♗d2 ♘f6 is seen in the notes to
Black's 6th move, but 6 f3 ♘f6 7 e3 h6 8
♘h3 may be self-standing.
A.Beliavsky-V.Bagirov, Minsk 1983,
continued 8...♗xc3+ 9 bxc3 d6 10 ♗e2
0-0 11 0-0 b6 12 ♘f4 ♘a5 13 ♕c2 c5 14
♗d2 ♗d7 15 ♘d5 ♘xd5 16 cxd5 ♕e7 17
dxc5 dxc5 18 c4 ♘b7 19 f4 ♘d6 20 a4 a5
21 ♖fb1 ♖a6 22 ♗c3, with good
chances.

6 e3

A major alternative which may well
also suffice for an edge is 6 ♘h3, but I
rather like Marin's approach.

6...h6

Black allows himself to be provoked. He might also try 6...♗b4 7 ♗d2
♕e7, but this has been under a cloud
since the game L.Polugaevsky-
Y.Balashov, Leningrad 1977, which
continued 8 ♘h3 ♘d8 9 a3 (Uhlmann
later contended that 9 c5!? ♗xc3 10
♗xc3 d5 11 cxd6 ♕xd6 12 d5!, or
11...cxd6 12 d5, would have been even
better) 9...♗xc3 10 ♗xc3 d6 11 ♘f4 0-0
12 ♗e2 c6 13 d5 c5 14 h4 ♘f7 15 b4 b6
16 g3 ♘e5 17 bxc5 bxc5 18 ♖b1 ♘fg4 19
♔f1, and with his king safe on g2,
White eventually made inroads into
Black's position down the b-file and on
e6.

7 ♘h3 g5 8 ♘g1!

What a wonderful concept and a serious test! Black has gained some time
and space, but White can play to undermine Black's weakened kingside
pawns with h4 and f3. White's knight

will re-emerge, either on e2, or, after h4, on h3. The course of the main game also indicates a more hidden point, namely that Black's advanced kingside pawns can become a source of great weakness in many endgames, not least if they become fixed, as they often do, on h5, g4, f5 and e4.

8...&g7

The extended fianchetto is best. Alternatively:

a) The slower 8...&e7 gave White a dangerous attack after 9 h4 g4 (neither did the convoluted 9...&g6 10 hxg5 hxg5 11 &xh8 &xh8 help Black after 12 &b3 d6 13 &d2 c6 14 0-0-0 &b6 15 &c2 &d7 16 f3 d5 17 g4 exf3 18 &xf3 fxg4 19 &xg5 dxc4 20 &xc4 0-0-0 21 &e6, with a clear advantage in C.McNab-S.Weeramantry, Gibraltar 2005) 10 &ge2 h5 11 &f4 &f7 12 &d2 c6 13 d5 &g6 14 &xg6 &xg6 15 &c2 cxd5 16 0-0-0 dxc4 17 &xc4 a6 18 &d5 &xd5 19 &xd5, in J.Timman-Z.Krnic, Amsterdam 2000.

b) Black also suffered after in 8...&b4 in G.Schwartzman-D.Vest, Kissimmee 1997, which continued 9 h4

&f7 (9...&xc3+ 10 bxc3 g4 11 c5 is good for White too) 10 &d2 a5 11 a3 &xc3 12 &xc3 d5 13 cxd5 &e7 14 d6! cxd6 15 d5 g4 16 &c4 &d7 17 &e2 b5 18 &b3 h5 19 &f4 &g6 20 &e6 &xe6 21 dxe6+ &e7 22 &c1 &c8 23 0-0 &e5 24 &d2 a4 25 &xe5 dxe5 26 &b4+ &d6 27 &xb5, and White won.

9 h4

9...g4

Black usually tries to block the game like this. The advance weakens key kingside dark squares, but Black hopes that his extra kingside space will markedly reduce White's scope for effective pawn breaks. Instead White was better after both 9...&e7 10 hxg5 hxg5 11 &xh8+ &xh8 12 &h3 g4 13 &f4 c6 14 d5, G.Zaichik-A.Reprintsev, Philadelphia 1996, and 9...&f7?! 10 f3 d6 11 &h3 in G.Schwartzman-T.Wolski, Las Vegas 1996, which abruptly concluded: 11...g4 12 fxg4 fxg4 13 &f4 h5 14 g3 &f5 15 &g2 &d7 16 0-0 &ae8 17 &fd5 &g6 18 &xf6 &xf6 19 &f4 1-0.

10 &ge2 h5

Black only loses time after 10...&h5!? 11 &d5 &e7 12 &ef4 &xf4 13

♘xf4 h5. C.McNab-D.Mason, British League 2004, powerfully continued 14 ♕b3 ♖h6?! 15 c5! ♔f8 16 ♗c4 ♖b8 17 ♗f7 b6 18 ♗xh5 ♖f6 19 f3 exf3 20 gxf3 ♗b7 21 c6 ♘xc6 22 ♗d2 ♘a5 23 ♗xa5 ♗xf3 24 ♗b4+ c5 25 dxc5 ♗xh1 26 c6+ d6 27 0-0-0 ♕c7 28 ♖xd6 1-0.

11 b3!?

This is safe but perhaps over-cautious. Marin suggests that 11 ♘f4, and if 11...d6 12 d5 ♘e5 13 ♘b5 ♗h6 14 ♘d4 ♗xf4 15 exf4 ♘g6 16 ♗e3 0-0 17 ♗e2, may be better.

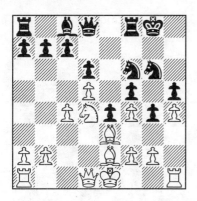

He considers that White may then be able to continue favourably with moves such as g3, ♔f1-g2, ♕d2, ♘c2, ♗d4, ♘e3 and b4.

11...♘e7 12 ♘f4 d6 13 ♗e2 ♔f7 14 ♗b2 ♘g6 15 ♘xg6 ♔xg6 16 ♕c2 c6 17 g3 d5?!

Without this move, which weakens the queenside dark squares, it would be much more difficult for White to make queenside progress. Black should have preferred Marin's 17...a6, intending ...b5.

18 a4 ♗e6 19 a5 ♖c8!?

Black now has to make some tricky

decisions. 19...a6 20 ♕d2, followed by ♘a4, might certainly have worried Black, but it would have drawn White's knight well away from the even more powerful f4-square.

20 a6 b6 21 0-0 ♘d7 22 cxd5 ♗xd5

Better than 22...cxd5 when White will be able to build on his light-square control, target b5 as a possible entry square and make use of the c-file.

23 ♗a3 ♘f6 24 ♗c4 ♗f8?

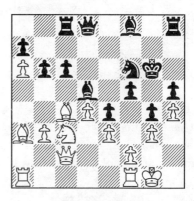

Inviting the exchange of this piece is a serious misjudgement. Now White's knight can get to f4 without challenge.

25 ♗xf8 ♕xf8 26 ♘e2 ♕d6 27 ♘f4+ ♔h6 28 ♖ac1 ♕d7

Or 28...b5?! 29 ♗xd5 ♘xd5 30 ♘xd5 cxd5? (the awful 30...♕xd5 is now essential) 31 ♕xc8 ♖xc8 32 ♖xc8 ♕xa6 33 ♖fc1 and wins, as analysed by Marin.

29 ♕b2 ♖hd8!?

Black's fixed and far-flung kingside pawns are now a fatal liability. If White can achieve any decent sort of queen-side or central breakthrough, Black will be hard put to defend his f- and h-pawns as well as his vulnerable king. After 29...♗xc4 30 bxc4 Black will be unable to prevent an eventual d5 breakthrough, and White should also win after 29...b5 30 ♗xd5 ♘xd5 31 ♘xd5 cxd5 32 ♖c5 (Marin).

30 ♖c2

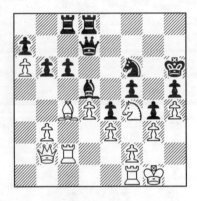

30...b5!?

This ruinous move fatally weakens c5, but otherwise White doubles rooks on the c-file and plays b4, followed by ♕b3 and if need be b5.

31 ♗xd5 ♘xd5 32 ♘xd5 cxd5

Or 32...♕xd5 33 ♖c5, and White wins by tripling on the c-file and playing d5.

33 ♖fc1 b4 34 ♖c5 ♖xc5 35 dxc5 ♕c6 36 ♕e5 ♖d7 37 ♕xf5 1-0

Game 16
A.Mikhalchishin-A.Skripchenko
Dortmund 2000

---

1 c4 e5 2 ♘c3 ♘c6 3 ♘f3 f5 4 d4 e4 5 ♗g5

This line seeks to exchange White's potentially bad bishop. It is far from a bad try, although it is questionable whether it is quite as testing or as rich

in ideas as 5 ♘g5.

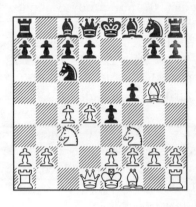

5...♗e7

Black's main move, but he also has 5...♘f6 and now:

a) 6 ♘d2 is the simple approach,

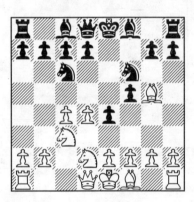

and leads to a further divide:

a1) White developed a queenside initiative and play in the centre after 6...♗e7 7 e3 d6 (White can also play for a kingside attack based on castling queenside and the plan h3 and g4, as he did in F.Rayner-D.Howell, Swansea 2002: 7...0-0 8 ♗e2 d6 9 ♕b3 a6?! 10 0-0-0 ♖b8 11 h3 ♘a5?! 12 ♕a4 c5 13 dxc5 ♗d7 14 ♕c2 dxc5 15 g4 b5 16 gxf5 ♗xf5 17 cxb5 ♕c8 18 ♗f4 ♖a8 19 ♘c4, and White won; in this line, V.Inkiov-V.Bagirov, Jurmala 1985, saw the superior 9...♔h8 10 0-0-0 a6 11 h3 b5 12 g4 ♘a5 13 ♕c2 c6 14 f4 bxc4 15 ♘xc4, with no more than a minimal pull) 8 b4 0-0 9 ♕b3 ♔h8 10 ♗e2 ♗d7 11 0-0 h6 12 ♗xf6 ♗xf6 13 ♘d5 ♗g5 14 f4 exf3 15 ♘xf3 ♗e7 16 ♘f4 ♕e8 17 ♖ae1 ♗f6 18 ♘d2 a5 19 b5 g6 20 ♗f3 c6 21 a4 (*see following diagram*) with a pull in the game W.Uhlmann-K.Arakhamia Grant, Aruba 1992.

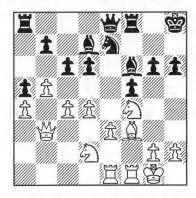

a2) After the provocative 6...h6 7 ♗xf6 ♕xf6 8 e3 ♘e7, H.Liebert-V.Kupreichik, Stary Smokovec 1975, continued 9 g4! g6 10 gxf5 gxf5 11 ♕h5+ ♔d8 12 f3! exf3 13 ♘xf3 d6 14 ♗d3 ♖g8 15 0-0-0 f4 16 ♘d5 ♘xd5 17 ♕xd5 ♖g7 18 e4, with dangerous threats.

a3) Even worse is 6...♘xd4?! 7 ♘dxe4 fxe4 8 ♕xd4, when White is ahead in development and Black's e-pawn tottering.

b) 6 ♘e5!? ♗b4 (6...♗e7 7 e3, and if 7...d6 8 ♘xc6 bxc6 9 f3, also looks a little better for White) 7 e3 ♕e7 8 ♕b3 a5 9 ♘xc6 bxc6 10 c5 d5 11 cxd6 cxd6 12 d5 c5 13 ♗b5+ ♔f7 14 0-0 ♗xc3 15 bxc3

h6 16 ♗xf6 ♔xf6 17 ♗c6 ♗a6 18 ♗xa8 ♗xf1 19 ♖xf1 ♖xa8 20 ♖b1, with a clear advantage, was D.Bronstein-V.Arbakov, Moscow 1981.

Returning to 5...♗e7:

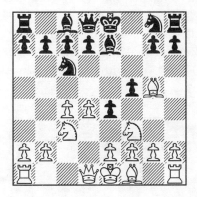

6 ♗xe7 ♘cxe7

Again there are less common alternatives:

a) After the relatively unexplored 6...♘gxe7, best is probably 7 ♘g5. D.Cramling-J.Furhoff, Stockholm 1993, continued 7...♘g6 8 ♘h3 0-0 9 e3 d6 10 ♕d2 ♘ce7 11 ♗e2 c6 12 0-0 d5 13 f3 ♗e6 14 b3 ♕d6 15 c5 ♕c7 16 b4 exf3 17 ♖xf3 ♔h8 18 ♗d3 ♘g8 19 ♖af1 ♘h4 20 ♖f4 ♘g6 21 ♖4f2 ♘h6 22 ♘f4 ♘g4 23 ♖e2 ♗d7 24 h3 ♘f6, and now 25 ♖ef2 looks a little better for White.

b) Black can also consider 6...♕xe7!?, especially since White achieved little in A.Miles-V.Liberzon, Buenos Aires 1979, after 7 ♘d5 (perhaps 7 ♘g1!?, after which 7...e3!? 8 f4 ♘f6 9 ♘f3 0-0 10 g3 ♕b4 11 ♕b3 b6 12 ♗g2 ♕xb3 13 axb3 ♗b7 14 0-0 ♘a5 15 ♖a3 saw White getting somewhere in J.Tarjan-J.Speelman, Malta Olympiad 1980) 7...♕d6 8 ♘d2 ♘ge7 9 ♘xe7 ♕xe7

10 e3 d6 11 ♕h5+ g6 12 ♕h6 ♘b4 13 ♔d1 c5.

7 ♘d2 ♘f6

The ambitious 7...e3?! only rebounds on Black. S.Palatnik-J.Benjamin, Philadelphia 1991, continued 8 fxe3 ♘f6 9 ♕b3! ♘g4 10 g3 ♘xe3 11 ♘d1 ♘xf1 12 ♖xf1 0-0, and now Palatnik suggests 13 ♘c3, and if 13...d6 14 0-0-0 c6 15 e4, with the better game.

8 e3

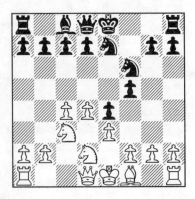

8...d6!?

With Black's pawn on d6, Black's e-pawn is less well protected, giving White a little more time and freedom of action to begin play on the queenside or in the centre. Black can and perhaps therefore should prefer either 8...c6 or 8...0-0, followed by ...c6, attempting to get in ...d5 in a single move. However, matters are not entirely clear after this plan either:

a) After 8...c6 White cut across Black's plan by playing 9 c5!? (Adamski's 9 b4 d5 10 b5 0-0 11 bxc6 bxc6 12 ♗e2 may also promise an edge) 9...d5 10 cxd6 ♕xd6 11 ♘c4 ♕c7 12 ♕b3 in D.Zagorskis-A.Matthaei, Porz 1993.

b) 8...0-0 9 ♗e2 c6 10 0-0 (White can also consider 10 b4, and if 10...d5 11 b5) 10...d5 11 ♕b3!? ♔h8 12 f4 exf3 13 ♘xf3 ♘g4 14 ♘d1 dxc4 15 ♗xc4 was pretty complicated in J.Sunye Neto-G.Sax, Rio de Janeiro 1979. However, 11 b4!? or a simpler plan, such as 11 ♘b3, and if 11...b6 12 cxd5 cxd5 13 a4, might be better.

9 ♗e2

Immediate central action is also possible. After 9 f3!? exf3 10 ♕xf3 c6 11 ♗d3 d5, all French Defence players will recognize White's position as a very active form of the defence, with an extra tempo.

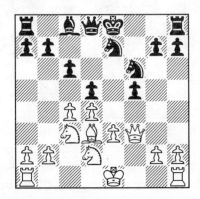

Black can occupy e4, but White's dynamic chances down the c- and f-files, potential to attack Black's pawns on d5 and f5, free piece play and opportunities on the h2-b8 diagonal, particularly the e5-square, give him a pull. L.Kavalek-F.Blatny, Luhacovice 1968, for example, continued 12 cxd5 cxd5 13 0-0 0-0 14 ♕g3 ♗d7 15 ♘f3 ♖c8 16 ♖ac1 ♘e4 17 ♕e1 ♕a5 18 ♘e5 ♗e6 19 ♘b5 ♕b6 20 ♖xc8 ♖xc8 21 ♕h4 ♘c6 22 ♘xc6 bxc6 23 ♗xe4 dxe4 24 ♘d6 ♕d8 25 ♕g3

罝c7 26 b3 c5 27 豐e5, and White won.

9...c6

Black plays to give herself the option of ...d5. She could also have sought to justify her last move with the development 9...0-0 10 0-0 (White might well prefer to prevent Black's next with Tarjan's 10 b4) 10...c5. J.Mellado Trivino-L.Fressinet, French League 2001, continued 11 ♘b3 b6, and now Raetsky and Chetverik suggest 12 f3 and if 12...♗b7 13 a4 exf3 14 ♗xf3 ♗xf3 15 豐xf3 豐d7 16 a5 罝ac8 17 axb6 axb6 18 罝a6 ♘e4 19 罝xb6 cxd4 20 exd4 ♘xc3 21 bxc3 罝xc4 22 ♘d2 罝c6 23 罝b4, with a slight pull.

10 f4

This standard blocking move also has its roots in the French Defence. It aims to stabilize the centre and leave White free to operate on the flanks with a highly secure king position. The advantage in such positions generally goes to the better developed player, best able to support flank action. Here White fits that bill well. White can, of course, also develop play based on 10 b4 or 10 0-0.

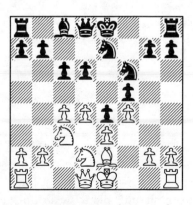

10...exf3!?

Black should have preferred 10...d5. Although White is then a little better, he is far from having yet achieved any significant advantage on either flank and Black's game will be hard to break down.

11 ♘xf3

White can hope for an edge both with this move and 11 ♗xf3. White has the same sort of advantage already referred to in the note to his 9th move and the game Kavalek-Blatny. Black's d-pawn is not (yet) on d5, which helps Black cover the e5-square, but on d6 it exerts no pressure on e4. Because White's pieces are very active, Black constantly has to be on guard against a favourable e4 break by White at any time.

11...♘e4 12 豐c2

Black may have been banking on making something of her knight's occupation of the e4 square, but it proves unstable there. White mustn't, however, rush things and after 12 ♘xe4? fxe4 13 ♘d2 ♘f5, Black is better.

12...豐a5

Black can only support her knight on e4 by weakening her hold on e5. White has an edge too after 12...d5 13 ♘e5.

13 0-0 ♘xc3 14 bxc3 豐c7 15 ♗d3 0-0 16 罝ae1 g6!?

This wasn't an easy choice as it weakens Black's kingside dark squares. However, 16...♗d7 17 e4 opens the centre to the advantage of White's better developed pieces.

17 豐f2 ♔g7 18 豐h4 d5!?

This was another tough decision, weakening e5 permanently and inviting White's dangerous response on the flank. But Black can't complete her queenside development easily and White is better after 18...♗e6!? 19 e4, and possibly also 19 ♘g5!? ♗g8 20 g4.

19 g4 b6

Black's defence is very difficult. After 19...fxg4?! Mikhalchishin planned 20 ♘g5 ♖xf1+ (or 20...h5 21 ♖xf8 ♔xf8 22 ♖f1+ ♔g8 23 ♖f6) 21 ♖xf1 h5 22 ♖f7+ ♔g8 23 ♘e6, and wins.

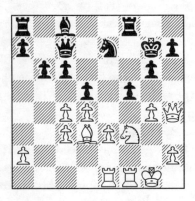

20 e4!

And this is a sublime attacking thrust. Even if there is a hidden saving course, it is very hard to defend positions like this over the board.

20...dxe4

After the game, Mikhalchishin gave the brilliant fantasy variation 20...fxe4?! 21 ♘g5 ♖xf1+ (or 21...h5 22 ♖xf8 ♔xf8 23 ♘xe4 dxe4 24 ♕f6+ ♔g8 25 ♖xe4) 22 ♖xf1 h5 23 ♖f7+ ♔g8 24 gxh5 ♘f5 25 h6! and wins.

21 ♗xe4 ♘g8?!

This makes it relatively easy for White, who now gets a clear, risk-free

attack at no material cost. Ribli suggests that Black might have struggled on with 21...fxe4!? and if 22 ♘g5 h5 23 ♖xf8 ♔xf8 24 ♕f2+ ♘f5 25 gxf5 gxf5 26 ♘xe4, although lines like this are still rather better for White.

22 gxf5 ♗xf5

Or 22...gxf5 23 ♘e5!.

23 ♗xf5 ♖xf5 24 ♘g5 ♔h8 25 ♖xf5 gxf5 26 ♔h1

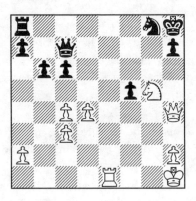

White has a clear lead in development, many positional advantages and attacking threats. In the final moves, he manages to convert these into a win against ever more back-to-the-wall defence by a despairing Skripchenko.

26...b5 27 d5 ♕g7 28 d6 h6 29 ♘e6 ♕xc3 30 d7 bxc4 31 d8♕ ♖xd8 32 ♘xd8 ♕d2 33 ♘e6 c5 34 ♕g3 1-0

Game 17
E.Bareev-V.Bologan
Ajaccio 2006

---

1 c4 e5 2 ♘c3 d6

The best way of heading for an ...f5 set-up should Black wish to do so without an early ...♘c6. Otherwise White achieves a very pleasant initiative in all variations after the immediate 2...f5!? 3 d4! exd4 (or 3...e4 4 ♘h3 and White has simply gained two tempi over our main game in which his knight only reaches h3 via f3 and g5) 4 ♕xd4:

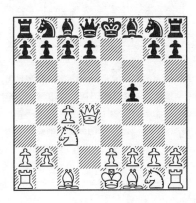

a) White has a definite advantage after 4...♘c6 5 ♕e3+!; for example, 5...♔f7 6 ♘h3 ♘f6 7 ♘g5+ ♔g8 8 ♘d5 h6 9 ♘f3 ♘e4 10 ♕b3 d6 11 g3 ♘e7 12 ♗g2 c6 13 ♘c3 ♘xc3 14 ♕xc3 was promising in the game B.Damljanovic-V.Tseshkovsky, Vrnjacka Banja 2005, as was 5...♕e7 6 ♘d5 ♕xe3 7 ♗xe3 ♗d6 8 0-0-0 ♘ge7 9 ♘f3 ♘xd5 10 cxd5 ♘e7 11 g3 b6 12 ♗g2 ♗b7 13 ♘d4 in the game W.Uhlmann-G.Braun, Naumburg 2002.

b) 4...♘f6 is a better move, but White also has a pull after 5 g3 ♘c6 6 ♕e3+. For example, C.Matamoros Franco-L.Vera, Rio de Janeiro 2003, continued 6...♕e7 7 ♗g2 ♕xe3 8 ♗xe3 ♗b4 9 ♗d2 ♗xc3 10 ♗xc3 0-0 11 ♘h3 d6 12 b3 h6 13 ♘f4 ♘e7 14 0-0, with the upper hand.

3 ♘f3 f5 4 d4 e4

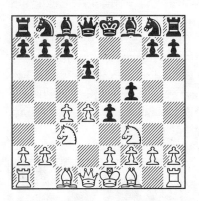

5 ♘g5

This is almost certainly White's best move. With Black's pawn on d6, 5 ♘g5 is even livelier than it is with Black's knight on c6, as in Game 15. After the knight's eventual retreat to h3, White can play two very distinct systems: one based on e3 and the other on g3. White can also play 5 ♗g5, but this has less bite with Black's pawn on d6 as Black benefits from not having a knight on c6 to be kicked by a white pawn, or simply getting in the way of his c-pawn. Indeed, after the sample line 5 ♗g5 ♗e7 6 ♗xe7 ♕xe7 7 ♘d5 ♕d8 8 ♘d2 c6 9 ♘c3 ♘f6 10 e3 0-0 11 ♗e2 ♗e6 12 0-0 ♘bd7 13 f3 d5 14 fxe4 fxe4 15 cxd5 cxd5 16 ♕b3 ♕b6, White has nothing.

5...♘f6

It is helpful not to get too confused by transpositions at this point. Black's most usual choice is a system based on development with ...♘f6, ...♗e7 and ...c6. He also sometimes chooses a system based on ...♘f6, ...g5 (or ...g6), ...♗g7 and ...c6, and there are various ways to reach the same set-ups. These will be separated out in this note, as well in the notes to Black's 6th and White's 7th and 9th moves below.

Black's second system (with an extended fianchetto) generally occurs now, and after 5...h6 6 ♘h3 g5 7 ♘g1! we meet a familiar position from Game 15 with Black's pawn on d6 and his knight still on b8.

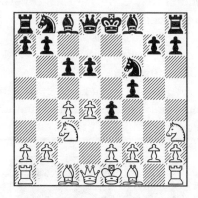

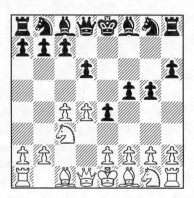

White can quickly play h4, secure his king and play on the queenside. V.Lazarev-F.Velikhanli, Geneva 2001, continued 7...♗g7 (the same h4 idea is also favourable after 7...♘f6: 8 h4 ♖g8 9 hxg5 hxg5 10 ♘h3 g4 11 ♘f4 c6 12 e3 ♘a6 13 ♗d2 ♘c7 14 ♕b3 ♕e7 15 0-0-0, favoured White in M.Illescas Cordoba-J.Hodgson, Spanish Team Championship 1993) 8 h4 g4 9 e3 c6 10 ♘ge2 ♗e6 11 ♘f4 ♗f7 12 ♗d2 ♘f6 13 ♗e2 h5 14 g3 ♘a6 15 a3 ♘c7 16 ♔f1 0-0 17 ♔g2 ♘e6 18 ♕c2 ♘xf4+ 19 exf4 d5 20 c5 ♘e8 21 ♗e3 ♘c7 22 b4, with good play for White.

6 ♘h3 ♗e7

Black frequently delays a decision on this bishop's development by playing 6...c6, which leaves White with three options:

a) 7 ♗g5 sees White preparing to exchange his slightly worse bishop. Black's best reply may be 7...♗e7 transposing into lines considered in note 'b' to White's 7th move. Instead the aggressive 7...h6 8 ♗xf6 ♕xf6 9 e3 g5 10 ♘g1! gives White good chances, not just on the kingside, where Black has long-term weaknesses, but even more critically on the queenside and in the centre. Y.Seirawan-E.Torre, Zagreb 1987, continued energetically 10...♘d7 11 h4 ♖g8 12 hxg5 hxg5 13 ♘ge2 ♘b6 14 ♕b3 ♕f7 15 d5! ♗d7 16 a4 ♗c8 17 a5 ♘d7 18 ♘d4 ♘c5 19 ♕a3 ♕c7 20 ♖d1 ♗d7 21 b4 ♘a6 22 b5, and White won.

b) 7 e3 will normally transpose to our main game after 7...♗e7. Instead 7...g6 8 ♗e2 ♗g7 9 f3 0-0 10 0-0 ♘a6 11 fxe4 fxe4 12 ♘f4 ♘c7 13 ♗d2 ♕e8 14 b4 left White with a small plus in W.Uhlmann-J.Hickl, German League 1997.

c) 7 g3 can transpose after 7...♗e7 to note 'a' to White's 7th move, below. Once again Black might also fianchetto, but after 7...g6 8 ♗g2 ♗g7 White effectively combined space-gaining play in the centre with an f3 break in H.Machelett-V.Jansa, German League 2003, which continued 9 0-0 ♘a6 10 f3 exf3 11 exf3 0-0 12 d5 c5 13 ♘f4 ♘c7 14 ♖e1 ♖e8 15 ♗d2 g5 16 ♘d3, with a slight pull.

7 e3

White plays for a closed structure based on an e3 and d4 pawn centre. He has a major alternative in 7 g3 and can also play 7 ♗g5:

a) 7 g3 sees White plan d5, followed by f3, to open lines for his pieces and support play on the e-file. Play usually continues 7...0-0 8 ♗g2 c6 9 0-0 ♘a6 10 d5 ♘c7 11 a4...

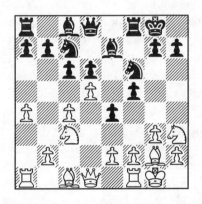

...after which White's d5 and f3 strategy was successful in D.Khismatullin-A.Kosteniuk, Kazan 2005, which continued 11...cxd5 (Black's best may be 11...a5!?, planning ...♘a6, but White might still have a pull after 12 f3, and if 12...cxd5 13 cxd5 ♘a6 14 ♗e3!, preventing ...♕b6) 12 cxd5 ♖b8 13 a5 ♖e8 14 f3 exf3 15 exf3 b5 16 axb6 ♖xb6 17 ♘f4 ♗f8 18 ♖e1 a6 19 ♗f1 ♗d7 20 ♗c4 ♕c8 21 b3 ♘b5 22 ♘a4 ♖b8 23 ♗b2 ♕b7 24 ♕d2 ♗e7 25 ♔g2 ♘c7

26 ♘c5 ♕c8 27 ♖ac1 ♕d8 28 ♘ce6 ♗xe6 29 ♘xe6 ♘xe6 30 ♖xe6, with a clear advantage.

b) 7 ♗g5 prepares to exchange White's slightly worse bishop to reduce Black's scope for counterplay and underscore White's structural advantages. White cleverly countered a plan to bring Black's knight to e6 in V.Popov-A.Utkin, St Petersburg 2001, which continued 7...c6 (B.Grachev-P.Svidler, Moscow (blitz) 2006, varied with 7...0-0 8 e3 c5 9 ♘f4 ♘c6, and now 10 dxc5 dxc5 11 ♗e2 retains a slight edge) 8 e3 0-0 9 ♘f4 ♘a6 10 h4 ♘c7 11 ♕b3! ♘e6 (or 11...♖b8 12 ♗e2 ♘e6 13 c5 d5 14 ♘xe6 ♗xe6 15 ♗f4, with an edge in S.Lputian-R.Tischbierek, Dortmund 1992) 12 c5 d5 13 ♘xe6 ♗xe6 14 ♕xb7, with a good extra pawn.

7...0-0 8 ♗e2 c6

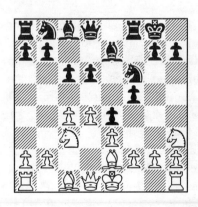

9 d5

White plays for space in the centre before deciding on any specific kingside configuration. He can also play both 9 0-0, with the idea of breaking in the centre with f3, and 9 ♘f4, with the idea of h4:

a) 9 0-0 ♘a6 10 f3 prepares to play French Defence-like positions with an extra tempo:

a1) W.Uhlmann-H.Knoll, Linz 1997, saw an effective transposition into a fully reversed French Defence after 10...d5!? 11 cxd5 cxd5 12 fxe4 fxe4 13 ♘f4 ♘c7 14 ♗d2 ♗d7 15 b4 ♗e8 16 ♕b3 ♗f7 17 b5 ♘ce8?! 18 b6!, and White enjoyed some advantage.

a2) If Black exchanges on f3, White can play on the queenside and in the centre. E.Ubilava-M.Rivas Pastor, Spanish Team Championship 1993, continued comfortably for White after 10...exf3 11 ♗xf3 ♘c7 12 ♕b3 ♔h8 13 ♗d2 d5 14 cxd5!? ♘cxd5 15 ♘xd5 ♘xd5 16 ♗xd5 ♕xd5 17 ♕xd5 cxd5 18 ♘f4 ♖d8 19 ♖ac1 b6 20 ♖c2 g5?! 21 ♘h5 ♗a6? 22 ♖c7 ♗xf1 23 ♖xe7 ♗d3 24 ♘f6 f4 25 exf4 g4 26 f5 ♗xf5 27 ♗f4 ♖f8 28 ♘xg4 1-0.

b) 9 ♘f4!? fights for more kingside and central ground. C.McNab-P.Gayson, Gibraltar 2003, for example, continued 9...♘a6 10 h4 ♘c7 11 d5 c5 (E.Gausel-V.Bologan, Manila Olympiad 1992, had seen 11...♘d7 12 h5 c5 and now perhaps 13 ♕c2 and ♗d2 is again best, whereas the game became pretty unclear after 13 b3!? ♗f6 14 ♗b2 ♘e5 15 ♕d2 ♗d7 16 ♖d1 ♕e7 17 ♔f1 ♖fd8 18 a4 a6 19 a5 ♖ab8 20 ♖a1 b5) 12 h5 ♕e8 13 ♕c2 ♗d7 14 a4 ♕f7 15 ♗d2 ♖fb8 16 f3 exf3 17 gxf3 b6 18 ♗d3 ♘fe8 19 ♘ce2 ♗g5 20 ♘g3 ♗xf4 21 exf4 g6 22 hxg6 hxg6 23 ♗c3 ♘f6 24 0-0-0, with a strong attack.

Returning to 9 d5:

9...♘bd7

Under changed circumstances, Black's knight heads for e5.

10 b3 ♘e5 11 ♗b2

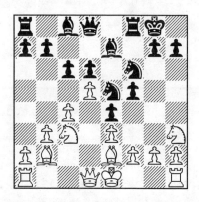

11...a5

White now achieves an edge with a small combination. Instead D.Cummings-W.Watson, Norwich 1994, saw the slightly unusual 11...♘fg4!? 12 ♕d2 ♗h4, to which White should probably react calmly with 13 0-0, and if 13...c5 14 f4 exf3 15 gxf3 ♘f6 16 ♘f4. If Black plays 11...c5, White should probably reply 12 ♘f4.

12 dxc6 bxc6 13 c5!

This neat lever slightly weakens Black's centre pawns and dark squares.

13...d5 14 ♘xd5 ♘xd5 15 ♗xe5 ♗xc5 16 0-0 ♕e7 17 ♗d4 ♗d6 18 ♖c1 ♗d7 19 ♗c4 ♗e6 20 ♗xd5!

White correctly plays for an opposite-coloured bishop middlegame. He has the better bishop and many pieces still remain on the board in a position where he has some realistic attacking chances on both flanks. By eliminating Black's powerful knight, White also solves the problem of getting his own knight into play.

20...♗xd5 21 ♘f4 ♗xf4 22 exf4

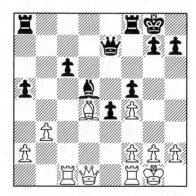

White's pawns now offer his bishop a potentially strong outpost on e5 and create possibilities for an attack down the g-file. Although a long way off, if White were, say, to combine pressure by a rook on g3 with an h3 and g4 pawn break, he might cause problems. As Black's split a- and c-pawns also give some cause for concern, White clearly has something to work on.

22...♖fd8 23 ♕c2 ♕e6 24 ♗e5 h6 25 ♖fe1 ♔h7 26 h3 g5?!

Black decides to defend actively, but passive defence may have been better. Black's king certainly seems a lot more open after this decision.

27 ♖cd1 ♖g8 28 g3 ♖af8 29 ♕c3 ♕g6 30 ♔h2 ♕h5 31 ♖d2 ♕e8

White's prospects have brightened remarkably. Black's active attempt to create kingside counterplay has completely backfired and White now wins Black's a-pawn cheaply. Black can no longer defend his abandoned queenside. He is lost after both 31...♖a8 32 ♖xd5 cxd5 33 ♕c7+ ♔g6 34 ♕d6+ ♔h7 35 ♕e7+ ♔g6 36 ♖c1 ♖a6 37 ♖c7, in-

tending 37...gxf4 38 ♕f7+ ♔g5 39 ♗xf4 mate, and 31...a4 32 bxa4 ♗xa2 33 ♕xc6.

32 ♕xa5 h5 33 ♕c3 h4 34 fxg5 ♖xg5 35 ♗f4 ♖h5 36 ♖g1 hxg3+ 37 ♖xg3

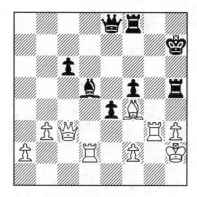

Black's plight has only got worse. With the black rook on h5 playing no real part in the game, White's rooks dominate.

37...♖g8 38 ♖d1 ♖xg3 39 ♕xg3 ♕g6 40 ♕e3 ♕f7 41 ♖g1 ♖h4 42 ♕g3 ♖h5 43 ♕c3 ♖h4 44 ♗e5 ♕h5 45 ♖g7+ ♔h6 46 ♖g3 ♕f7 47 ♗g7+ ♔h7 48 ♗f6 ♕h5 49 ♗xh4 1-0

Game 18
M.Marin-M.Narciso Dublan
Solsona 2004

---

1 c4 e5 2 ♘c3 ♗b4 3 ♘d5

White can play many third moves, but this occupies a strong central outpost, attacks Black's bishop, avoids positions with doubled c-pawns and intuitively feels best. One of its merits is that it forces Black to play the game in accordance with White's intentions.

Moves such as 3 g3, 3 ♘f3, 3 ♕c2, and 3 e3 allow Black to choose from a range of playable alternatives to re-entering the main lines of the Four Knights after ...♘f6 and ...♘c6.

3...♗e7

This is Black's usual choice, but he can also play:

a) 3...a5 is slightly weakening and gives White several good replies, including 4 ♘f3 (4 a3 ♗e7 5 d4 d6 6 e3, intending 6...♘f6 7 ♘xe7 ♕xe7 8 ♘e2 with a bishop-pair advantage, is also favourable) 4...♘c6 (or 4...e4!? 5 a3 c6 6 axb4 cxd5 7 ♘d4 dxc4 8 d3 ♕b6 9 dxc4 ♕xb4+ 10 ♗d2 ♕c5 11 ♘b5 ♘e7 12 ♗e3 ♕b4+ 13 ♕d2 ♘a6 14 ♘d6+ ♔f8 15 ♖xa5, and White won in M.Gurevich-C.Kennaugh, British League 1998) 5 a3 ♗c5 6 e3 e4 7 d4 exd3 8 ♗xd3 ♘f6 9 ♕c2 d6 10 ♗d2 ♘e5 11 ♘xe5 dxe5 12 0-0-0 h6 13 ♗c3 ♘d7 14 ♗f5 c6 15 ♘f4! ♕e7 16 ♘d3 ♗d6 17 f4!, with good chances in M.Marin-J.Estrada Nieto, Andorra 2001.

b) The main line was once 3...♗a5, but White's centre gives him an edge after 4 b4! c6 5 bxa5 cxd5 6 cxd5 ♕xa5

(White also keeps an edge after 6...♘f6 7 ♕a4; for example, 7...♘xd5 8 ♕e4 ♘e7 9 ♕xe5 0-0 10 ♗b2 f6 11 ♕d6 ♘bc6 12 e3 ♔h8 13 ♘f3 ♘f5 14 ♕f4 ♘fe7 15 a6 b5 16 ♗d3, favoured White in R.Slobodjan-M.Bluvshtein, Havana 2004) 7 e4 ♘f6.

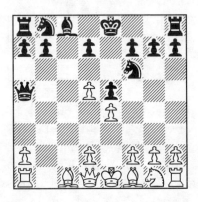

White plays for d4 and for strong e4- and d5-pawns as a basis for play on the flanks. This plan of action for White worked well in the instructive encounter V.Tukmakov-A.Raetsky, Lausanne 2005, after 8 f3 0-0 9 ♔f2 d6 10 d4 ♘bd7 11 ♗b2 ♖e8 12 ♘e2 b5 13 a4 b4 14 ♘c1 ♗a6 15 ♘b3 ♕b6 16 a5 ♕b7 17 ♖c1 ♖ac8 18 ♗xa6 ♕xa6 19 ♕e2 ♕b7 20 dxe5 dxe5 21 ♖xc8 ♖xc8 22 ♖c1 ♘e8 23 a6 ♕b8 24 ♔f1 ♖xc1+ 25 ♗xc1 ♘d6 26 ♗e3 ♕c7 27 ♕d3 f6 28 ♔e2 ♔f7 29 g4 g6 30 h3 h5 31 ♗f2 hxg4 32 hxg4 ♔e7 33 ♔d1 ♔f7 34 ♕c2 ♕xc2+ 35 ♔xc2, and White won.

c) 3...♗c5 is Black's best alternative to the text:

c1) White can hope for a slight pull with 4 e3. A.Kharlov-J.Piket, French League 2001, for example, continued, 4...♘f6 5 b4 ♘xd5 6 bxc5 ♘f6 7 ♗a3 0-0

8 c6 罝e8 9 cxb7 皇xb7 10 罝b1 豐c8 11
②e2 ②c6 12 ②g3 a5 13 皇b2 d6 14 皇e2
②e7 15 0-0, with an edge.

c2) Also good is 4 ②f3, after which
D.Poldauf-R.Kasimdzhanov, Rethymnon 2003, continued 4...e4 5 ②g5 e3!? 6
d4 exf2+ 7 含xf2 皇e7 8 ②xe7 豐xe7 9 e4
d6 10 h3 (or 10 皇d3 ②c6 11 皇c2 ②f6 12
h3! with an edge – Lautier) 10...②c6 11
②f3 f6 12 皇d3 豐f7 13 罝f1 ②ge7 14 含g1
豐h5 15 a3 0-0 16 b4 a6 17 罝a2 豐e8 18
罝e2, with good play.

Returning to 3...皇e7:

4 d4

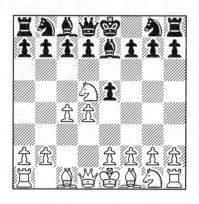

4...d6

White stands well after the riskier
4...e4 5 皇f4 and following 5...c6 (or
5...d6 6 e3 ②f6 7 豐c2 ②bd7 8 ②c3 c6 9
a3 豐b6 10 ②ge2 0-0 11 ②g3 d5 12 ②f5,
with an edge in Z.Azmaiparashvili-
E.Schmittdiel, Dortmund 1992) 6 ②c7+!
豐xc7 7 皇xc7 皇b4+ 8 豐d2 ②a6 9 皇d6
皇xd2+ 10 含xd2 ②h6 11 e3 ②f5 12 皇a3
d6 13 f3 exf3 14 ②xf3, White enjoyed
the better game in L.Psakhis-
P.Martinez Rodriguez, Mondariz 1997.

Likewise 4...exd4 is provocative and
allows White to consider the promising

gambit 5 ②f3!, and if 5...c5 6 e3 dxe3 7
皇xe3 d6 8 皇f4. B.Alterman-
M.Oratovsky, Israel 1995, continued
8...②f6 9 ②xe7 豐xe7+ 10 皇e2 ②e4 11
0-0 g5!? 12 ②xg5! ②xg5 13 皇xd6 豐e4
14 罝e1 皇e6 15 皇g4 豐d4 16 皇xe6 豐xd1
17 罝axd1 ②xe6 18 f4 ②c6 19 f5 ②cd4 20
fxe6 ②xe6 21 皇xc5, and White won.

5 e4 ②c6

Black has a major alternative in
5...②f6, after which 6 ②xe7 豐xe7 7 f3 is
critical.

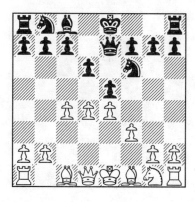

Here White has secured the centre
and has the bishop-pair, but Black has
a solid game and is ahead in development. Practice does though tend to favour White:

a) 7...0-0 8 d5 (White can delay this
too, preferring 8 ②e2 c6 9 ②c3) 8... ②h5
9 皇e3 ②f4 10 豐d2 f5 11 0-0-0 fxe4 12
fxe4 皇g4 13 罝e1 c6 14 g3 ②g6 15 皇g2
cxd5 16 cxd5 ②a6 17 含b1 gave White
the upper hand in M.Marin-J.Ramiro
Ovejero, Solsones 2004.

b) 7...exd4 8 豐xd4 ②c6 was another
Marin game, M.Marin-E.Dizdarevic,
Istanbul 2003, which continued 9 豐c3
0-0 10 ②e2 ②d7 (or 10...②h5 11 g4

♕h4+ 12 ♔d1 ♘f6 13 ♘g3 ♗e6 14 ♗e3 ♘d7 15 ♗e2 a5 16 ♔d2 ♘c5 17 b3 ♖fe8 18 ♖ag1 f6, as in B.Lalic-A.Shirov, Moscow Olympiad 1994, and now 19 ♔d1, threatening g5, is better for White according to Lalic) 11 ♘f4 ♘b6 12 a4 a5 13 ♗e3 ♘d7 14 ♘d5 ♕d8 15 ♖d1 b6 16 ♗d3 ♘c5 17 ♗c2 ♗e6 18 0-0 ♗xd5 19 cxd5 ♘b4 20 ♗d4, with good chances.

c) 7...♘h5 8 ♗e3 exd4 9 ♕xd4 ♘c6 10 ♕c3 ♕e5 11 ♘e2 ♗d7 12 0-0-0 0-0 13 g4 ♘f6 14 h4

14...♖fe8 15 ♖g1 a5 16 h5 a4 17 h6 a3 18 b3 ♘b4 19 ♔b1 ♗c6 20 ♕xe5 dxe5 21 ♗c5 ♘a6 22 ♗xa3 with a clear advantage was another example of powerful and effective White play in I.Smirin-O.Lehner, Vienna 1998.

d) Not dissimilar was P.H.Nielsen-S.Pedersen, Aalborg 2000, which continued 7...c6 8 d5 ♘h5 9 ♗e3 0-0 10 g4 ♘f4 11 ♘e2 cxd5 12 cxd5 ♕h4+ 13 ♗f2 ♕f6 14 ♘xf4 exf4 15 ♕d4 ♕e7 16 0-0-0 ♘d7 17 ♕d2 g5 18 h4, with advantage.

Finally, we should note that neither does 5...c6 equalize. G.Kasparov-A.Shirov, Novgorod 1994, continued 6 ♘xe7 ♕xe7 7 ♘e2 f5 8 dxe5 ♕xe5 9 exf5 ♘f6 10 ♕d4 ♗xf5 11 ♗f4 ♕a5+ 12 ♕c3 ♕xc3+ 13 ♘xc3 0-0 14 0-0-0 d5 15 ♗d6 ♖c8 16 f3 ♘bd7, and now Kasparov gives 17 cxd5 cxd5 18 ♗d3 as the most accurate.

Returning to 5...♘c6:

6 ♘e2

6...f5

Black must try to shake White's formidable central grip. Another try is 6...exd4 7 ♘xd4 ♘f6, after which J.Hjartarson-J.Hodgson, Clichy 1995, continued 8 ♘xc6 (8 ♘xe7 ♕xe7 9 f3 is also a reasonable alternative) 8...bxc6 9 ♘c3 0-0 10 ♗e2 ♘d7 11 ♗e3 ♗f6 12 ♕d2 ♘c5 13 f3 ♗e5 14 ♖c1 ♕h4+ 15 ♗f2 ♕f6 16 0-0, with an edge.

7 exf5

This may be more accurate than 7 dxe5 dxe5 8 exf5 ♗xf5 which robs White of d5 possibilities. D.Reinderman-D.Howell, Gausdal 2005, then continued 9 ♘g3 ♗e6 10 ♗d3 ♘f6 11 ♘xf6+ gxf6 12 0-0 ♕d7 13 ♕h5+ ♗f7, with unclear play.

7...♗xf5 8 ♗e3 ♘f6

After 8...♗f6!?, J.Banas-M.Kubala, Martin 1996, saw 9 ♘xf6+ ♘xf6 10 ♘g3

exd4 11 ♗xd4 ♘xd4 12 ♕xd4 c5 13 ♕d2
♗g6 14 ♗e2 d5 15 cxd5 ♕xd5 16 ♕e3+
♔f7 17 0-0 ♖he8 18 ♕c3 ♔f8 19 ♗f3
♘e4 20 ♕a3, with a strong attack.

9 ♘g3

White should avoid 9 ♘xf6+?! ♗xf6
10 d5 ♘d4!, and if 11 ♗xd4 exd4 12
♘xd4 ♕e7+ 13 ♗e2 ♗xd4 14 ♕xd4 0-0,
with good play for Black.

9...♗g6 10 ♘xf6+ ♗xf6 11 d5

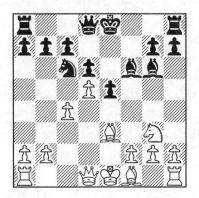

11...♘e7

Now if 11...♘d4, White simply
plays 12 ♗d3.

12 ♗d3 ♗f7

White has extra space, good light-
square control and a clear initiative. He
is better too after 12...e4?! 13 ♘xe4
♗xb2 14 ♖b1 ♗xe4 15 ♗xe4 ♗c3+ 16
♔f1 b6 17 ♕d3 (Marin).

13 ♘e4 c6

Or 13...♘f5?! 14 ♕a4+! ♔f8 15 ♘xf6
♕xf6 16 0-0.

**14 dxc6 ♘xc6 15 0-0 ♗e7 16 ♕g4 0-0
17 ♖ad1 ♕c8 18 ♕g3 ♔h8 19 ♗e2 ♖d8
20 ♘c3 ♘b4 21 a3 ♘c2 22 ♘d5 ♗xd5
23 ♖xd5 ♕e6 24 ♗d3 ♘xe3 25 ♕xe3**

Black's game is cramped, while
White controls the central light squares

and can create threats on the flanks.
White has a clear advantage, but still
faces considerable technical difficulties,
especially because the presence of opposite-coloured bishops offers some
hope for Black.

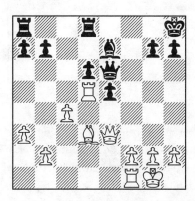

**25...♖f8 26 ♗e4 ♖ac8 27 ♕d3 ♕h6 28
♖a5 ♖c7 29 g3!?**

White missed 29 ♖xa7! and if 29...d5
30 ♕xd5 ♗c5 31 ♖xb7 ♗xf2+ 32 ♔h1
with a winning advantage, as Marin
later pointed out.

**29...b6 30 ♖d5 ♕h3 31 ♗g2 ♕g4 32 b3
♖f6 33 ♖e1 ♗f8 34 ♖e4 ♕c8 35 ♖h4 g6
36 ♖e4 ♖c5 37 ♖e2 ♕a6 38 ♖a2 ♕c8 39
♖c2 ♕a6 40 b4 ♖c7 41 ♕b3 ♕c8 42
♖dd2 ♗e7 43 ♗d5 ♗f8 44 ♔g2 ♗e7 45
♖e2 ♖f8 46 ♕d3 ♕d7 47 h4 ♔g7 48 ♖e3**

It isn't easy for White to make progress, but according to Marin his best
plan was probably 48 b5!?, followed by
moves such as ♗c6, ♖e4, ♖ce2, a4-a5
and f4.

**48...b5 49 cxb5 ♖xc2 50 ♕xc2 ♕xb5 51
♕e4 ♗d8 52 ♗c6 ♕a6 53 a4 ♗b6 54
♖f3 ♕xf3 55 ♕xf3 ♕c8 56 a5 ♗d4 57 b5
♕f5 58 g4 ♕xf3+ 59 ♔xf3 h6 60 ♔e2
♔f6 61 ♗d5 g5 62 h5**

62...♚e7?!

White's queenside pawns still provide some practical winning chances. However, some Romanian analysis indicates that Black could probably have saved the half-point by playing the bold 62...e4! and if 63 ♗xe4 ♚e5 64 ♗c6 d5. Black then has the dominant

king and his bishop can stay on the a7-g1 diagonal, covering possible breakthrough threats on the queenside.

63 f3 ♗c3?!

This is weak, but Black is lost too after 63...♚d7? 64 ♚d3 ♚e7 (or 64...♚c7 65 ♚e4 ♗c3 66 ♚f5 ♗xa5 67 ♚g6) 65 ♚e4 ♗c5 66 ♗b7 ♚e6 67 ♗c8+ ♚f6 68 ♚d5 ♚e7 69 ♗f5 ♚d8 70 ♚c6, and wins (Marin). It also seems too late even for 63...e4!? in view of 64 ♗xe4 ♚e6 65 ♚d3 ♚e5 66 ♚c4 ♗f2 67 b6 axb6 68 a6 b5+ 69 ♚xb5 d5 70 ♗c2 ♗a7 71 ♚c6 d4 72 ♚b7 ♗c5 73 a7 ♗xa7 74 ♚xa7 ♚f4 75 ♗d1 ♚e3 76 ♚b6 ♚d2 77 ♗b3 ♚e3 78 ♚c5 ♚xf3 79 ♗d1+ ♚e3 80 ♚c4, and if 80...♚d2 (or 80...d3 81 ♚c3) 81 ♗a4 d3 (or 81...♚e3 82 ♚d5) 82 ♚d4 ♚e2 83 ♚e4 d2 84 ♚f5.

64 b6 axb6 65 a6 1-0

Summary

This chapter comprehensively concludes coverage of 1 c4 e5 systems. In those lines in which Black plays ...f5, following up 3 ♘f3 with 4 d4 is both in keeping with our repertoire approach and is the key response, allowing White to press. Following both 2...♘c6 3 ♘c3 f5 4 d4 e4 and 2...d6 3 ♘c3 f5 4 d4 e4, the most critical try is 5 ♘g5, although White can also hope to outmanoeuvre Black in the former with 5 ♗g5.

A fashionable option is 2...♗b4, but with 3 ♘d5 White kicks Black's bishop with tempo and takes the game unreservedly to Black.

1 c4 e5 2 ♘c3 *(D)* **2...♘c6**
        2...♘f6 3 ♘f3 d6 – *Game 13*
        2...d6 3 ♘f3 f5 – *Game 17*
        2...♗b4 – *Game 18*
3 ♘f3 *(D)* **3...f5**
        3...g6 – *Game 14*
4 d4 e4 *(D)*
        5 ♘g5 – *Game 15*
        5 ♗g5 – *Game 16*

    2 ♘c3   *3 ♘f3*   *4...e4*

Chapter Four

Symmetrical Four Knights, 3...d5 and Keres-Parma

1 c4 c5 2 ♘f3 ♘f6 3 ♘c3

The six games in this chapter consider a number of key lines after 1...c5. These variations can also arise after 1...♘f6, followed by ...c5, and from some other move orders. Against all of these variations, we will consider d4 antidotes, aimed at activating White's pieces in the centre. Black plays ...e6 in most of these lines. Although two involve an early ...d5.

Game 19 introduces the main line of the Symmetrical Four Knights: **1 c4 c5 2 ♘f3 ♘f6 3 ♘c3 ♘c6 4 d4 cxd4 5 ♘xd4 e6**. Against this my primary recommendation is to prevent ...♗b4 with **6 a3**, which generally leads to battles against a range of Hedgehog-like defences. After **6...♗e7 7 e4 0-0 8 ♘f3** Black tends to play ...d6 eventually, leading to our first Hedgehog structure.

After ...d6, Black has a typically tough, defensive pawn barrier along his third rank, and develops his pieces

flexibly behind it. He keeps a weather eye open for counterattack, usually based on ...b5 and ...d5 pawn breaks, but on the whole his position is essentially defensive. White seeks to build on his extra space and attacking potential, but must take care not to overstretch his forces.

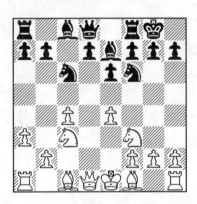

Game 20 sees Black preferring to meet 6 a3 with a simplifying exchange: **6...♘xd4 7 ♕xd4 b6 8 ♕f4!**

This line also leads to Hedgehog structures, but with three pairs of minor pieces on the board rather than the four in Game 19.

This doesn't lead to any substantive change in either side's main objectives: White still has an edge, while Black plays an early game of containment. Note White's 8th move which is a refinement introduced by Viktor Korchnoi. Before playing e4, White first plays his queen via f4 to g3, causing Black some development problems down the g-file.

A good alternative to 6 a3 is **6 g3**; the subject of Game 21.

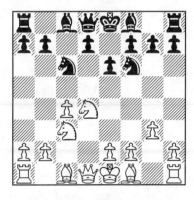

Play becomes especially rich when, with the critical 6...♕b6, Black seeks

undermining piece play before looking to free his game with ...d5.

Game 22 introduces us to 3...d5 systems by Black, but first begins with an examination of a couple of important move order issues after 2...♞c6. Following **2...♞f6 3 ♞c3 d5 4 cxd5 ♞xd5** my main repertoire choice is the promising counter in the centre with **5 d4**.

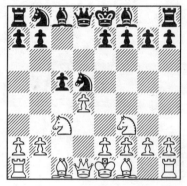

This gives White good chances of a slight, nagging pull in the middlegame after **5...cxd4** 6 ♕xd4 ♞xc3 7 ♕xc3 ♞c6 8 e4, as we'll see in Game 22. Black is looking for equality, but he is slightly behind in development.

Grünfeld players will prefer **5...♞xc3 6 bxc3 g6**, but White needn't transpose to a main line Grünfeld with 7 e4. Instead 7 e3 (Game 23) might appear outwardly quiet, but contains its own venom. White secures his pawn centre and long-term chances of playing e4 under more controlled circumstances in the middlegame. He first completes his development and constrains Black's game on the queenside.

Finally, in Game 24 we examine the Keres-Parma System with **2...♞f6 3**

♘c3 e6 4 g3 d5 5 cxd5 ♘xd5. A testing reply is 6 ♗g2 ♘c6 7 d4 ♗e7 8 0-0 0-0 9 ♘xd5 exd5 10 dxc5 ♗xc5 11 ♗g5, reaching an IQP position and one similar to the Tarrasch Defence.

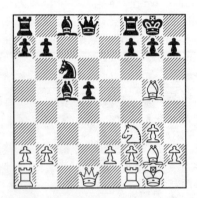

Black takes some risk playing the Tarrasch with only three pairs of minor pieces rather than the usual four, as simplification tends to emphasize the weakness of his isolated queen's pawn. Indeed, White has an early initiative and a promising game.

Game 19
L.Bruzon-K.Miton
Skanderborg 2005

---

1 c4 c5 2 ♘f3 ♘f6 3 ♘c3 ♘c6 4 d4 cxd4 5 ♘xd4 e6

Black's main move. It is also very important to be aware that his main alternative, 5...g6, transposes after 6 e4 to the Maróczy Bind Variation of the Accelerated Dragon, which unfortunately must lie outside our coverage.

Lesser alternatives:

a) 5...♕b6!? transposes after 6 ♘b3

e6 7 a3 to note 'b' to White's 6th move (or after 7 g3 to the notes to White's 7th move in Game 21). However, White can also try the interesting 6 ♘b3 e6 7 ♗g5.

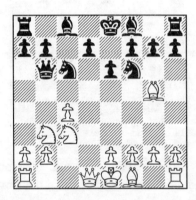

J.Lautier-Zhang Zhong, Turin Olympiad 2006, continued 7...♗e7 (or 7...♗b4 8 ♗xf6 gxf6 9 ♖c1 0-0!? 10 e3 ♘e5?! 11 a3 ♗e7 12 c5! ♕d8 13 f4 ♘g6 14 h4 ♖e8 15 h5 ♘f8 16 ♘b5 f5, as in the game Y.Pelletier-E.Schmittdiel, German League 2001, and now Pelletier gives 17 ♘d6 ♗xd6 18 cxd6, with a clear advantage) 8 e3 a6 (preparing ...d5 with Palliser's calm suggestion of 8...0-0!? may improve) 9 ♗e2 ♘e5?! (misguided, but even 9...♕c7 runs into 10 c5!) 10 ♗f4 d6 11 c5! ♕c7 12 cxd6 ♕xd6 13 0-0 ♗d7 14 ♘d2 ♗c6 15 ♕c2 ♘fd7 16 ♘c4, with a pleasant plus.

b) 5...e5 is possible, but asks a lot of Black's position. Z.Azmaiparashvili-H.Urday Caceres, Oviedo (rapid) 1993, continued 6 ♘db5 d6 7 ♘d5 (both 7 g3 and 7 ♗g5 a6 8 ♗xf6 gxf6 9 ♘a3 also have a good reputation) 7...♘xd5 8 cxd5 a6 9 ♘c3 ♘e7 10 e4 g6 11 ♗e3 f5 12 ♕b3 ♘g8 13 exf5 gxf5 14 ♗e2 ♘f6 15

0-0 ♗g7 16 f4, with advantage.

c) White has an easy edge too after 5...d5 6 cxd5 ♘xd5 7 ♘xc6 bxc6. D.Komljenovic-A.Prados Barrios, Seville 2006, continued 8 ♗d2 e5 9 ♕a4 ♗d7 10 ♕e4 ♘f6 11 ♕xe5+ ♗e7 12 e4 0-0 13 ♗c4, with an extra pawn.

6 a3

The main point of this modest, but tough little move is to deny Black's king's bishop access to its most active post on b4. Game 21 considers White's main alternative, 6 g3.

6...♗e7

This move generally leads to Hedgehog-type positions. Related variations are 6...♗c5 7 ♘b3 ♗e7 and 6...♕b6 7 ♘b3 ♗e7 which we will consider here, whereas 6...♘xd4, 6...d5 and 6...♕c7 can be found in our next illustrative game. Those alternative Hedgehog-like possibilities:

a) 6...♗c5 7 ♘b3 ♗e7 8 e4 0-0 9 ♗e2 b6 10 0-0 reaches a further divide, although in both cases White generally plays actively, usually involving both ♗e3 and f4:

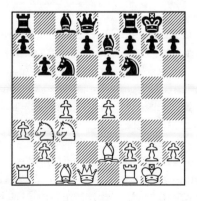

a1) 10...♗a6!? attacks c4, hoping to divert White's attention from the centre. White's best reply is 11 f4 (11 ♗f4 is sound, but less ambitious), denying e5 to Black's queen's knight and raising the prospect of e5. Black got into trouble in V.Chuchelov-L.Gofshtein, French League 2001, after 11...♖c8 12 ♗e3 d6 13 ♖c1 ♕d7 (Black's best may be 13...♘b8!?, re-routing the knight to its ideal Hedgehog formation square on d7, after which S.Agdestein-J.Emms, Cappelle la Grande 1993, continued 14 ♘d2 ♗b7 15 ♗f3 ♘bd7 16 ♕e2 a6 17 ♗f2, with only a minimal pull; note too that in this line 14...d5?! is premature due to 15 cxd5 and then 15...♗xe2 16 ♘xe2 exd5 17 ♖xc8 ♕xc8 18 e5! or 15...exd5 16 ♗xa6 ♘xa6 17 ♘xd5 ♘xd5 18 ♖xc8 ♕xc8 19 exd5) 14 ♕e1 ♕b7 15 ♘d2 ♘a5 16 e5! dxe5 17 fxe5 ♘d7 18 ♕g3 ♕b8 19 ♘f3 ♖fd8 20 ♘b5 ♗xb5 21 cxb5, with an excellent game.

a2) 10...♗b7 sees Black head for a straightforward Hedgehog. White can again set up an f4 and ♗e3 clamp and Black couldn't break White's grip in U.Andersson-H.Steel, Gibraltar 2007, after 11 ♗e3 ♖c8 12 ♖c1 d6 (U.Andersson-V.Bologan, French League 2002, varied with 12...♘e5!? 13 ♘b5 ♘xe4 14 ♘xa7 ♖a8 15 ♘b5 f5, with unclear play, but White can avoid this line by playing f4 on move 11 or 12) 13 f4 ♕c7 14 ♗f3 ♖fd8 (or 14...♕b8 15 ♕e2 ♕a8 16 g4 ♖fe8 17 g5 ♘d7 18 h4 a6 19 ♘d2 ♗f8 20 b4 g6 21 ♖fd1 a5 22 b5 ♘e7 23 ♘a4 ♕a7 24 ♘b3, with a plus in K.Georgiev-A.Kolev, Elenite 1993) 15 ♕e2 ♕b8 16 ♖fd1 ♗f8 17 ♗f2 ♘e7 18 ♘d2 ♘g6 19 g3 ♕a8 20 ♖e1 d5!? 21

cxd5 exd5 22 e5 d4 23 ♗xb7 ♕xb7 24 exf6 dxc3 25 ♖xc3 ♖xc3 26 bxc3 gxf6 27 ♗d4 f5 28 a4, with continuing pressure.

b) 6...♕b6 7 ♘b3 leads to another split:

b1) 7...♗e7 8 e4 0-0 9 ♗e2 ♕c7 10 0-0 b6 11 ♗e3 reaches by now familiar Hedgehog structures.

White again generally plays actively, usually involving both ♗e3 and f4, particularly if Black plays an early ...d6. If Black doesn't play ...d6, White has a second promising plan, based on playing ♖ac1 and c5:

b11) 11...♗b7 12 ♖c1 ♖ac8 13 c5! bxc5 14 ♘xc5 ♗a8 (or 14...♖fd8 15 ♘xb7 ♕xb7 16 b4) 15 b4 d6 16 ♘b3 ♕b8 17 f3!? (bolstering e4, but Stohl points out that there's also nothing wrong with 17 f4 ♗d8 18 ♕d2 ♗b6 19 ♔h1) 17...♖fd8 18 ♗a6 ♖c7 was Bu Xiangzhi-Zhang Zhong, Taiyuan 2004, and now Stohl suggests 19 f4, and if 19...d5!? 20 e5 (or 20 exd5) 20...d4 21 ♘xd4 ♘xd4 22 ♗xd4 ♖cd7 23 ♘e2 ♘e4 24 ♕d3, with the better chances

b12) T.Sammalvuo-B.Lalic, Cappelle la Grande 2002, varied with 11...♗a6!?

12 ♖c1 ♖ac8 13 f4! ♖fd8 (Palliser's 13...d6 would restrict White to a typical edge) 14 e5 (both 14 ♗d3 and 14 ♕e1 are also good) 14...♘e8 15 ♘d5 ♕b8 16 ♘xe7+ ♘xe7, and now I again like Stohl's recommendation of 17 ♗d3 which looks better for White.

b2) The isolated queen's pawn positions after 7...d5!? 8 ♗e3 ♕d8 9 cxd5 exd5 (or 9...♘xd5 10 ♘xd5 exd5 11 g3 ♗e7 12 ♗g2 ♗f6!? 13 ♕d2 d4 14 ♗xc6+ bxc6 15 ♗xd4 ♕d5 16 0-0-0 ♗g5 17 f4 ♕xb3, as in J.Speelman-G.Sax, Hastings 1990/91, and now 18 fxg5 0-0 19 ♕c3 is strong as shown by Speelman) are promising for White, who is well developed.

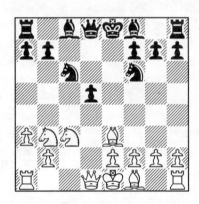

V.Chuchelov-V.Lazarev, French League 1998, continued 10 g3 ♗e7 11 ♗g2 ♗e6 12 0-0 0-0 13 ♖c1 ♖e8 (Z.Izoria-Z.Almasi, Bled Olympiad 2002, improved with 13...♖c8!? 14 ♖c2 ♘e5! 15 ♘d4 ♘c4 16 ♗g5 ♔h8, and Black defended, but 14 ♗c5!?, trying to weaken Black's hold on the dark squares, looks better) 14 ♖c2 ♘e4? 15 ♘xe4 dxe4 16 ♖d2 ♕c8 17 ♗xe4, and White won.

Returning to the immediate 6...♗e7:

7 e4 0-0

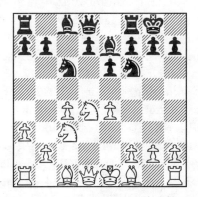

8 ♘f3

White can no longer play for the more critical anti-Hedgehog structures, based on ♗e2, ♗e3 and f4 after this move, or if he does, by playing 8 ♘b3, he is a tempo down on the line 6...♗c5 7 ♘b3 ♗e7. This is a minor concession, but White must avoid 8 ♗e2 d5! which is clearly dead level.

8...b6

Black generally holds back his d-pawn. Sometimes he prefers 8...♕c7, which prevents 9 ♗f4. V.Korchnoi-R.Ponomariov, 8th matchgame, Donetsk 2001, continued 9 ♗g5 b6 10 ♗d3 (10 ♗h4!? and if 10...♘h5 11 ♗xe7 ♘xe7 12 ♘b5 ♕f4!? 13 ♘d2 can also be considered) 10...h6 11 ♗h4 ♘h5 12 ♗xe7 ♘xe7 13 0-0 (13 ♘b5!?, and if 13...♕b8 14 0-0 ♘f4 15 ♗c2, might improve) 13...♗a6 14 ♖c1 ♘f4 15 ♘b5 ♗xb5 16 cxb5 ♕d6 17 ♗b1 ♕xd1 18 ♖cxd1 d5 19 e5 g5 20 ♖fe1 ♖ac8 21 h4 g4 22 ♘h2 h5 23 f3!? g3!? 24 ♘f1, with a slight pull.

9 ♗e2

White can also keep the option of

playing ♗d3 open, by playing 9 ♗f4. V.Korchnoi-R.Ponomariov, 2nd match-game, Donetsk 2001, instructively continued 9...d6 (if the immediate 9...♗b7!? White should perhaps reply 10 ♗e2 or 10 ♖c1 because Black obtained good chances on the dark squares in R.Pogorelov-A.Greenfeld, Navalmoral de la Mata 2006, after 10 ♗d3 ♘h5!? 11 ♗e3 ♗c5) 10 ♗e2 ♗b7 11 0-0 ♖c8 12 ♖e1 a6 13 ♗f1 ♕c7 14 b4 ♖fd8 15 ♖c1 ♘e5 16 ♘d2 ♕b8 17 h3 ♗c6 18 ♕e2 ♘g6 19 ♗g3 ♕b7 20 ♘b3 h6 21 ♖b1! (in the long term White is looking to get in a4-a5 or possibly c4-c5) 21...♗f8 22 f3 ♖e8 23 ♗f2 ♕b8 24 ♕e3 ♘d7 25 ♖ed1 ♗b7?! 26 ♘a4!

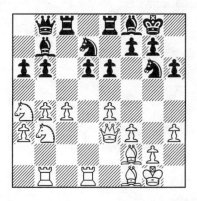

26...♘ge5 27 ♘xb6 ♘xb6 28 ♕xb6 ♘xc4 29 ♗xc4 ♖xc4 30 ♘a5 ♖c7 31 b5 ♗a8, and now Korchnoi gives 32 ♕xa6 ♖c2 33 b6 d5 34 b7, winning.

Going back to the position in Korchnoi-Ponomariov after 11...♖c8, Black defended better in I.Cheparinov-S.Karjakin, Wijk aan Zee 2005, with 12 ♖c1 ♘e5!? 13 ♘d2 a6 14 ♖e1 ♖c7 15 ♗e3 (15 ♗f1!? and if 15...♕a8 16 ♗g3 à la Korchnoi is also possible) 15...♘ed7

16 b4 ♛a8 17 ♞a4 ♜c6! 18 ♛b3 ♝d8 19 f3 ♜c8 20 ♔h1 ♝c7 21 ♝f1 ♔h8

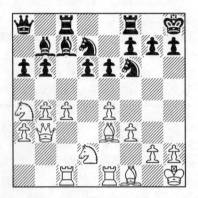

22 ♛b2 ♜g8 23 ♞b3 ♝c6 24 ♞c3 ♝b7, with a high tension balance. Black has achieved a well-known Hedgehog formation, first worked out by Bobby Fischer, and his forces support a potential kingside diversion with ...g5.

Returning to 9 ♝e2:

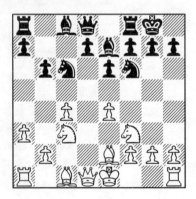

9...♝b7 10 0-0

This move and 10 ♝f4 are often interchanged. If you want to stop ...♛c7, play the bishop move.

10...♜c8

Black can, of course, also play 10...♛c7. White achieved a favourable

exchange of light-squared bishops in another instructive encounter, A.Delchev-A.Graf, Batumi 2002, which continued 11 ♝g5 ♜ad8 12 ♛d2 (F.Vallejo Pons-V.Anand, Monaco (rapid) 2005, varied with 12 ♜c1 ♛b8 13 ♜e1 h6 14 ♝h4 d6 15 ♝f1 ♜fe8, and now 16 h3, safeguarding g3 for White's bishop, may retain a very slight edge) 12...d6 13 b4 ♞b8 14 ♝d3 ♞bd7 15 ♜fe1 ♜fe8 16 h3 ♞f8 17 ♜ac1 ♛b8 18 ♝c2 ♜c8 19 ♝a4 ♜ed8 20 ♛e2 ♞g6 21 ♞d2 ♝a6 22 ♝b5! ♝xb5 23 ♞xb5 ♛b7 24 ♞f3 h6 25 ♝d2 a6 26 ♞bd4 ♞d7 27 b5! ♜e8 28 ♞c6 ♝f8 29 ♞fd4, with good play.

11 ♝f4 ♞a5 12 ♞d2!

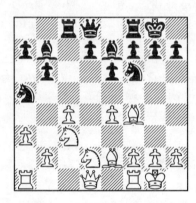

White correctly allows Black to play ...d5. In the concrete circumstances of this game, it's doubtful whether this freeing move is actually better than heading for a standard Hedgehog formation with ...d6. As we shall see, playing ...d5, even in one move, isn't always a panacea for Black.

12...d5!? 13 cxd5 exd5 14 e5 ♞e4 15 ♞cxe4

Black's adventure on the e4-square is to say the least risky, but if he hadn't played this way, he would have simply have had a cramped game with little counterplay.

15...dxe4 16 b4 ♗g5

Black clearly intended this to improve on 16...♘c6?! 17 ♗g4 ♖a8 (Bruzon points out that 17...♖c7 18 ♗f5 ♘d4 19 ♗xe4 ♕a8 20 ♗xb7 ♕xb7 21 e6 ♖cc8 22 exf7+ ♖xf7 23 ♗e3 ♗f6 is also better for White), played in M.Krasenkow-K.Miton, Warsaw 2003, which had continued 18 ♗f5! ♗g5 19 ♕h5 g6 20 ♗xg5 gxh5 21 ♗xd8 ♖axd8 22 ♘xe4 ♘xe5 23 ♘f6+ ♔h8 24 ♘xh5 ♖g8 25 ♘g3 h5 26 ♖fe1 f6 27 ♗e4, and White won.

17 ♗xg5 ♕xg5

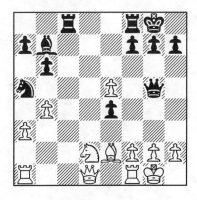

18 h4!

This is a fine concept, whose idea is to deflect the Black queen's attention away from White's knight on d2, whereas White is only a little better after 18 bxa5 ♖fd8 19 ♗g4 ♖xd2 20 h4! ♖xd1 21 hxg5 ♖xa1 22 ♖xa1 ♖c5 23 axb6 axb6 24 ♖b1 (Bruzon).

18...♕xh4

Not, of course, 18...♕xe5? 19 bxa5 ♖fd8 20 ♖c1 e3 21 ♘f3 exf2+ 22 ♔xf2! and wins.

19 bxa5 ♖c6

But what about this move, no doubt part of Miton's prepared home analysis? Black threatens an attack on the h-file. White can force perpetual check but is there more?

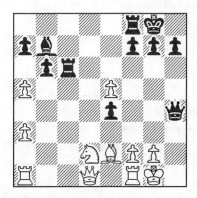

20 ♕b3?

Bruzon gets cold feet and takes the half-point. Back home and after much analysis, he concluded that White could have played on either by playing 20 ♘xe4, and if 20...♕xe4 21 ♗f3 ♕xe5 22 ♗xc6 ♗xc6 23 axb6 axb6 24 ♕g4 h6 25 ♖ac1 ♕f6 26 ♖fd1, or even better 20 f3!, intending 20...e3 21 ♘c4 ♖h6 22 ♘xe3 ♕h2+ 23 ♔f2 ♕h4+ 24 g3 ♕h2+ 25 ♘g2 ♖h3 26 ♖h1 ♕xg3+ 27 ♔g1 ♖xh1+ 28 ♔xh1 ♕xe5 29 axb6 axb6 30 ♖c1.

20...♖h6 21 f3 ♕h2+ 22 ♔f2 ♕h4+ 23 ♔g1 ♕h2+ ½-½.

Game 20
F.Vallejo Pons-S.Karjakin
Dos Hermanas 2003

---

1 c4 c5 2 ♘f3 ♘c6 3 d4 cxd4 4 ♘xd4 ♘f6 5 ♘c3 e6 6 a3 ♘xd4

This move leads to Hedgehog defences with three pairs of minor pieces rather than the usual four. This creates some novel problems for both sides but no change in their main objectives. We have already considered 6...♗e7, 6...♗c5 and 6...♕b6 in Game 19, but Black also has 6...d5 and 6...♕c7. Neither has an especially good reputation, but some strong players have played them:

a) 6...d5 7 cxd5 exd5 reaches an isolated queen's pawn position with White's knight on d4 a valuable resource. White then usually continues with 8 ♗g5, giving the game an active Semi-Tarrasch Defence character, in which e3 combined with a3 and b4 is a common structure:

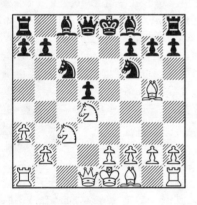

a1) After 8...♗e7 9 e3 0-0 10 ♗b5, all White's forces bristle with energy. M.Krasenkow-S.Mamedyarov, Antalya 2004, continued 10...♘e5 (White was also much better after 10...♘xd4 11 ♕xd4 ♗e6 12 0-0 a6 13 ♗e2 h6 14 ♗h4 ♘e4 15 ♗xe7 ♘xc3 16 ♕xc3 ♕xe7 17 ♕d4 in J.Speelman-N.De Firmian, Moscow 1990) 11 0-0 a6 12 ♗e2 ♗e6 13 ♕b3

♕b3 b5 14 ♖ad1 ♕b6?! 15 ♗xf6 ♗xf6 16 ♘xd5 ♗xd5 17 ♕xd5 ♖ad8 18 ♕b3 ♘c6 19 ♘xc6 ♕xc6 20 ♖c1 ♕d5 21 ♕xd5 ♖xd5 22 ♖c2, with a clear advantage.

a2) Black's best may be 8...♗c5, addressing White's grip on d4. L.Van Wely-V.Ivanchuk, Foros 2007, continued 9 e3 0-0 10 ♗e2 ♗xd4!? (10...♘xd4 11 exd4 ♗e7 is slightly better for White) 11 exd4 h6 12 ♗h4 ♕d6 13 ♗g3 ♕e7 14 0-0 ♘e4 15 ♖c1 ♘xc3 16 ♖xc3 ♕f6, and now Van Wely suggests 17 ♗f3, with advantage.

b) 6...♕c7!? is a tactical idea which can lead to fireworks, as it did in J.Timman-J.Polgar, Hoogeveen 1999, after 7 ♘db5 ♕b8 8 g3 a6 9 ♘d4 ♘xd4! 10 ♕xd4 b5 11 e4! e5 12 ♕e3 ♕c7 13 cxb5 ♗c5 with an extremely unclear position. A simpler approach is 7 ♗g5...

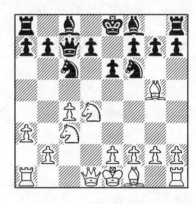

...and then 7...♗e7 (Black's best may be 7...♘xd4!? 8 ♕xd4 ♗c5, after which A.Delchev-N.Ninov, Tsarevo 2001, continued 9 ♕d2 b6 10 e4 ♗b7 11 ♗d3 ♗c6 12 ♖c1 a5 13 ♕e2 h6, and now White could perhaps keep a very slight edge by playing 14 ♗h4) 8 ♘db5!? (Tukmakov's 8 e3 b6 9 ♗e2 ♗b7 10 0-0

is also possible) 8...♕b8 9 e3 a6 10 ♘d4 b6 11 ♗f4 ♕a7 12 ♘xc6!? dxc6 13 e4 ♗b7 14 e5 ♖d8 15 ♕e2 gave White an edge in E.Agrest-D.Cramling, Swedish League 2004.

Returning to 6...♘xd4:

7 ♕xd4 b6

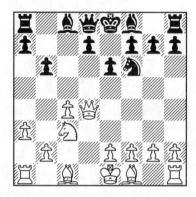

8 ♕f4!

Viktor Korchnoi introduced this positionally deep move in his 1991 Candidates match with Gyula Sax. White aims to transfer his queen to the kingside before setting up his usual e4 and c4 pawn centre. Korchnoi's subtle refinement continues to test Black, whereas other moves lead to no more than balanced play.

8...♗b7

Alternatively:

a) 8...♗e7 9 e4 d6 10 ♕g3 0-0 11 ♗h6 ♘e8 has some similarities with our main game and after 12 ♗f4 ♗b7 (White was also somewhat better after 12...e5?! 13 ♗d2 f5 14 ♕d3 ♗e6 15 exf5 ♗xf5 16 ♕e3 ♘f6 17 ♗e2 ♖c8 18 0-0 in J.Nogueiras-J.Caceres Cortes, Montreal 2002) 13 ♖d1 ♗h4 14 ♕h3 ♕f6 (or 14...f5?! 15 exf5 ♗xf2+ 16 ♔xf2 ♖xf5 17

g3 ♗xh1 18 ♗d3 ♗c6 19 ♗xf5 exf5 20 ♕xf5, with advantage as given by Kasparov, while Ribli's 14...♗g5 15 ♗xg5 ♕xg5 16 ♕g3 supplies an edge) 15 ♗e3 ♗g5 16 ♗e2 ♗xe3 17 ♕xe3 ♕e7 18 0-0 ♘f6 19 ♖d2 ♖fd8 20 ♖fd1 ♗c6 21 f4 h5 22 ♗f3 ♕c7 23 h3 e5!? 24 f5 h4?! 25 ♕f2 ♗b7 was G.Kasparov-L.Van Wely, Moscow 2004, and now Kasparov suggests 26 b3 a6 27 a4, with a clear advantage.

b) 8...♗a6 9 e4 ♖c8 (probably better is 9...d6, after which 10 ♗d2 ♗e7 11 ♗e2 0-0 12 0-0 ♖c8 13 b3 gave White a slight pull in G.Tunik-A.Obukhov, St Petersburg 2005) 10 e5! ♘g8 11 b3 f5?! (Ribli suggests 11...♘e7!?, and if 12 ♗b2 ♘g6 13 ♕g3 ♕h4 14 ♕xh4 ♘xh4 15 0-0-0, but this still looks a bit better for White) 12 h4 d6 13 ♗b2

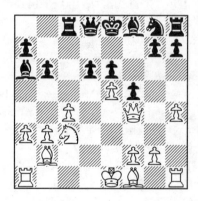

13...♕c7?! (13...dxe5 14 ♕xe5, and if 14...♕f6 15 ♘b5 ♕xe5+ 16 ♗xe5 ♗xb5 17 cxb5 ♘f6 18 ♗c4 is also better for White, as pointed out by Ribli) 14 c5! ♗xf1 15 cxd6, and White won in the game M.Krasenkow-B.Macieja, Warsaw 2004.

9 e4 d6 10 ♗d3

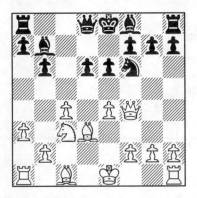
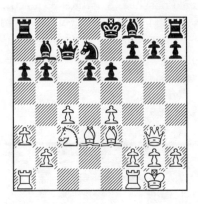

10...a6

Deviating from V.Korchnoi-G.Sax, 5th matchgame, Wijk aan Zee 1991, which had seen 10...♗e7 11 ♕g3! 0-0 (White repulsed a bold attempt by Black to turn defence into attack on the kingside in T.Harding-L.Andersen, correspondence 2004, which continued 11...h5!? 12 h3 ♘d7 13 0-0 g5 14 ♗c2 g4 15 ♖d1 gxh3!? 16 ♘b5! a6 17 ♘xd6+ ♗xd6 18 ♖xd6 ♕e7 19 ♗f4 0-0-0 20 ♖ad1 ♘c5 21 ♕g7 ♖xd6 22 ♖xd6) 12 ♗h6 ♘e8 13 ♗d2 ♖c8 14 0-0 ♗f6 15 ♖ac1 g6 16 b3 a6, and now Korchnoi suggests that 17 ♖fd1, and if 17...♗g7 18 ♗g5, is better for White.

11 0-0 ♘d7 12 ♕g3 ♕c7

J.Lautier-V.Topalov, Cannes (rapid) 2002, had previously gone 12...g6 13 ♗f4 ♕c7 14 ♗c2 (14 ♖ad1 has been suggested as a possible improvement) 14...h5 15 ♗a4 ♗c6 16 ♗xc6 ♕xc6, with a rough balance. In this sequence Vallejo Pons would probably have played 13 ♗e3!?, and if 13...♘e5 14 ♗d4, as he clearly intended in the main game.

13 ♗e3

13...g6?!

Black has difficulty completing his kingside development. The text doesn't help, although 13...♘e5 14 ♗d4 is also awkward to meet, because 14...♘xc4?! 15 ♖ac1 looks strong for White.

14 ♗d4!

White exploits Black's lack of development and weakness on the long a1-h8 diagonal, and stands well.

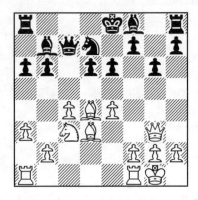

14...e5

Black weakens d5 significantly, but all moves have drawbacks. According to Ribli, quoting Ftacnik, White is also better after both 14...♘e5 15 f4 ♘xd3 16 ♕xd3, and if 16...e5 17 fxe5 dxe5 18 ♗f2

&c5 19 b4, and 14...♖g8 15 ♖ad1 ♗g7 16 ♗e2.

15 ♗e3 ♗g7 16 ♘d5 ♕d8 17 h4!

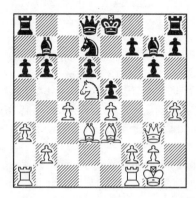

White's powerful grip on the centre enables him to make gains on the flanks. Black can't really prevent the further advance of this pawn, as playing 17...h5 would now allow White to conquer too many dark squares with 18 ♗g5.

17...0-0 18 h5 ♘c5!?

Perhaps Black should have played 18...♖e8 to allow his bishop to retreat to f8, but Karjakin lacks space and counterplay and his choices are all difficult.

19 h6! ♗h8 20 b4!

Having pinned Black down on the kingside, White now drives him back on the other flank.

20...♘d7

Not, of course, 20...♘xd3? allowing the amusing finish 21 ♗xb6 and if 21...♘f4 22 ♗xd8 ♘e2+ 23 ♔h2 ♘xg3 24 ♘e7 mate. Ribli also gives 20...♗xd5 21 bxc5 ♗b7 22 cxb6, intending 22...f5 23 exf5 e4 24 ♗c2 ♗xa1 25 ♖xa1 ♖xf5 26 ♖d1, with a clear advantage.

21 ♗g5 f6 22 ♗e3 ♖f7 23 ♗e2 ♔f8 24

♖ad1 f5!?

Black has such a miserable game that he might as well throw caution to the winds with this move.

25 exf5 gxf5 26 f4!

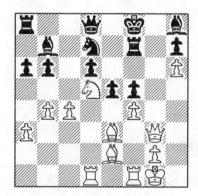

White halts all Black's activity with this blocking move. He now threatens 27 ♗h5, inducing Black to exchange his light-squared bishop, with catastrophic consequences for his already fragile hold on the central light squares.

26...♗xd5 27 ♖xd5 ♘f6 28 ♖d3 ♘e4 29 ♕h3 ♕c8

Black's cause is quite lost. His knight may look well placed, but nothing else is in Black's position. Karjakin's queen abandons the defence of b6 to support f5, but that fails to help.

30 ♗h5 ♖f6 31 ♗xb6 ♕xc4 32 fxe5 dxe5 33 ♖xf5 ♕c1+ 34 ♖d1 ♕xh6 35 ♗e3 ♕g7 36 ♗f3 ♘c3 37 ♗h6 1-0

> *Game 21*
> **B.Gelfand-L.Nisipeanu**
> *Bled Olympiad 2002*

1 c4 c5 2 ♘f3 ♘c6 3 d4 cxd4 4 ♘xd4

♘f6 5 ♘c3 e6 6 g3

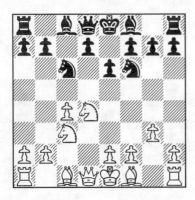

6...♕b6!

Black aims to chase White's knight from its strong d4 outpost. Quieter responses don't really challenge White. The simple 6...d5, for example, 7 ♗g2 ♗b4 8 0-0 0-0 9 cxd5 ♘xd5 10 ♘xd5 exd5 11 ♗e3 leads to comfortable White play against an indifferent form of Tarrasch Defence. Best of the rest are the slightly more ambitious moves 6...♗c5 and 6...♗b4, but practice favours White and none of Black's alternatives to the text are popular nowadays.

a) 6...♗c5 7 ♘b3 gives Black a choice since White hasn't covered the b4-square.

a1) 7...♗b4 8 ♗g2 d5 9 cxd5 is, though, very pleasant for White. His pieces were very active after 9...exd5 10 0-0 ♗e6 11 ♗e3 0-0 12 ♖c1 ♖c8 13 a3 ♗e7 14 ♘b5 in Z.Ribli-E.Schmittdiel, Austrian League 1998, and 9...♘xd5 10 0-0! is a promising gambit. J.Lautier-P.Leko, Cap d'Agde 1994, continued 10...♘xc3 11 ♕xd8+ ♔xd8 12 bxc3 ♗xc3 13 ♖b1 a5 14 ♗e3 ♗b4 15 ♖fc1 ♔e7 16

♘d4 ♗d7 17 ♘b5 ♔f6 18 a3 ♗e7 19 h4, with advantage.

a2) Some strong players have tried 7...♗e7 8 ♗g2 0-0 9 0-0 b6, but White is slightly better after 10 ♗f4. O.Romanishin-G.Kuzmin, Alushta 2004, continued 10...♗b7 (or 10...♗a6 11 ♘b5 ♖c8 12 ♘d6 ♗xd6 13 ♗xd6 ♘e7 14 ♘d2, and White had the upper hand in U.Andersson-Z.Hracek, Berlin 1996) 11 ♖c1 d6 12 ♘b5 ♘e8 13 ♕d2 a6 14 ♘c3 b5!? 15 cxb5 axb5 16 ♘d4 d5 17 ♘xd5! ♘xd4 18 ♘xe7+ ♕xe7 19 ♕xd4 ♗xg2 20 ♔xg2 ♖xa2 21 ♖a1, with the better game.

b) 6...♗b4 generally leads after 7 ♗g2 0-0 8 0-0 to slightly more lively positions. Recently 8...♕e7 (8...a6 9 ♗f4 ♖e8 10 ♘xc6 bxc6 11 ♗d6 ♗xd6 12 ♕xd6 ♕e7 13 ♕xe7 ♖xe7 14 e4 gave White a pull in G.Kasparov-P.Ricardi, Buenos Aires simul 1992) has been popular, but White has been scoring well with 9 ♘a4!?.

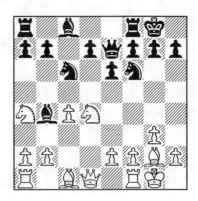

J.Stocek-T.Petrik, Tatranske Zruby 2004, continued 9...d5 (Black did better after 9...♖d8 10 a3 ♗d6 11 b4!? ♗e5 12 ♗b2 ♗xd4 13 ♗xd4 ♘xd4 14 ♕xd4 d6

15 ♘c3 e5 in S.Atalik-N.Short, Turin Olympiad 2006, when perhaps White should try 16 ♕d3) 10 cxd5 exd5 11 ♗f4 ♗g4 12 h3 ♘xd4 13 ♕xd4 ♗xe2 14 ♖fe1 ♗xe1 15 ♖xe1 a5 16 ♘c3 ♕b4 17 ♕xb4 axb4 18 ♘xe2 ♖fe8 19 ♗e3 ♖xa2 20 ♗d4, and White won.

Returning to the more challenging 6...♕b6:

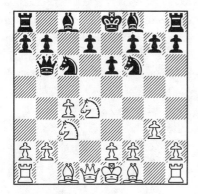

7 ♘db5!?

White has a more common option in 7 ♘b3, which leads to a long and critical variation that is still unclear today. After 7...♘e5 (not forced, but after 7...♗b4 8 ♗g2 d5 White has the dangerous gambit 9 cxd5 ♘xd5 10 0-0!; instead A.Karpov-C.Pritchett, Nice Olympiad 1974, saw 9 ♘d2 d4 10 ♘a4 ♕c7 11 0-0 ♗e7 12 a3 0-0 13 b4 e5 14 ♕c2 ♗e6 15 ♘b3 ♖ad8 16 ♘ac5 ♗c8 17 e4 ♗xc5! 18 ♘xc5 d3 19 ♘xd3 ♘d4 20 ♕b2 ♗g4 21 ♖e1 ♖fe8 22 f4?!, and now 22...♘e2+! and if 23 ♖xe2 ♗xe2 24 ♕xe2 ♕xc4 25 ♗f1 ♕d4+ should win, as pointed out by Bobby Fischer) 8 e4 ♗b4 9 ♕e2 d6 10 f4 ♘c6 11 ♗e3 ♗xc3+ 12 bxc3 ♕c7 13 ♗g2, we reach a tense position that has been contested many

times in top-class chess. Black can't easily prevent White playing c5 and exchanging one of his doubled c-pawns. White's extra space and bishop-pair give him some chances of a long-term pull, although he does have to nurse split a- and c-pawns. Practice has suggested that this theoretical position is probably about equal, but it is rich enough in resources that some readers may still wish to consider it.

7...♘e5

This counterattacking move is again critical, but Black has two alternatives:

a) 7...♗c5 is the better option and now:

a1) White achieves little with the over-cautious 8 ♘d6+ ♔e7 9 ♘de4 ♘xe4 10 ♘xe4, as Black can achieve a dynamic isolated queen's pawn position after 10...♗b4+ 11 ♗d2 d5 12 cxd5 exd5 13 ♘c3 ♗e6 14 ♗g2 ♖hd8 15 0-0 ♔f8, as he did in P.Schlosser-L.Ftacnik, Austrian League 2006.

a2) White should instead play 8 ♗g2! offering a gambit that should probably be declined:

a21) Black has no clear follow-up after 8...♗xf2+?! 9 ♔f1 ♘g4 10 ♕d6 and this line is suspect. A.Greenfeld-V.Yemelin, Israel 1998, continued 10...♔d8 11 ♗g5+ f6 12 ♘a4 ♕a6 13 h3 ♕xa4 14 hxg4 ♗b6 (or 14...♗xg3 15 ♗xf6+ gxf6 16 ♕xg3) 15 ♖xh7 ♖e8, and now Yemelin suggests 16 ♗h4! and if 16...g5 17 ♖d1 ♘e7 18 b3 ♕a6 19 b4! winning.

a22) White was better after 8...a6?! 9 ♘d6+ ♔e7 10 ♘de4 ♘xe4 11 ♘xe4 ♗b4+ 12 ♔f1! in M.Marin-M.Sion Castro, Benasque 1999.

a23) White also has good play after 8...d5 9 0-0 dxc4 10 ♘d6+ ♗xd6 11 ♕xd6.

For example, 11...♘e7 (11...♘b4!? may improve, but 12 ♕f4 ♕a6 13 ♗e3 ♘c2 14 ♗c5 ♘d7 15 ♖ad1 ♘xc5 16 ♕c7, kept an edge in the game M.Mulyar-A.Moiseenko, Edmonton 2005) 12 ♕a3 ♘fd5 13 ♘e4 0-0 14 ♘d6 c3 15 e4 ♘b4 16 ♘c4 ♕c5 17 ♕xc3 b5 18 ♘a3 ♕xc3 19 bxc3 ♘d3 20 ♘xb5, and White won in A.Rustemov-S.Karjakin, Dos Hermanas 2003.

a24) Black gets closer to equality with 8...♘e5!? 9 0-0 ♘xc4 10 ♕a4 a6 11

♕xc4 axb5 12 ♕xb5 ♕xb5 13 ♘xb5, but White's queenside pawn majority and slight lead in development still count for something.

b) 7...d5?! is risky. White developed a dangerous initiative in G.Kasparov-R.Vaganian, Skelleftea 1989, after 8 ♗g2 d4 9 ♘a4 ♕a5+ 10 ♗d2 ♗b4 (or 10...♕d8 11 e3 e5 12 exd4 exd4 13 0-0 a6 14 ♕e1+ ♗e6 15 ♗xc6+ bxc6 16 ♗a5, and White won in R.Vera-I.Herrera, Ubeda 2001) 11 ♘c5 0-0 12 ♘d3 ♗xd2+ 13 ♕xd2 ♕xd2+ 14 ♔xd2 ♖d8 15 c5 ♘e8 16 ♘a3 f6 17 f4, with some advantage.

Returning to 7...♘e5:

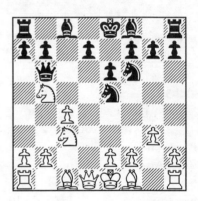

8 ♗g2

This natural move is better than 8 ♗f4, which leads after 8...♘fg4 9 e3 a6 to a position where White has no apparent advantage.

8...a6

In the case of 8...♘xc4 9 ♕a4 a6 10 ♕xc4 axb5 11 ♕xb5 ♗c5, play transposes to note 'a24' to Black's 7th move.

9 ♘a3!

White continues in gambit style, whereas after 9 ♕a4 ♖b8 10 ♗e3 ♗c5 11

♗xc5 ♕xc5 12 ♕a3 ♕xa3 13 ♘xa3, he achieves no more than balanced chances.

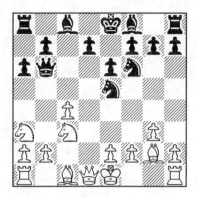

9...♗e7

Black heads for a solid, if slightly cramped Hedgehog defence. He might be able to accept the gambit and survive, but it is a very high risk strategy. After 9...♗xa3!? 10 bxa3 ♘xc4 11 ♗g5 Black is behind in time and has many weaknesses. White has good compensation, but the outcome remains uncertain. Black has now tried many moves in a relatively small number of top-class games:

a) 11...♕d8 12 ♖c1 d5 13 0-0 ♘e5 was B.Gelfand-B.Macieja, Bermuda 2004, and now Gelfand suggests 14 e4 d4 15 ♕a4+ ♕d7 16 ♖fd1 ♘c6 17 e5, with a clear advantage.

b) E.Agrest-V.Ivanchuk, Swedish League 2003, continued 11...d5 12 0-0 ♗d7!? (trying to improve over the 12...0-0 13 ♖c1 ♖d8 14 ♗xf6 gxf6 15 e4! d4 16 ♘a4 ♕b5 17 ♖xc4 ♕xc4 18 ♘b6 ♕c5 19 ♘xa8 ♗d7 20 ♕g4+ ♔f8 of E.Agrest-T.Wedberg, Skara 2002, and now 21 e5! ♖xa8 22 exf6 is in White's

favour), and now 13 e4 ♘xe4 14 ♘xe4 dxe4 15 ♖b1 ♕c5 16 ♖xb7 0-0 was fairly acceptable for Black. However, other 13th moves also need to be examined...

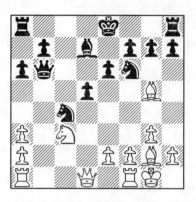

...including 13 ♗xf6!? gxf6 14 ♗xd5 exd5 15 ♘xd5, intending 15...♕c6 16 ♕d4 (or 16 ♖c1 ♗e6 17 ♘xf6+ ♔e7 18 ♕d4) with dangerous threats, and 13 ♖b1!? ♕c5 (or 13...♕a7 14 ♗xf6 gxf6 15 e4) 14 ♖xb7, and if 14...♗c6 15 ♖c7 0-0 (and not 15...♕d6? 16 ♖xc6 ♕xc6 17 ♗xf6 gxf6 18 ♘xd5! when White wins after 18...exd5 19 ♗xd5 ♕c8 20 ♗xa8 ♕xa8 21 ♕a4+) 16 ♗xf6 gxf6 17 e4.

c) 11...h6?! 12 ♗xf6 gxf6 13 0-0 ♖b8 was B.Gelfand-L.Van Wely, Bled Olympiad 2002, and now 14 ♘e4! is strong, intending 14...f5 (or 14...♗e7!? 15 ♖b1 ♕c7 16 ♕d4 e5 17 ♕a7 d5 18 ♘c3 ♗e6 19 ♘xd5+ ♗xd5 20 ♗xd5) 15 ♖b1 ♕c7 16 ♕d4 ♕e5 17 ♘d6+ ♔e7 18 ♕h4+ ♔xd6 19 ♖fd1+ ♔c7 (and not 19...♔c5? 20 ♕e7+) 20 ♕xc4+ ♔d8 21 ♖b3, with a miserable position for Black.

d) E.Agrest-J.Hall, Swedish League 2004, saw Black try 11...♕c5!?, but after 12 ♗xf6 gxf6 13 0-0 (13 ♖c1!? is another option) 13...♘e3!

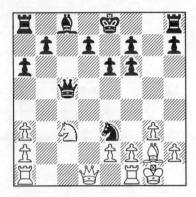

14 ♕d3!? (14 fxe3 ♕xe3+ 15 ♔h1 ♕xc3 16 ♖c1 ♕e5 17 ♖c4 also needs a test) 14...♘xf1 15 ♘e4 ♕e5 16 ♘d6+ ♔e7 17 ♖d1 ♘xg3 18 hxg3 a5 19 a4 ♔f8 20 ♖b1 ♔g7 21 ♖b5 ♕a1+ 22 ♔h2 ♖a6 23 ♖c5, White enjoyed decent attacking chances for the exchange.

We should also note that White pressed energetically after 9...♘fg4 10 0-0 ♗c5 11 ♘e4 ♗xa3 12 bxa3 ♘xc4 13 ♗f4 d5 14 ♘c3 ♕a5 15 ♖c1 0-0 16 e4! in D.Yevseev-D.Shchukin, St Petersburg 2005.

Returning to the calm 9...♗e7:

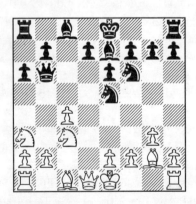

10 0-0 d6 11 ♕b3 ♕c7

After 11...♕xb3 12 axb3 ♖b8 13 b4

White has a slight pull due to his extra space and without any complicating counterplay on Black's part.

12 ♗f4 0-0 13 ♖fd1 ♘g6 14 ♗e3 ♘d7 15 ♘a4

White battles to control the queenside dark squares. He might also play 15 ♖ac1!? and if 15...♖b8 16 ♗a7 ♖a8 17 ♗d4.

15...♖b8 16 ♗a7 ♖a8

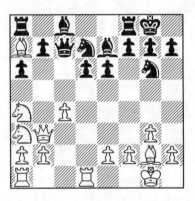

17 ♕e3

Gelfand suggests that White should have played 17 ♗d4!, and that the positions after 17...♖b8 18 ♕c3! ♗f6 19 ♖ac1 b6 remain slightly better for White. Now Nisipeanu makes a series of fine defensive moves that considerably loosen White's dark-square control and achieve a rough balance.

17...♗d8! 18 ♖ac1 ♕a5! 19 b3 ♘e7! 20 g4

White must attend to the threat of ...♘f5, but now Black's knight reaches c6, reinforcing Black's pressure on the queenside dark squares and forcing White into playing an unclear exchange sacrifice.

20...♘c6! 21 ♗xc6 bxc6 22 ♖xd6 ♕c7

Both sides are walking something of a positional tightrope here. After 22...♗e7 Gelfand intended 23 ♖xd7 ♗xd7 (or 23...♗xa3 24 ♖cd1 ♗xd7 25 ♗b6 ♕b4 26 ♗c5 with the better game) 24 ♖d1! with good compensation for the exchange.

23 ♗c5 ♘xc5 24 ♕xc5 ♗e7 25 ♖cd1

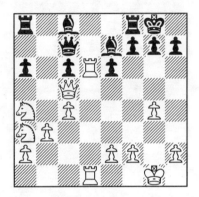

25...♗xd6

Black might also have tried 25...e5!? and if 26 h3 ♗xd6 27 ♕xd6 ♕xd6 28 ♖xd6 f5.

26 ♕xd6 ♖a7!?

It was still possible to play 26...♕xd6 27 ♖xd6 e5, and if 28 f3 e4. Now Gelfand finds time to make a valuable pawn move on the queenside that both strengthens his dark-square control and prepares a path for his knight on a3 to recentralize.

27 c5! e5 28 ♘c4?!

Here Gelfand points out that he should have preferred 28 f3 and if 28...e4 29 ♘c4.

28...f6?

This move is unnecessarily passive. After 28...♗xg4 29 f3 (or 29 ♘xe5 ♗xe2 30 ♖e1 ♗b5 31 ♘b6 ♕xd6 32 cxd6 ♖d8

33 a4 f6) 29...♗h3! 30 ♘xe5 ♕e7, Black completely repulses White's forces and even stands a little better, as given by Gelfand and Notkin.

29 f3 ♕f7 30 ♘ab6 ♖c7 31 ♘a5

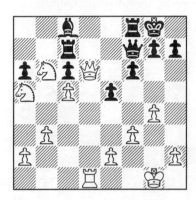

31...h5?!

Black's kingside counterattack comes too late. Gelfand suggests that Black had to try either the ugly 31...♗b7 or 31...♖e8!? 32 ♘xc6 ♖e6 33 ♕xc7!? ♕xc7 34 ♖d8+ ♔f7 35 ♖xc8 ♕xc6 36 ♖xc6 ♖xc6 37 b4, when White is better.

32 gxh5 ♗h3 33 ♘xc6 ♔h7

Or 33...♕xh5 34 ♔h1 and Black will have great difficulty dealing with White's rampant knights combined with the rapid advance of his c-pawn.

34 ♔h1 ♖fc8 35 ♕d3+ e4 36 ♕xe4+ f5 37 ♕h4 ♖e8 38 ♘d4 ♕e7 39 ♕xh3 ♕xc5 40 ♘c4 ♖d8 41 e3 f4 42 ♖g1 1-0

Game 22
Z.Izoria-S.Maze
European Ch., Warsaw 2005

1 c4 c5 2 ♘f3 ♘f6

Before moving on to systems characterized by ...d5, we should be aware that Black can also try to play 2...♘c6 3 ♘c3, and now either 3...♘d4!? or 3...e5. However, for our repertoire purposes, we need only know that White can bypass both of these tricky lines by playing 3 d4 cxd4 4 ♘xd4.

Then Black usually takes play back into games 19-21 with 4...♘f6 or consents to defend a Maróczy Bind Accelerated Dragon Sicilian after 4...g6 5 e4. Occasionally he also tries something independent:

a) 4...e6 and now:

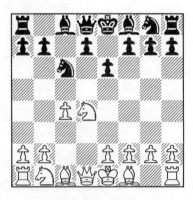

a1) 5 ♘c3 ♗b4!? (rather than again

transpose to games 19-21 with 5...♘f6) cuts out a3 systems for White. On the other hand, 6 g3 ♘f6 now leads to one of White's more comfortable g3 systems (see note 'b' to Black's 6th move in Game 21). White can also consider 6 ♘db5!?:

a11) 6...♘f6 7 ♗f4 reaches a promising position, with good play down the d-file, that usually occurs after 1 c4 c5 2 ♘f3 ♘f6 3 ♘c3 ♘c6 4 d4 cxd4 5 ♘xd4 e6 6 ♘db5 ♗b4!? (with this move order 6...d5 7 ♗f4 e5! is the critical main line) 7 ♗f4. B.Macieja-J.Gdanski, Warsaw 2004, continued 7...0-0 8 ♗d6 ♗xd6 9 ♘xd6 ♕b6 (or 9...♘e8 10 e3 ♕b6 11 ♖b1 ♕b4 12 ♘xe8 ♖xe8 13 ♗e2, with an edge) 10 ♕d2 ♘d4 11 0-0-0! ♕xd6 12 ♕xd4 ♕xd4 13 ♖xd4 b6 14 e4 ♖d8?! (or 14...e5 15 ♖d2 ♗b7 16 f3) 15 e5! ♘e8 16 ♗e2 ♗b7 17 ♖hd1 f6?!, and now Macieja gives 18 ♗g4! and if 18...f5 19 ♗f3 ♗xf3 20 gxf3 ♖ac8 21 ♖xd7 ♖xd7 22 ♖xd7 ♖xc4 23 ♖xa7, winning. He also considers 17...♗xg2 18 f3 f6 19 ♖h4 g5 20 ♖h5 ♔g7 21 exf6+ ♔g6 22 f4 g4 23 ♗xg4 ♗c6 24 f5+ exf5 25 ♖xf5 ♘xf6 26 ♖d6 ♖f8 27 h4 to be in White's favour.

a12) 6...a6 7 ♘d6+ ♚e7 8 ♗f4! ♕a5 (or 8...♘f6 9 a3 ♗xc3+ 10 bxc3 ♕a5 11 ♕d2 ♕c5 12 ♖d1 ♘e5 13 e3 ♖d8 14 ♗e2, with a clear advantage in L.Polugaevsky-P.Cramling, Aruba 1992) 9 ♖c1 ♘e5 10 c5! f6 11 ♗d2 ♘h6 12 a3 ♗xc3 13 ♗xc3 ♕c7 14 g3 ♕c6 15 ♖g1 ♘hf7 16 ♗g2 ♕c7 17 ♕d2 ♘c6 18 ♖d1 ♖b8 19 ♕f4, with good chances, was A.Beliavsky-S.Sale, Bled 1999.

a2) 5 g3 should be employed by fans of Game 21. Black usually transposes to that, but he does also have the risky 5...♗b4+ 6 ♘c3 ♕a5!?.

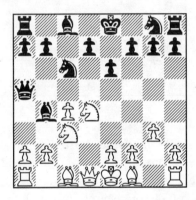

V.Ivanchuk-P.Eljanov, Fuegen 2006, continued 7 ♘db5 ♘f6 (against 7...d5 White can play 8 ♗f4, and if 8...e5 9 ♗d2, with good chances, or 8 a3!? ♗xc3+ 9 bxc3 ♘f6 10 ♘d6+ ♚e7 11 cxd5 ♘xd5 12 ♗d2) 8 a3 ♗xc3+ 9 ♘xc3 ♘e4 10 ♗d2 ♕f5 11 f4! ♘xc3 (or 11...♘a5!? 12 ♘xe4 ♕xe4 13 ♗xa5 ♕xh1 14 ♕d6 ♕c6 15 ♗b4 ♕xd6 16 ♗xd6, with an edge according to Notkin) 12 ♗xc3 ♕e4 13 ♖g1 ♕e3 (or 13...♕xc4 14 ♗xg7 ♖g8 15 ♗c3 d5 16 ♖c1) 14 ♖g2 0-0 15 ♕d6 b6 16 g4 ♗a6 17 ♖g3 ♕c5 18 ♕xc5 bxc5, and now Notkin recommends 19 e3

with advantage.

b) 4...♕b6 usually transposes after 5 ♘b3 e6 6 ♘c3 ♘f6 to Game 19 in the event of 7 a3. If, however, White wishes to play g3 systems with ♘db5 rather than ♘b3, he must play 5 ♘db5!?, which has some novel features and was perhaps a little underestimated by Richard Palliser when he recommended this move order for Black in his *Beating Unusual Chess Openings*. After 5...♘f6 (note that 5...a6 6 ♘5c3 e6 7 g3 ♘e5 8 ♗g2 ♘f6 9 ♘a3! transposes to Game 21; in this line 6 ♗e3!? is possible too and 6...♘e5 7 b3 ♕c6 8 ♖g1 deserves a test) 6 g3 a6 7 ♘5c3 ♘e5 (V.Topalov-S.Karjakin, Leon 2003, varied with 7...g6 8 ♗g2 d6 9 0-0 ♗g7 10 b3 0-0 11 ♗b2 ♕a5 12 ♘d2 ♕h5 13 e4 ♕xd1 14 ♖fxd1 ♘d7 15 ♖ab1 ♘c5 16 ♘d5 ♗e6 17 ♗xg7 ♚xg7 18 ♘f1 b5 19 b4 ♘d7 20 ♘fe3, with an edge) 8 b3 ♕c6 9 ♖g1, White has to keep his king in the centre.

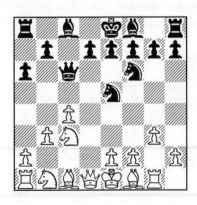

However, he nevertheless held the centre and assumed a kingside attack in B.Gulko-K.Mekhitarian, Cali 2007, which continued 9...e6 10 ♗g2 ♕c7 11

♗b2 ♗e7 12 ♘d2 0-0 13 ♖c1 d6 14 h3
♖b8 15 f4 ♘g6 16 e3 b6 17 ♕e2 ♗b7 18
g4 ♗xg2 19 ♕xg2 ♘d7 20 g5 f5 21 gxf6
♘xf6 22 ♘f3 ♕d7 23 ♘h4, and White
won.

Returning to 2...♘f6:

3 ♘c3 d5 4 cxd5 ♘xd5 5 d4 cxd4

Our next game will focus on
5...♘xc3 6 bxc3 g6. Black can also
transpose to a Semi-Tarrasch Defence
with 5...e6. Then 6 e4 ♘xc3 7 bxc3 cxd4
8 cxd4 has long been considered to give
White a pleasant edge and he can also
aim with 6 g3 to reach lines considered
in Game 24.

6 ♕xd4

6...♘xc3

6...e6 is more interesting at this
stage. After 7 e4 ♘xc3 8 ♕xc3 play
simply transposes, but Black can also
consider 7...♘c6 8 ♗b5 ♘xc3 9 ♕xc3,
which leads to 9 ♗b5 systems (see note
'a' to White's 9th move). This restricts
both sides' options.

7 ♕xc3 ♘c6 8 e4

8...e6

White is ahead in time, but the
pawns are symmetrical and neither
side has any structural weakness, so
this quiet, but sound move, looking
ahead to establishing gradual equality,
is a good one. Black can also consider
8...♗g4, so that this bishop's scope is
not restricted after ...e6, or 8...a6. However, Black may have to concede the
bishop-pair and delaying his kingside
development entails some risk to king
safety:

a) White has good chances after
8...♗g4 9 ♗b5 ♖c8 10 ♗e3 (promising
too is 10 ♗f4). V.Topalov-A.Beliavsky,
Linares 1994, continued 10...a6
(L.Portisch-R.Hübner, Montreal 1979,
had previously gone 10...♗xf3?! 11 gxf3

a6 12 ♖d1 ♕c7 13 ♗xc6+ ♕xc6 14 ♕d4 f6 15 0-0 e5 16 ♕a7, with some advantage) 11 ♖d1 ♕c7 12 ♗a4 b5 13 ♗b3 e6 14 0-0 ♗xf3 15 gxf3 ♗d6 16 ♕xg7 ♗xh2+ 17 ♔h1 ♗e5 18 ♕h6, and White stood well.

b) 8...a6 9 ♗c4 ♗g4 (V.Korchnoi-A.Karpov, Riga 1970, varied with 9...♕a5 10 ♗d2 ♕xc3 11 ♗xc3 e6 12 0-0 ♖g8 13 ♖fd1 b5 14 ♗d3 f6 15 a4 b4 16 ♗d4! ♘xd4 17 ♘xd4, with an edge) 10 0-0 e6 11 ♘e5 ♘xe5 12 ♕xe5 ♖c8 13 ♗b3 ♗e2?! (13...♕d6 14 ♕g5 ♗e2 15 ♖e1 h6 16 ♕e3 ♗b5 may be better, but after 17 a4 ♗c6 18 e5, and if 18...♕b4 19 ♗d2 ♕g4 20 f3 ♕g6 21 ♖ac1, White still has a pull) 14 ♖e1 ♗b5 15 ♗xe6! fxe6 16 ♕h5+ g6 17 ♕e5 ♔f7 18 ♕xh8 saw White win in Bu Xiangzhi-N.Miezis, Reykjavik 2004.

9 a3!?

White must attend to the threat of ....♗b4. In addition to the text-move, White can also play for an edge with 9 ♗b5, which is his most frequently played move, and 9 ♗d2. Black remains behind in development, but White must play energetically if he is to make anything of this slight advantage as play moves into the middlegame:

a) 9 ♗b5 ♗d7 (Black can also try 9...♕b6, but he must then be prepared to defend stubbornly after 10 ♗xc6+ ♕xc6 11 ♕xc6+ bxc6 12 0-0 ♗a6 13 ♖e1) 10 0-0 ♕b6 11 a4 ♕c5 12 ♕d3 ♕d6 13 ♕e2 reaches a position in which White can hope to build some pressure on Black's kingside, usually after an eventual e5, gaining space and pivotal use of e4.

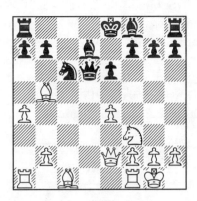

White often presses on the b1-h7 diagonal to coax ...g6, weakening the kingside dark squares, and he also has h-file prospects based on the pawn push h4-h5. Meanwhile Black generally tries to create diversionary play in the centre. Practice has seen:

a1) 13...a6 14 e5 ♕c7 15 ♗d3 ♗e7 (J.Piket-L.Van Wely, Dutch League 1998, varied with 15...♘b4 16 ♗e4 ♗c6 17 ♗d2 ♗xe4 18 ♕xe4 ♘d5 19 ♖fc1 ♕d7 20 h4! h5 21 ♗g5 ♗e7 22 ♗xe7 ♕xe7 23 ♖a3 0-0 24 ♘g5 g6 25 ♖f3 ♔g7 26 g4! hxg4 27 ♕xg4 ♔h6!? and now Piket gives 28 ♘e4, and if 28...♖ac8 29 ♖xc8 ♖xc8 30 ♘d6 ♖f8 31 a5 ♔g7 32 ♖b3, with excellent chances) 16 ♗d2 0-0 17 ♕e4 g6 18 h4 ♖fd8 19 ♖ac1 ♗e8 20 ♗b1 ♕b6 21 ♗c3 ♘b4 22 a5 ♕b5 23 ♘d4 ♕d5 24 ♕f4 ♘a2 25 ♗e4 ♕d7 26 ♖cd1 ♘xc3 27 bxc3 ♕c7 28 ♖d3 ♕xa5 29 h5 ♖ac8 30 hxg6 hxg6 31 ♖h3 ♖xc3 32 ♘f3 ♖xf3 33 gxf3 ♗f8 34 ♗xg6! saw White's kingside attacking plans prevail in A.Iljin-P.Ponkratov, St Petersburg 2007.

a2) Perhaps a tougher choice is 13...♕c7. P.Eljanov-R.Zelcic, Ljubljana

2002, continued 14 e5 ♗e7 (or 14...♗c5, as in V.Anand-M.Adams, FIDE World Championship, Groningen 1997, and now Adams suggests 15 ♗e3 ♗xe3 16 ♕xe3 and if 16...♕b6 17 ♕g5 0-0 18 ♖fd1, with an edge) 15 ♗d2 0-0 16 ♕e4 ♖fd8 17 ♗c3 ♗e8 18 h4 g6...

...and now White would retain a slight pull with 19 h5 or 19 ♖fc1.

a3) Against 13...♗e7, White achieved a pull with some opportunistic dark-square play in J.Piket-M.Brodsky, Wijk aan Zee 1995, which continued 14 b3 ♕c7 15 ♗b2 0-0 16 ♖ac1 a6!? (Ftacnik gives 16...♕b6 17 ♖fd1 ♖fd8 18 ♘d2, with an edge) 17 ♗xc6 ♗xc6 18 ♘e5 ♗f6 19 ♘xc6 ♗xb2 20 ♕xb2 bxc6, and now Piket advocates 21 ♖c5! followed by ♖fc1-c3, with a clear advantage.

b) The modest 9 ♗d2 also has bite. Black failed to solve the problem of his vulnerable g-pawn, fatally neglecting his kingside development in G.Cabrilo-V.Klasan, Belgrade 2006, which continued 9...♗d7 10 ♗e2 ♕b6 (or 10...♕f6 11 e5 ♕g6 12 0-0 ♗b4 13 ♕e3 0-0 14 ♖fd1 ♖fd8 15 ♖ac1, with an edge in I.Tsesarsky-A.Kapengut, Sofia 1988) 11

0-0 ♖c8 12 ♖fd1 f6 13 ♗e3 ♕c7 14 ♖ac1 ♗e7 15 ♕b3 ♕b8?! 16 ♖xd7! ♔xd7 17 ♗c4 ♔e8 18 ♗xe6 ♖d8 19 h3 ♔f8 20 ♗d5 ♘b4 21 ♘d4, and White won.

Returning to 9 a3:

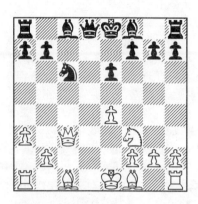

9...♗d7

Black usually plays this move followed by ...♖c8 quickly, not least to encourage White's queen to move, relieving the pressure on g7 that makes the completion of Black's kingside development difficult. Quite wrong is 9...♕a5?! 10 b4! when White is already clearly better and he won after 10...♘xb4? 11 ♗d2 in S.Knott-F.Rayner, Douglas 2005.

10 ♗e2 ♖c8

Black has no quick fix in 10...♕f6?! which is always a temptation in this line, because after 11 e5! ♕g6 12 0-0 ♗e7 13 ♖d1, Black has simply lost time and misplaced his queen.

11 0-0 ♘a5

This is a very logical idea. Black drives White's queen from c3 and finds play on the queenside light squares. Once again 11...♕f6?! 12 e5! is not to be trusted.

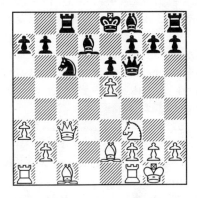

J.Gustafsson-D.Milanovic, online blitz 2004, continued 12...♕g6 13 ♗f4 ♘b4?! 14 ♕b3 ♘d5 15 ♗g3 ♕c2 16 ♗d1!, with a significant plus.

12 ♕d3!

This move appears to cause Black the most problems. Despite having the freer game, White made little real headway in V.Topalov-M.Adams, Linares 1997, after 12 ♕e3 ♗c5! 13 ♕f4 ♘b3 14 ♕g3 ♘xc1 15 ♖axc1 0-0 16 ♘e5 f6 17 ♘xd7 ♕xd7 18 ♕b3 ♔h8 19 ♗c4 e5 20 ♖fd1 ♕e7, and Black defended.

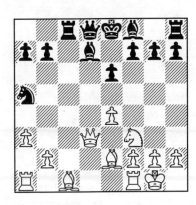

12...♗c6!?

Black attempts to improve on the most heavily played move in this posi-

tion, namely 12...♗a4. He still intends to move his bishop to a4, but only after first dissuading White from exchanging queens on d8 by targeting White's e-pawn. After 12...♗a4 13 ♕xd8+ (White can also consider 13 ♕e3!?, after which E.Weinzettl-H.Penz, Austrian League 2002, continued 13...♗c5 14 ♕f4 ♘b3 15 ♕g4 ♘xc1 – or 15...♘xa1 16 ♕xg7 ♖f8 17 b4 ♗d6 18 ♕xa1 – 16 ♖axc1 0-0 17 e5! with attacking chances) 13...♖xd8, White can very quickly develop a serious queenside initiative with 14 ♗e3:

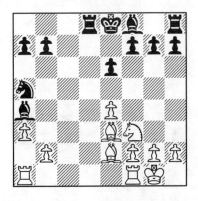

a) White's rooks penetrated on the c-file with fatal consequences in R.Ruck-A.Grosar, Bled 2002, which continued 14...b6?! 15 ♖ac1 ♗d6 16 e5! ♗e7 17 ♖c7 ♖d7 18 ♖c8+ ♖d8 19 ♖fc1 ♖f8 20 b4 ♘b7 21 ♖8c7 ♖d7 22 ♘d4 a5 23 ♗b5 ♗xb5 24 ♘xb5 ♘d8 25 ♖xd7 ♔xd7 26 ♖c7+ ♔e8 27 ♘d6+ ♗xd6 28 exd6 1-0.

b) Black's knight occupied, but was quickly eliminated from b3, in V.Anand-V.Korchnoi, Tilburg 1998, which saw 14...♘b3 15 ♗d1! b5?! (V.Kramnik-L.Van Wely, Monaco (blindfold) 1998, the brilliant stem game in the line, had earlier seen 15...a6 16 ♗xb3 ♗xb3 17 ♖ac1 ♗d6 18 ♗b6 ♖a8 19 ♘d4! ♗a4 20 ♖c4 ♗d7 21 ♖d1 0-0 22 e5, with a serious advantage) 16 ♗xb3 ♗xb3 17 ♖fc1 e5!? 18 ♘xe5 a6 19 ♘c6 1-0.

13 ♕e3

Now if White exchanges queens on d8, he has to take time out to defend his e-pawn and Black would be fine. On the other hand, this is a perfectly good attacking alternative plan.

13...♗a4

Black continues the battle to secure b3 for his knight. He of course, can't allow 13...♕b6? 14 b4 ♕xe3 15 ♗xe3 ♘b3 16 ♖ab1, winning.

14 b4

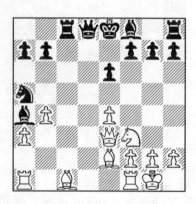

This and White's next move are highly convincing. White gains queenside space and control of b3. Black's queenside light square strategy falls about his feet in total ruin. If Black doesn't now proceed to occupy b3, he is simply in trouble. After 14...♘c4, White can simply take on a7 either immediately or after exchanging

Black's knight. Or 14...♘c6 15 ♗b2, and White has a considerable lead in development.

14...♘b3 15 ♗d1! ♘c5

This is Black's only move. The queen sacrifice 15...♕xd1?! 16 ♖xd1 ♘xa1 17 ♖d3! just loses.

16 ♗b2 ♗b5 17 bxc5 ♗xc5 18 ♕c3

Now clearly better, White invites Black to win his queen and two pawns for rook and two minor pieces. It may be that 18 ♕f4!?, and if 18...♗xf1 19 ♔xf1 0-0 20 ♕e5, is even stronger.

18...♗xf2+ 19 ♖xf2 ♖xc3 20 ♗xc3 0-0 21 ♗b4 ♖e8 22 ♖c1 a5 23 ♗c3 ♕e7 24 a4!

White establishes control of b5 and either forces Black to allow White's knight to be exchanged for Black's active bishop or permit a dangerous attacking breakthrough on the f-file.

24...♗c6 25 ♘e5 ♕g5!?

Or 25...♗xe4 26 ♘xf7 ♖f8 27 ♗e5 ♕b4 28 ♗h5, with a clear advantage.

26 ♗b2 ♗xe4 27 ♘xf7 ♕e3 28 ♗h5 ♖f8 29 ♖c7?

But here White fails to convert, overlooking 29 ♘h6+! ♔h8 (neither do

29...♕xh6 30 ♖xf8+ ♔xf8 31 ♗a3+ ♔g8 32 ♖c8 mate, nor 29...gxh6 30 ♗f7+! ♖xf7 31 ♖c8+ defend) 30 ♘g4 ♕b6 31 ♔h1, and Black's game is about to collapse.

29...h6!

Now Black scrambles together a real defence.

30 h4 ♕e1+ 31 ♖f1

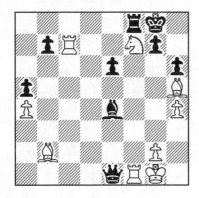

31...♕g3?

But Black also misfires, failing to see the not too difficult draw by perpetual check after 31...♕e3+! 32 ♖f2 ♕e1+ etc. White can't play 32 ♔h1? since 32...♕h3+ wins, and if 32 ♔h2 ♕d2 33 ♘xh6+ ♕xh6 34 ♖xf8+ ♔xf8 35 ♗xg7+ ♕xg7 36 ♖xg7 ♔xg7 37 ♗e8, Black should hold. Izoria now takes full advantage of his reprieve with an immediately crushing knight sacrifice.

32 ♘xh6+! ♔h7

If instead 32...gxh6 then the reply 33 ♗f7+! ♖xf7 (33...♔h7 is no better: 34 ♗g6+ ♔xg6 35 ♖g7+) 34 ♖c8+ ♔h7 35 ♖xf7+ ♔g6 36 ♖g7+ wins, as shown by Ribli.

33 ♖xg7+ ♕xg7 34 ♗xg7 ♖xf1+ 35 ♔xf1 ♔xg7 36 ♘f7 ♗d3+ 37 ♔e1 1-0

Game 23
B.Gulko-M.Bengtson
World Open, Philadelphia 2003

1 c4 c5 2 ♘f3 ♘f6 3 ♘c3 d5 4 cxd5 ♘xd5 5 d4 ♘xc3

The immediate 5...g6 is also possible, but gives White more options, including the critical 6 dxc5! (6 e3 ♗g7 7 ♗b5+ ♗d7 8 ♕b3 ♘xc3 9 bxc3 transposes to the notes to White's 8th move) 6...♘xc3 7 ♕xd8+ ♔xd8 8 bxc3, which seems better for White.

His pieces are very active and Black's king is insecure. White gave back material to gain a positional stranglehold in B.Kurajica-B.Rogulj, Rabac 2004, which continued 8...♗g7 (Black also struggled after 8...f6 9 ♗a3 ♔c7 10 0-0-0 e5 11 ♘d2 ♗e6 12 e3 ♘d7 13 ♘e4 f5 14 ♘d6 ♗e7 15 ♗b5, in M.Stean-N.Short, Hastings 1979/80) 9 ♘d4! ♗d7?! (or 9...♘c6 10 ♗a3! ♗d7 11 0-0-0! and if 11...a6 12 e4 ♔c7 13 ♗e2 e5!? 14 ♘b3, and White is better) 10 ♖b1! ♗c6 11 f3 ♘d7 12 e4! ♘xc5 13

♘xc6+ bxc6 14 ♗e3 ♘e6 15 ♗a6 ♗xc3+ 16 ♔f2 ♗d4 17 ♖hd1 c5 18 ♖b7 ♔e8 19 ♗c4 a5 20 a4 g5 21 ♖db1 h5 22 ♗d5, with advantage.

6 bxc3 g6

The exotic 6...cxd4 7 cxd4 e5 is not entirely convincing. I.Nester-M.Oleksi-enko, Lvov 2006, continued 8 dxe5 ♕xd1+ 9 ♔xd1 ♘c6 10 e3 ♗g4 11 ♗b5 0-0-0+ 12 ♔e2 ♘xe5 13 ♗b2 f6 14 h3 ♗xf3+ 15 gxf3 ♘c6 16 ♖ac1, with an edge. Black sometimes prefers 6...e6 when 7 e4 is a main line Semi-Tarrasch and White can also consider both 7 g3, along the lines of our next illustrative game, and 7 e3 ♗e7 8 ♗d3 ♘c6 9 0-0 0-0 10 ♗b2.

7 e3

7 e4 transposes into one of White's main lines against the Grünfeld Defence, but this modest move is also good. White holds back e4 until he has completed his development and secured his position in the centre and on the queenside. A more recent idea is 7 ♗g5!? ♗g7 8 ♕d2:

J.Sadorra-T.Vakhidov, Manila 2006, which continued 8...h6 9 ♗f4 cxd4 10 cxd4 ♘c6 11 e3 0-0 12 ♖b1 ♕a5 13 ♗d3 g5!? 14 ♗g3 f5 15 ♗c4+ ♔h7 16 ♗e5 ♕xd2+ 17 ♔xd2 ♘xe5 18 ♘xe5 ♗xe5 19 dxe5 ♖d8+ 20 ♔e2 b6 21 ♖hd1 ♗b7 22 ♗e6 f4 23 exf4 gxf4 24 ♖bc1, with advantage.

b) Matters were less clear in Bu Xiangzhi-A.Timofeev, Taiyuan 2006, after 8...cxd4!? 9 cxd4 ♘c6 10 e3 0-0 11 ♖c1 h6 12 ♗h4 ♗e6 13 ♗d3 (or 13 ♗c4 ♗xc4 14 ♖xc4 ♕d6) 13...♕d6 14 0-0 ♖ac8 15 ♖b1 ♕d5 16 e4 ♕xa2 17 d5 ♕xd2 18 ♘xd2 ♘e5 19 ♗xe7 ♖fe8 20 ♖xb7 ♘xd3 21 dxe6 fxe6 22 ♖xa7 ♖c2, with compensation.

c) Finally, we should note that the stem game in this line was marred by a blunder: 8...♕a5 9 ♖c1 h6 10 ♗h4 ♗f5 11 e3 ♘c6 12 ♗e2 0-0 13 0-0 ♖fd8 14 ♕b2 ♕b6 15 ♕a3 ♕a5? 16 ♕xa5 ♘xa5 17 ♗xe7 and White won, V.Kramnik-L.Van Wely, Monaco (blindfold) 2001.

Returning to 7 e3:

7...♗g7

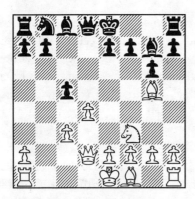

a) White made his good development and strong centre work well in

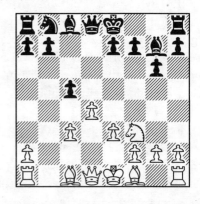

8 ♗d3

White leaves e2 free for his queen to

support any future advance by White's e or c-pawn. Instead after 8 ♗c4 0-0 9 0-0 ♕c7 play transposes into Keres' Variation against the Grünfeld Defence, which is considered at some length in Timothy Taylor's *Beating the King's Indian and Grünfeld*. Suffice to say here only that Taylor suggests that the further moves 10 ♕e2 ♗g4 11 ♗a3 lead to equality, and that he considers possible improvements, including the move he believes most promising, 11 ♗d5.

A more important alternative is 8 ♗b5+ which creates some confusion in the black camp:

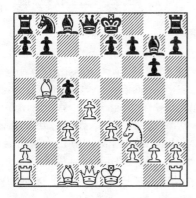

a) Arguably Black's ideal development involves posting his knight on c6 and his bishop somewhere like g4 or b7, but 8...♘c6 9 0-0 0-0 10 a4, followed by ♗a3, allows White to put pressure on c5. This usually results in an early exchange on d4 leaving White in control of exploitable queenside space. G.Arsovic-D.Antic, Banja Koviljaca 2002, for example, continued 10...♗d7 11 ♗a3 cxd4 12 cxd4 a6!? 13 ♗d3 ♖e8 14 ♘d2 ♗e6 15 ♖b1 ♗d5 16 ♗c5 f5!? 17

♗c4 ♖b8 18 ♗b6 ♕d7 19 ♗xd5+ ♕xd5 20 ♕b3 e6 21 ♕xd5 exd5 22 g3, with a clear advantage.

b) Black therefore tends to block White's check and after 8...♗d7 both sides' light-squared bishops seem to be on transient squares, but it isn't at all clear who this favours.

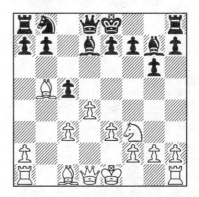

White has tried a range of different 9th moves without agreement on which may be the best one:

b1) P.Schlosser-A.Shirov, German League 2000, continued 9 ♗d3 0-0 10 0-0 ♗c6 11 ♖b1 ♘d7 12 e4 e6 13 ♕e2 ♖c8 14 ♗e3 ♕a5 15 ♘d2!? cxd4 (not 15...♕xc3? 16 ♘c4! and if 16...♖xe4 17 ♗xe4 cxd4 18 ♘d6 dxe3 19 ♘xc8 exf2+ 20 ♔h1 ♖xc8 21 ♕xf2 ♘f6 22 ♗xb7, but can White do more than draw after 15...♕xa2!? 16 ♖a1 ♕b2 17 ♖fb1 ♕xc3 18 ♖c1 ♕b4 19 ♖cb1?) 16 cxd4 ♘b6 17 ♘b3 ♕h5 18 ♕xh5 gxh5 19 ♘a5 ♖fd8 20 ♖b4 ♗f8 21 ♘xc6 ♖xc6 22 ♖b3 ♖dc8 23 ♖fb1 ♖c3 24 ♔f1 ♗e7 25 ♗d2 ♖3c7 26 ♔e2 ♖d7 27 ♗e3, with a slight pull.

b2) 9 a4 ♕a5 10 ♕b3 cxd4 11 exd4 0-0 12 0-0 ♕c7 13 ♖e1 e6 14 ♘g5 ♘c6 15 ♗a3 ♖fe8 16 ♘e4 ♘a5 17 ♕a2 ♗c6 was roughly equal in V.Anand-P.Leko, Linares 1999.

b3) Perhaps the best course is the simple 9 ♗e2 ♘c6 10 0-0...

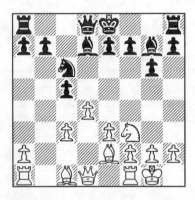

...after which 10...0-0 11 ♖b1 (promising too was 11 a4!? ♗g4 12 h3 ♗xf3 13 ♗xf3 ♖c8 14 ♗a3 b6!? 15 dxc5 bxc5 16 ♗xc5 ♕a5 17 ♗a3 ♖fe8!? 18 ♗xc6 ♖xc6 19 ♕d7 ♖ec8 20 ♗xe7, with a clear advantage in Z.Franco Ocampos-R.Ruiz Escobar, Pamplona 2000) 11...♕c7 12 e4 ♗g4 13 d5 ♘e5 14 c4 ♗xf3 15 gxf3 g5!? 16 ♗xg5 ♘g6 17 ♔h1 ♔h8 18 ♖g1 b6 19 ♗e3 ♗e5 20 ♕d2 ♗xh2 21 ♖g4 f5? 22 ♖xg6 hxg6 23 f4 saw White win in B.Ostenstad-D.Madsen, Trondheim 2004.

c) Black can also block with 8...♘d7. L.Bruzon-W.Arencibia, Santa Clara 2006, continued 9 0-0 0-0 (or 9...a6!? 10 ♗d3 0-0 11 a4 b6, as in Zhang Zhong-E.Najer, Ergun 2006, when White might consider 12 ♗a3, and if 12...♗b7 13 e4) 10 ♗a3 ♘f6 11 ♖c1 b6 12 ♘e5!? (Bruzon later preferred 12 e4, and if 12...♗h6!? 13 e5 ♘h5 14 ♖b1 ♗f5 15 ♗d3 ♗xd3 16 ♕xd3 ♘f4 17 ♕e4, with a pull, or 13...♗xc1?! 14 ♕xc1 ♘h5 15

♕h6 f6 16 ♗c4+ e6 17 g4) 12...♕c7 13 ♕e2 ♗b7 14 ♘d3 ♖fd8 15 e4 ♖ac8, and now Bruzon considers 16 f4 to be slightly better for White.

Returning to 8 ♗d3:

8...0-0 9 0-0

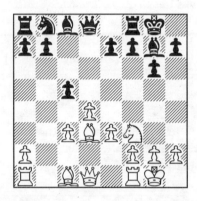

9...♕c7

This is Black's usual choice. Instead 9...♘c6 10 ♗a3 puts pressure on c5, and seems promising for White. If Black exchanges pawns on d4, White obtains free play on the queenside, but otherwise Black may have to gambit his c-pawn. V.Anand-M.Krasenkow, Canada de Calatrava (rapid) 2007, continued 10...b6 11 dxc5 ♕c7 (or 11...bxc5 12 ♗e4) 12 ♗e4 ♗b7 13 ♘d4! bxc5 14 ♗xc5 ♘e5 15 ♗xb7 ♕xb7 16 ♘b3 ♖ac8 17 ♕e2, with a pull.

10 ♕e2

On e2, White's queen supports e4 and a range of possible queenside piece developments. Black can defend c5 and complete his queenside development with ...♘d7, ...b6 and ...♗b7, so that 10 ♗a3 may not achieve much. But 10 ♖b1!? has more bite and Black had to defend well in S.Dyachkov-A.Naiditsch,

Moscow 2006, which continued 10...♘d7!? 11 e4! b6 12 ♗g5 e6 13 ♕d2 ♗b7 14 ♕e3 ♖ac8 15 ♖fd1 cxd4 16 cxd4 ♕d6 17 ♗b5, with some pressure.

10...b6

Black defends c5 and plans a queenside fianchetto. He avoids exchanging pawns on d4 before he is ready to counterattack in the centre and contest the queenside. White eventually plans to play e4, but d4 must be secure before he does this. The main battle is thus likely to be focused primarily on the c5- and d4-squares. The reader should note that while transpositions do abound, Black has two alternative plans:

a) 10...♖d8!? targets d4. Sharp play ensued in V.Filippov-J.Lautier, Rethymnon 2003, which continued 11 ♖d1 (Ribli's 11 ♖b1!? b6 12 ♖d1 may be better; after the 12...♗b7 13 e4 cxd4 14 cxd4 ♘c6 15 d5 ♘d4 16 ♘xd4 ♗xd4 17 ♗c4 ♗e5 of Z.Ribli-M.Tal, Reykjavik 1988, according to Tal, 18 g3 is better for White) 11...b6 12 ♗b2 ♘c6 13 ♖ac1 ♗b7 14 e4 e6 15 ♕e3 ♖d7! 16 h4 h6 17 ♗a3!? ♖ad8 and now White should

have settled for 18 ♗e2 or 18 dxc5 bxc5 19 ♗e2, with a rough balance.

b) 10...♘c6!? sees Black taking risks with c5. V.Kramnik-L.Van Wely, Monaco (rapid) 1999, continued 11 ♗a3 b6 12 ♖ab1 ♖d8 (maybe 12...♘a5!?, although then White has 13 dxc5 bxc5 14 ♖b5) 13 ♗e4!? (13 ♖fd1 transposes into Ribli-Tal, above) 13...♗b7 14 dxc5 ♗xc3 15 ♖fc1 ♗f6, and the game was drawn.

11 ♖d1

White is angling for e4 and ♗e3, and this rook plays a useful indirect role in support of d4, whereas Black has good play after the immediate 11 e4!? ♗g4!, undermining d4.

11...♗b7

After 11...♘c6 all of 12 ♗a3, 12 ♖b1, and perhaps even 12 ♗b2 are good candidate moves.

12 e4

White controls d4 and ...♗g4 isn't possible, so the time is now right for this move.

12...e6

This move isn't very dynamic, though it isn't entirely bad either. But Black can safely play 12...♘c6!?, which may be critical. M.Tal-Lin Ta, Manila 1990, continued brilliantly: 13 ♗e3 ♖ad8!? 14 ♖ac1 ♘a5!? 15 d5! ♗c8 16 ♗g5! (threatening c4 and e5) 16...f6 17 ♗d2 e5?! 18 ♖b1 ♗d7 19 ♗a6 ♘b7 20 ♗xb7! (eliminating Black's best minor piece) 20...♕xb7 21 ♗e3 ♗a4 22 ♖e1 ♕e7 23 ♘d2 f5 24 f3 f4 25 ♗f2 g5 26 g4! (neutralizing threats based on ...h5 and ...g4) 26...fxg3!? 27 hxg3 ♖f7 28 ♗e3 h6 29 ♔g2 ♖df8 30 ♖h1 ♕d6 31 ♖bf1 ♕g6 32 g4 ♗d7 33 ♖f2 ♖f6 34 ♔g1 ♖6f7 35 ♘f1 ♕d6 36 ♘g3 ♖e8 37 ♘f5 ♗xf5 38 gxf5 ♖f6 39 ♕b5 ♖e7 40 a4!

40...♗f8 41 ♖g2 ♖g7 42 ♔f2 ♕e7 43 ♔e2! ♕d8 44 ♔d3 ♕c8 45 ♕c4 ♕d7 46 ♖gh2 ♕d6 47 ♕b5 ♖d7 48 a5! (making the decisive breakthrough) 48...♗g7 49 axb6 axb6 50 ♖a1 ♖d8 51 ♖ha2 ♖xf5?! 52 exf5 ♕xd5+ 53 ♔e2 g4 54 fxg4 ♕g2+ 55 ♔e1 ♕g3+ 56 ♗f2 ♕xc3+ 57 ♔e2, and White won.

13 ♗e3 ♘d7 14 e5!

This is a standard and strong way to proceed. White's centre pawns establish a dark-square wedge and free e4 for use by a minor piece. White threatens ♘g5, with ♕g4-h4 to follow.

White's knight, if attacked, can always fall back to e4, where it strengthens White's control on the key dark squares.

14...f6?!

Black radically challenges e5, but without really shaking White's central grip and weakens his kingside in the process. 14...h6 is better, but White can probe with h4-h5. Ideally Black would like to have his knight on the strong d5-square, rather than d7. By opening up the game, Black enables White's better and more aggressively posted pieces to launch a massive attack.

15 exf6 ♘xf6 16 ♘e5 ♘d5 17 ♕g4!

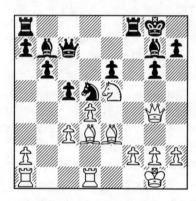

White not only threatens 18 ♕xe6+, but also raises the prospect of ♘xg6. Under serious pressure, Bengtson cracks.

17...♗xe5?! 18 ♕xe6+ ♔h8 19 dxe5 ♘xe3 20 fxe3 ♖ae8 21 ♕d6

This move kills the game. Black can't exchange queens, as White's passed d-pawn wins, so White retains his extra pawn and ongoing attack.

21...♕g7 22 e6 ♕h6 23 e4 ♕e3+ 24 ♔h1 g5 25 ♕e5+ 1-0

Game 24
Bu Xiangzhi-J.Polgar
Biel 2007

1 c4 c5 2 ♘f3 ♘f6 3 ♘c3 e6 4 g3 d5

Black by no means has to follow up 3...e6 with this central thrust. Instead 4...b6 reaches the pure Hedgehog, the subject of our next chapter.

5 cxd5 ♘xd5 6 ♗g2 ♘c6

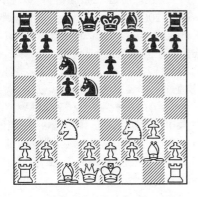

7 d4

7 0-0 ♗e7 8 d4 simply transposes, but playing this way also allows 8 ♘xd5!?, which has some distinct features. Black can reply:

a) 8...exd5 9 d4 0-0 transposes back into our main game. Black gains no advantage by playing 9...cxd4 10 ♘xd4 0-0 as these simplified IQP positions are slightly better for White: for example, 11 ♗e3 ♗e6 12 ♖c1 ♘xd4 13 ♗xd4 ♗f6 14 e3 ♗xd4 15 ♕xd4 ♕a5 16 a3 ♖ac8 17 ♖fd1 ♖xc1 18 ♖xc1 h6 19 ♗f3 a6 20 ♖c5 ♕e1+ 21 ♔g2 saw White building up a clear advantage in V.Tukmakov-F.Casagrande, Arco 2000.

b) 8...♕xd5 sees Black's queen becomes an early target. White has good chances after 9 d3 (and possibly also after the infrequent gambit 9 d4!?, after which A.Kosten-G.Schroll, Austrian League 2004, saw 9...♘xd4 10 ♘xd4 ♕xd4 11 ♕c2 0-0 12 ♖d1 ♕f6 13 ♗e3 a5 14 ♖d2 a4!? 15 ♗xc5 ♗xc5 16 ♕xc5 a3 17 ♕c3 axb2 18 ♕xf6 gxf6 19 ♖xb2 ♖d8 20 a4 ♖a7 21 f4! ♖d6 22 a5, with an edge), and 9...0-0 10 ♗e3 f5 11 ♖c1 ♖b8 12 a3 ♖d8 13 ♕c2 ♘d4 14 ♘xd4 cxd4 15 ♗f4 ♖a8 16 ♗c7 ♖d7 17 b4 h6 18 ♗e4 ♕b5 19 f4 g6 20 ♕c4 was promising in Y.Seirawan-V.Chuchelov, Vlaardingen (rapid) 2005.

7...♗e7 8 0-0

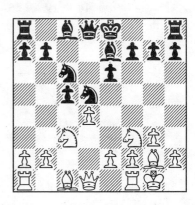

8...0-0

Bu's move order requires White to take into account several distinct lines, including:

a) 8...♘xc3 9 bxc3 0-0 gives White the opportunity to establish a mobile pawn centre, supported on the long h1-a8 diagonal by White's powerful king's bishop. White controls more space and has long-term chances either to achieve a passed d-pawn or to set up attacking chances after e5. He has good prospects after both after 10 e4 and 10 ♖b1:

a1) The direct approach has much to commend it. V.Tukmakov-F.Gheorghiu, Zurich 2000, continued 10 e4 b6 (or 10...cxd4 11 cxd4 b6 12 ♗b2 ♗a6 13 ♖e1 ♗b4 14 ♖e3 ♘a5 15 ♕a4 ♗e7 16 d5! ♗c5 17 ♗d4 ♖c8 18 ♖c3 ♗xd4 19 ♕xd4 ♖xc3 20 ♕xc3 exd5 21 ♖d1 d4 22 ♘xd4, with the more comfortable game in A.Greenfeld-R.Gwaze, Jersey 2004) 11 ♖e1 (an immediate 11 d5 has often worked out well too) 11...♗b7 12 d5 ♘a5 (White also stood well after 12...exd5 13 exd5 ♘a5 14 h4 ♖e8 15 ♘e5 ♗d6 16 ♗f4 ♕c7 17 ♕h5 ♖e7 18 ♖e3! in Z.Ribli-E.Anka, Hungarian League 2002) 13 ♗f4 exd5 14 exd5 ♗d6 15 ♗xd6 ♕xd6 16 ♘d2 c4 17 ♘f1 ♕f6 18 ♕d2 ♖ad8 19 ♖ad1

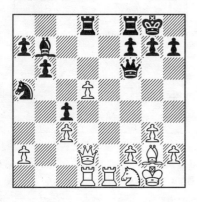

19...g6 20 ♘e3 h5 21 d6 ♗xg2 22 ♔xg2 ♔g7 23 d7, with a definite advantage.

a2) 10 ♖b1!? is slower but also promising. Black can't play ...b6, because the long light-squared diagonal remains open, and he has a problem with his queen placement.

H.Nakamura-B.Zisman, Virginia Beach 2004, continued 10...♕c7 (V.Smyslov-A.Tolush, Moscow 1961, a positional gem, varied with 10...♕a5 11 ♕b3 ♖d8 12 ♗f4 cxd4 13 ♘xd4 ♘xd4 14 cxd4 ♖xd4 15 ♗xb7 ♗xb7 16 ♕xb7 ♕d8 17 ♗b8! 1-0) 11 ♕a4 ♗d7 12 ♗f4 ♕c8 13 ♕d1 ♖d8 14 e4 b6 15 ♕e2 ♗e8 16 ♖fd1 cxd4 17 cxd4 ♗d6 18 ♗e3 ♕d7 19 e5 ♗e7 20 ♘g5 h6 21 ♘e4 ♖ac8 22 ♗xh6! gxh6 23 ♕g4+ 1-0.

b) 8...cxd4 hopes to achieve a rather passive equality, but White retains an edge due to his pawn centre and better development. After 9 ♘xd5, Black should probably content himself with 9...exd5 10 ♘xd4, transposing to note 'a' to White's 7th move, above. Instead Black's split a- and c-pawns proved a long-term weakness in V.Shushpanov-J.Krejci, Olomouc 2002, after 9...♕xd5?! 10 ♘xd4 ♕d7 11 ♘xc6 bxc6 12 ♗e3 0-0 13 ♕xd7 ♗xd7 14 ♖fd1 ♖fd8 15 ♖xd7 ♖xd7 16 ♗xc6, and White went on to win.

c) Also fairly rare is 8...♘xd4 9 ♘xd4 ♘xc3 10 bxc3, after which 10...cxd4 11 cxd4 0-0 12 ♖b1!...

...saw White maintain a pull well into a favourable double rook endgame that concluded with a picturesque mating attack in I.Rogers-R.Michiels, Vlissingen 2005: 12...♖b8 13 ♗f4 ♗d6 14 ♗xd6 ♕xd6 15 ♕a4 a6 16 e3 b5 17 ♕a5 ♗b7 18 ♗xb7 ♖xb7 19 ♖fc1 ♕b6 20 ♕xb6 ♖xb6 21 ♖c7 ♖fb8 22 ♖bc1 g6 23 ♖a7 ♖8b7 24 ♖c8+ ♔g7 25 ♖aa8 ♔f6 26 ♔g2 ♖d7 27 g4! e5 28 dxe5+ ♔xe5 29 h4 ♔e4 30 g5 f6 31 ♖c3 fxg5 32 hxg5 ♖bd6 33 ♔g3 ♔f5 34 f4 ♔e4 35 ♖e8+ 1-0.

Returning to 8...0-0:

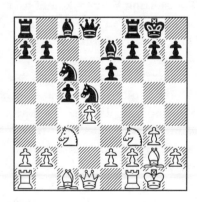

9 ♘xd5

This is simple and strong. White reaches Tarrasch Defence-like posi-

tions, with three minor pieces each on the board rather than four, where he can expect to achieve a slight, but lasting positional advantage.

White can also play for an advantage with 9 e4, after which 9...♘xc3 10 bxc3 transposes to variation 'a1' in the notes to Black's 8th move. Black can also play 9...♘db4, but 10 dxc5 (10 a3 cxd4 11 axb4 dxc3 12 bxc3 is the quieter alternative) 10...♗xc5 11 e5! is testing:

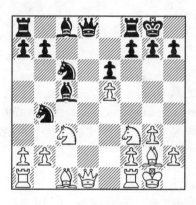

a) White established a clear space advantage and launched a dangerous kingside attack in T.Nyback-E.Romanov, Chalkidiki 2003, after 11...♘d3 12 ♕e2 ♘xc1 13 ♖axc1 ♗e7 14 a3 a6 15 ♖fd1 ♕a5 16 h4! ♖b8 17 ♕e4 ♘d8!? 18 ♗f1 b5 19 ♗d3 g6 20 ♕f4 ♗b7 21 ♘e4 ♕b6?! 22 ♘f6+ ♗xf6 23 exf6, and White won.

b) M.Sorokin-A.Obukhov, Krasnoyarsk 2003, saw the cagier 11...h6 12 a3 ♘d3 13 ♕e2 ♘xc1 14 ♖axc1 ♗e7 15 b4 a6 16 ♘a4 ♗d7 17 ♖fd1 ♕c7 18 ♕e3 ♖ad8 19 ♘d4 ♕b8 20 ♘xc6, with a very slight advantage.

9...exd5 10 dxc5

There are other moves, but this is

White's most consistent positional course, isolating Black's queen's pawn directly.

10...♗xc5 11 ♗g5

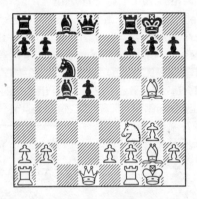

This direct move has more or less become established as the main line in a variation which has been heavily played and analysed over many decades.

11...♕d7

Black's queen blocks his light-squared bishop, but his two main alternatives, 11...f6 and 11...♕b6, also have downsides:

a) After 11...f6 12 ♗d2, Black's weakening of the a2-g8 diagonal and White bishop's post on d2 combine to make the ground-gaining b4 a persistent threat. White's opportunities on the queenside together with good play in the centre, aimed at and around Black's isolated queen's pawn, promise White good play. L.Psakhis-R.Har Zvi, Israeli League 2003, for example, continued 12...♖e8 (or 12...♗f5 13 b4! ♗b6 14 b5 ♘e7 15 ♗b4 ♗e4 16 ♗h3 ♔h8 17 ♘d4 ♖e8 18 a4 ♗xd4 19 ♕xd4 ♘f5 20 ♕d2, with advantage in V.Anand-

J.Timman, Prague (rapid) 2002) 13 e3 ♗f5 14 ♗c3 ♕d7 15 ♕b3 ♖ad8 16 ♖fd1 ♗b6 17 a4 ♗e4 18 a5 ♗c5 19 ♕b5 ♗f8 20 a6 b6 21 ♖d2 ♗c5 22 ♕a4 ♖b8 23 ♘e5 ♘xe5 24 ♗xe4, and White won.

b) 11...♕b6 12 ♖c1 also offers good chances for an edge. Cu.Hansen-P.H.Nielsen, Stockholm 1994, for example, continued 12...d4 13 ♘d2 ♖e8 14 ♘c4 ♕a6 15 a3 ♗f5 16 ♖e1 ♗e4 17 ♗xe4 ♖xe4 18 ♘d2 ♖e5 19 ♘f3, with good chances.

12 ♘e1!

Transferring White's knight to d3 is a common idea in this line. From d3, the knight exerts influence on the important central dark squares b4, c5, e5 and f4. It also supports a possible b4 thrust by White, brings his fianchettoed bishop into play and is a powerful blockading piece. Black's d-pawn can advance to d4 in this line, but is unlikely to progress further, at least in the short term. White's bishop on g5 can either play to d2 in support of queenside action or possibly find a more aggressive central role from f4.

12...♖e8

Black counterattacks against e2, seeking to improve on 12...d4 13 ♘d3 ♗b6, after which Black's defence is difficult. White's potential was powerfully demonstrated in L.Schandorff-A.Greenfeld, Saint Vincent 2005, which saw 14 ♗d2 ♖e8 15 ♖e1 ♕d6 16 a4 a6 17 ♕b3! ♘a5!? 18 ♕d5 ♕xd5 19 ♗xd5 ♗f5 20 b4 ♘c6 21 a5 ♗a7 22 b5! axb5 23 a6! ♖ad8 24 ♗g2 ♗e4 25 ♗xe4 ♖xe4 26 axb7 ♗b8 27 ♖ec1 ♖e6 28 ♖a8 1-0.

12...h6 13 ♗d2 also looks a bit better for White. J.Gustafsson-G.Hertneck, German League 2002, continued 13...♖d8!? 14 ♘d3 ♗b6 15 a4 a5 16 ♘f4! d4 17 ♘d5! ♖a6!? 18 ♖c1 ♗a7 19 ♗f4! ♔h7 20 ♘c7 ♖b6 21 ♘b5 ♗b8 22 ♗xb8 ♘xb8 23 ♖c4, and White won.

13 ♘d3 ♗b6 14 ♗d2 ♕d6 15 ♘f4 ♗g4 16 a4!

Black's energetic play has forced White to take great care down the e-file. However, he still seems to have a firmer grip on the game and this excellent flank move causes Polgar real problems on the queenside.

16...♖ad8 17 a5 ♗c5 18 ♖e1 a6 19 ♖c1

♘e5 20 h3 ♗f5 21 ♕b3 ♘c4 22 ♖ed1

The tension reaches its pitch with this move. Clearly Black's d-pawn is at risk and Polgar can find nothing better than to defend it with a docile retreat that signals an end to the extraordinary burst of energy she has displayed from the late opening.

22...♗e6!? 23 ♗e1!

White's game certainly looks more solid and threatening than Black's after this move.

23...b5 24 axb6 ♘xb6 25 ♕a2

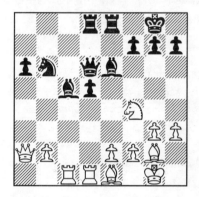

25...♗b4!?

Black is playing for broke now, but with a weakness on a6 in addition to all White's central pressure, there was no easy choice at this stage.

26 ♗xb4 ♕xb4 27 ♕xa6 ♘c4 28 ♘xd5 ♗xd5 29 ♖xd5 ♖xd5 30 ♗xd5 ♘b6 31 ♗a2 h6

The tactics all seem to work for Bu. Not only can he consolidate his extra pawn but he can also launch an attack aimed at Black's weak f-pawn. Of course, 31...♕xb2? 32 ♖b1 wins.

32 ♖c7 ♖d8 33 ♖xf7 ♔h8 34 ♕a3 1-0

Summary

This chapter covers the symmetrical Four Knights, 3...d5 and Keres-Parma Defences based on ♘f3 and d4 antidotes. However, detailed coverage of the Maróczy Bind Sicilian and Tarrasch Defence lines that Black can occasionally offer to enter must be sought elsewhere.

Against 2...♘f6 3 ♘c3 ♘c6 4 d4 cxd4 5 ♘xd4 e6 6 a3, Black can reach tough, counter-punching Hedgehog defensive formations. White can, however, use his extra space and attacking potential to probe. Should White wish to avoid these types of Hedgehog, 6 g3, and if 6...♕b6 7 ♘b5!?, is a complex and critical alternative.

White has good chances for an edge after 2...♘f6 3 ♘c3 d5 4 cxd5 ♘xd5 5 d4, no matter how Black reacts in the centre. Indeed, following 5...♘xc3 6 bxc3 g6 White can build on his strong pawn centre with the quiet but venomous 7 e3. Likewise, White should be happy to see the Keres-Parma System, which is perhaps a not entirely convincing form of the Tarrasch Defence. White's well-developed forces and central control give him a good game.

1 c4 c5 2 ♘f3 ♘f6 3 ♘c3 *(D)* **3...♘c6**

       3...d5 4 cxd5 ♘xd5 5 d4 *(D)*

              5...cxd4 – *Game 22*

              5...♘xc3 – *Game 23*

       3...e6 4 g3 d5 – *Game 24*

4 d4 cxd4 5 ♘xd4 e6 6 a3 *(D)*

       6 g3 – *Game 21*

              6...♗e7 – *Game 19*

              6...♘xd4 – *Game 20*

      3 ♘c3   **5 d4**   **6 a3**

Chapter Five

The Hedgehog

1 c4 c5 2 ♘f3 ♘f6 3 ♘c3 e6 4 g3 b6 5 ♗g2 ♗b7 6 0-0 ♗e7

The three games in this chapter complete our consideration of key lines after 1...c5. Once again d4 options figure prominently in our repertoire against the Hedgehog defences, in which an exchange of pawns on d4 defines all the main lines of the opening.

We begin by considering the main variations arising after 1 c4 c5 2 ♘f3 ♘f6 3 ♘c3 e6 4 g3 b6 5 ♗g2 ♗b7 6 0-0 ♗e7 (or 3...b6 4 g3 ♗b7 5 ♗g2 e6 6 0-0 ♗e7). From this position, White can either play indirectly for d4 with **7 ♖e1 d6 8 e4**, followed by d4 (Game 25), or play directly **7 d4 cxd4 8 ♕xd4** (Game 26).

Both lines press Black hard, but Black's game has all the considerable defensive attributes of Hedgehog structures, which we have already seen in certain sections of Chapter Four. White has extra space and attacking potential, while Black's game will bristle behind

the super-solid defensive Hedgehog line of pawns along his third rank with counterattacking potential should White overstretch.

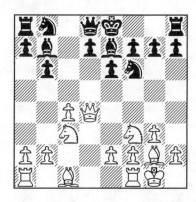

Black doesn't have to develop his king's bishop to e7 and he might prefer a double fianchetto with **3...b6 4 g3 ♗b7 5 ♗g2 g6 6 0-0 ♗g7 7 d4 cxd4 8 ♕xd4** (Game 27).

This double fianchetto form of the Hedgehog is also pretty resilient. White can expect to put pressure on Black's kingside, frequently combining play on the c1-h6 diagonal with the advance g4-g5 (often after ♗h3).

In the centre, d5 is more vulnerable to occupation by a White knight than when Black plays an early ...e6. White has a slight pull but Black's game also benefits from counterattacking potential, usually based on putting pressure on c4 and preparing ...b5.

A related opening is the immediate queenside fianchetto, 1...b6. White has several choices, including the challenging main lines 2 d4 ♗b7 3 ♘c3 e6 4 e4 and 4 a3, but the simpler 2 ♘f3 ♗b7 3 g3, which is in full accord with our repertoire, can also be played:

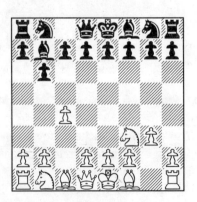

a) Play often transposes to the Hedgehog after 3...♘f6 4 ♗g2 e6 5 0-0 ♗e7 6 ♘c3 c5, and we're back in Games 25 and 26. Slightly more distinct is 6...0-0!?, although after 7 ♖e1 ♘e4 (7...c5 8 e4 d6 9 d4 cxd4 10 ♘xd4 reaches a favourable form of Hedgehog Defence, where White threatens e5, with a plus; or 7...d5 8 cxd5 ♘xd5 9 e4 ♘xc3 10 bxc3 c5 and we're in note 'a2' to Black's 7th move in Game 25) 8 ♘xe4 ♗xe4 9 d3 ♗b7 10 e4 c5 (10...d5 11 exd5 exd5 12 ♘e5! gives White an edge, due to the awkward pin on Black's d-pawn) 11 d4 cxd4 12 ♘xd4 we've transposed to note 'b2' to Black's 7th move in Game 25.

b) 3...♗xf3 4 exf3 c5 is playable, but conceding the bishop-pair in open play is positionally suspect. After 5 d4! cxd4 (or 5...♘c6!? 6 d5 ♘d4 7 ♘c3 g6 8 ♗g2 ♘h6 9 h4! ♗g7 10 h5, and White was better in B.Kelly-M.Simons, British League 2004) 6 ♕xd4 ♘c6, White's bishop-pair counts for more than the slight weakening of his kingside pawns.

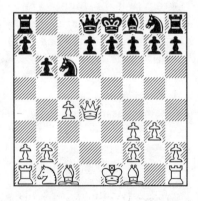

J.Werle-A.Bitalzadeh, Dutch League

2006, for example, continued 7 ♕d1 g6 8 ♘c3 ♗g7 9 ♗d2 ♖c8 10 f4 ♘h6 11 ♗g2 0-0 12 0-0 ♘f5 13 ♖c1 ♘b4 14 ♕a4, with a pull.

Game 25
M.Al Sayed-N.Kalesis
Athens 2006

---

1 c4 c5 2 ♘f3 ♘f6 3 ♘c3 e6 4 g3 b6 5 ♗g2 ♗b7 6 0-0 ♗e7

Black can transpose with 6...d6 7 ♖e1 ♗e7, but this move order also allows him some independent lines, especially 7...♘bd7 8 e4 ♖c8!? (taking aim at c4; instead 8...a6 9 d4 cxd4 10 ♘xd4 ♕c7 11 ♗e3 is likely to transpose to our main game). Then 9 d4!? (more challenging than 9 b3) 9...cxd4 10 ♘xd4

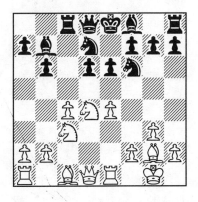

10...♖xc4 (greedy, but also better than 10...a6?! 11 e5! ♗xg2 12 exf6 ♗a8 13 fxg7 ♗xg7 14 ♘f5 0-0 15 ♘xg7 ♔xg7 16 ♕xd6 ♖xc4 17 b3 ♕c7 18 ♗h6+! and White won in V.Eingorn-D.Heinbuch, Bad Wörishofen 1997) 11 ♘xe6!? fxe6 12 e5 ♗xg2 (White regains his piece after 12...♘xd5!? 13 ♘xd5 because

13...♗xd5? 14 ♗xd5 exd5 15 ♕xd5 gives him a crushing attack down the central files) 13 exf6 ♘xf6 14 ♖xe6+ ♔d7 15 ♔xg2 ♕a8+ 16 f3 ♖xc3 17 ♖xf6 ♖xc1 18 ♖f7+ ♔e6 19 ♕b3+ d5 20 ♖xf8 ♖xa1 21 ♕e3+ was the dangerous course of A.Greenfeld-L.Ftacnik, Beer-sheva 1990, which was eventually drawn, but it's hard to believe that White's attack wasn't doing well.

Black can also play some unusual blocking plans based on meeting e4 with ...e5, but these have a poor reputation. J.Granda Zuniga-Y.Seirawan, Buenos Aires 1993, for example, continued 6...♘c6 7 e4 e5 (Black also failed to equalize after 7...d6 8 d4 e5!? 9 dxe5 dxe5 10 ♕a4 ♗d6 11 ♗g5 0-0 12 ♖ad1 ♘d4 13 ♘xd4 cxd4 14 ♘d5 ♗e7 15 ♗xf6 ♗xf6 16 f4!, in A.Belozerov-I.Lysyj, Sochi 2005) 8 d3 g6, and now White should probably play for a quick f4 with 9 ♘h4 (or perhaps 9 ♘e1), and if 9...♘h5 10 ♗f3 ♘g7 11 ♘d5, with the better chances.

7 ♖e1

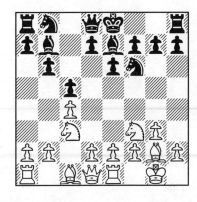

7...d6

Black can also radically change the

nature of the struggle with both 7...d5 and 7...♘e4:

a) 7...d5 8 cxd5 ♘xd5 (8...exd5 9 d4 0-0 leads to a variation of the Queen's Indian Defence, held to be slightly in White's favour) 9 e4 and now:

a1) 9...♘b4 10 d4 cxd4 11 ♘xd4 is close to equality, but White can still fight to make something of his slight lead in development and extra space, even after further piece exchanges. For example, 11...0-0 (after 11...♘8c6 12 ♘xc6 ♘xc6, 13 e5 is again promising) 12 a3 ♘8c6 13 ♘xc6 ♘xc6 14 e5! ♕xd1 15 ♖xd1 ♖fd8 16 ♗e3 ♖ab8 17 ♖xd8+ ♘xd8 18 ♘b5! ♗xg2 19 ♔xg2 saw White increasing his advantage in V.Kramnik-A.Karpov, Monaco (rapid) 1999.

a2) After 9...♘xc3 10 bxc3 0-0 11 d4 White's strong pawn centre is a weighty factor.

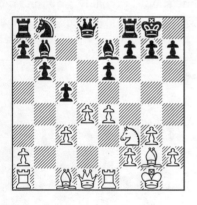

V.Kramnik-V.Anand, Las Palmas 1996, continued powerfully: 11...♘d7 12 ♗f4 cxd4 13 cxd4 ♘f6 14 ♘e5! ♗b4 (14...♖c8 15 ♕a4! a6 16 ♖ad1 b5 17 ♕b3 ♘d7 18 ♘xd7 ♕xd7 19 ♗h3 ♖c4 20 d5! was also pretty good in V.Chuchelov-V.Loginov, Moscow 2003) 15 ♖e3 ♖c8

16 d5! exd5 17 exd5 ♗d6 (after 17...♗xd5 18 ♖d3 ♗xg2 19 ♖xd8 ♖fxd8 20 ♕b3 ♗c3 21 ♕xf7+ ♔h8, Psakhis's 22 ♗h6! ♖g8 23 ♕xf6! is strong; so too is 17...♘xd5 18 ♖d3 ♘xf4 19 gxf4! ♗xg2 20 ♖xd8 ♖fxd8 21 ♕b3 ♗c3 22 ♔xg2 ♗xa1 23 ♘xf7 ♔f8 24 ♘g5, and wins – Kramnik) 18 ♘c6 ♗xc6 19 ♗xd6 ♗a4 20 ♗xf8 ♗xd1 21 ♗e7 ♕c7 22 ♖xd1 ♘d7 23 ♗h3 h6 24 ♗f5 b5 25 ♗b4, and White won.

b) 7...♘e4!? prevents White's planned e4 and seeks to simplify by an exchange of minor pieces. White can respond in two main ways.

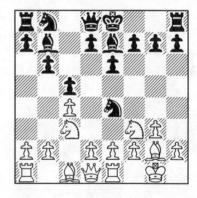

He can play the position arising after the ambitious but double-edged 8 d4 ♘xc3 9 bxc3 or the more careful 8 ♘xe4 ♗xe4 9 d3 ♗b7:

b1) After 8 d4 ♘xc3 9 bxc3 White's pawns are weak but he might quickly achieve good play, with moves such as e4 and d5. Following 9...♗e4 10 ♗f1! White prepares to move his knight and continue the battle for e4 without exchanging the light-squared bishops. Black must act nimbly if he is not to be rapidly wrong-footed:

b11) Bu Xiangzhi-A.Anastasian, Tripoli (rapid) 2004, continued radically: 10...♗xf3!? 11 exf3 ♘c6 12 d5! ♘a5 13 f4 0-0 14 h4 ♗f6 15 ♗d2 ♖e8 16 g4 g6 17 ♕f3 ♗g7 18 h5 f5 19 ♗d3 ♕f6 20 ♖e2 ♖f8 21 ♖ae1 ♖ae8 22 g5 ♕f7 23 h6, with the better chances.

b12) 10...d6 looks better. V.Topalov-M.Adams, FIDE World Championship, San Luis 2005, continued 11 h4!? (possibly too ambitious; instead 11 ♘d2 ♗b7 12 e4 ♘d7 13 ♗d3 ♘f6 14 ♘b3 0-0 15 a4 ♕c7 16 ♗e3, with a space advantage, was E.Miroshnichenko-V.Chuchelov, Kusadasi 2006) 11...♘d7 12 d5 0-0 13 a4 h6 14 ♗h3 exd5 15 cxd5 ♗f6 16 ♖a3 b5 17 axb5, and now Adams gives 17...♘e5, with at least equality.

b2) 8 ♘xe4 ♗xe4 9 d3 ♗b7 10 e4 (another try is 10 d4 cxd4 11 ♕xd4 0-0 12 ♗f4!?) prepares d4, planning to reach Hedgehog structures with only three pairs of minor pieces and a slight pull:

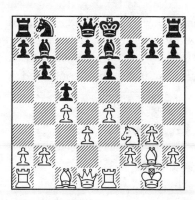

b21) A.Beliavsky-C.Lutz, Leipzig 2002, continued 10...♘c6 11 d4 cxd4 12 ♘xd4 ♘xd4 13 ♕xd4 0-0 14 ♖d1 d6 15 a4 ♕c7 16 ♖a2 ♗c6 17 b3 ♖fd8!? 18

♗a3, with an ongoing edge.

b22) 10...0-0 11 d4 cxd4 12 ♘xd4 ♘c6 13 ♘b5 d6 14 ♗e3 ♘e5 15 b3 a6 16 ♘c3 ♖c8 17 ♖c1 ♕c7 18 h3 ♘d7 19 ♖e2 ♕b8 20 ♖d2, also saw White maintaining a small pull in V.Chuchelov-M.Gurevich, German League 2000.

Returning to 7...d6:

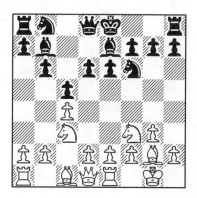

8 e4 a6

The alternatives are less stable.

a) White made considerable ground on the kingside in S.Krivoshey-K.Spraggett, Metz 2007, after 8...♘bd7 9 d4 cxd4 10 ♘xd4 ♕c7 11 ♘db5!? (also good is 11 ♗e3 ♖c8 12 ♖c1 ♕b8 13 b3 0-0 14 f4 a6 15 g4 ♕a8 16 ♔f2 g6 17 g5 ♘h5 18 ♕g4 ♖ce8 19 ♖cd1 ♕c8 20 ♘de2 ♗c6 21 ♘g3 ♘xg3 22 hxg3, with a powerful attack in J.Werle-A.Kabatianski, Dutch League 2006) 11...♕b8 12 f4 a6 13 ♘d4 0-0 14 g4 ♖c8 15 g5 ♘e8 16 ♕e2 ♕c7 17 ♗h3 ♘f8 18 ♗e3 ♕xc4 19 ♕f2 ♕c7 20 f5 e5 21 ♘f3 ♘d7 22 ♖ac1 ♕d8 23 ♕h4 ♗f8 24 f6, and stood well.

b) White can combat the blocking plan 8...e5!? by combinative means with 9 d4 cxd4 10 ♘xd4! exd4 11 e5!.

M.Mrva-J.Smolen, Piestany 2004, continued 11...♗xg2 12 exf6 gxf6 13 ♘b5 ♗b7 14 ♕xd4 0-0 15 ♗h6 ♔h8 16 ♖xe7 ♕xe7 17 ♗xf8 ♕xf8 18 ♕xf6+ ♕g7 19 ♕d8+ ♕g8 20 ♕e7 ♗c6 21 ♘xd6, and White won.

9 d4 cxd4 10 ♘xd4 ♕c7

Not 10...0-0? 11 e5! and wins.

11 ♗e3

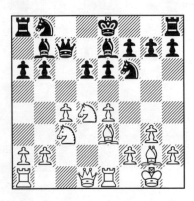

11...0-0

Black has no easy task in these lines. White's extra space, good development and potential kingside attacking chances tend to outweigh Black's opportunities for counterattack. White's pawn on c4 augments White's pressure in the centre. While White's c-pawn may provide Black with a possible target on the c-file, Black's overall game seems much less dynamic than White's.

Play transposes to our main game in the event of 11...♘bd7 12 ♖c1 0-0 13 f4 ♖fe8, but here Black can also try:

a) 13...♖ac8 14 ♗f2!? ♕b8 15 e5 ♘e8 16 ♗h3! ♘c5 17 b4 dxe5 18 fxe5 was promising for White in A.Summerscale-S.Buckley, Edinburgh 2003.

b) 13...♖fc8!? 14 g4! ♘f8 15 g5 ♘6d7 16 ♘d5! exd5 17 ♘f5 ♖e8 18 cxd5 ♕b8 19 ♗d4! f6 20 ♕g4 ♘e5 21 fxe5 fxe5 22 ♗e3, and White was rewarded for her powerful play with a large advantage in Zhu Chen-K.Bischoff, Pulvermuehle 2000.

12 f4

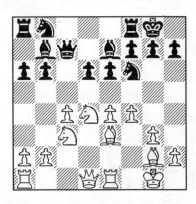

12...♖e8

Black sometimes seeks to counter White's kingside pressure by playing 12...♘bd7 13 ♖c1 h5. This might slow White down a bit, but it also weakens Black's kingside. White retained an edge by exploiting opportunities in the centre in B.Damljanovic-M.Zivanic, Belgrade 2002, which continued 14 h3 ♖fe8 15 ♗f2 ♗f8 16 ♘f3 ♖ac8 17 ♘d2 g6 18 ♕e2 ♗g7 19 e5! dxe5 20 fxe5 ♘h7 21 ♗xb7 ♕xb7 22 ♘f3 ♕c6 23 b3 ♖ed8 24 h4, with good chances.

13 ♖c1 ♘bd7

After 13...♗f8, White also has a promising game after both sharp continuations, 14 f5 and 14 g4:

a) 14 f5 h6 (Black should avoid 14...e5?! 15 ♘d5, but he can transpose with 14...♘bd7 to the notes to his 14th move, below) 15 ♖f1 (John's Watson 15 ♗h3!? deserves attention, intending 15...e5 16 ♘de2 ♘bd7 17 ♘d5 ♘xd5 18 cxd5 ♕d8 19 ♗g2 ♗e7 20 h4, with a pull) 15...♕e7 16 fxe6 fxe6 17 ♗h3 ♕f7 18 ♖xf6! ♕xf6 19 ♕g4 ♘c6 20 ♖f1 ♘e5 was V.Filippov-S.Shipov, Sochi 2004, and now Stohl gives 21 ♖xf6! ♘xg4 22 ♖xf8+ ♔xf8 23 ♗xg4, with an edge.

b) No less aggressive is 14 g4!? ♘fd7 15 g5 ♘c6 16 ♘de2 ♖ac8 17 ♘g3 ♕b8 18 h4 ♗a8 19 ♗f1 ♘a7 20 ♕e2 d5!? 21 cxd5 exd5 22 ♕g4 ♘c5 23 e5 ♘c6 24 ♗f2 ♖cd8 25 ♖cd1 d4 26 ♘ce4 ♘xe4 27 ♘xe4 b5 28 h5, with a strong attack in N.Davies-P.Sowray, British League 2000.

14 f5

As Black can maintain control of e6 after this move, this may be premature. White can play the sound 14 ♗f2, but 14 g4!? is critical.

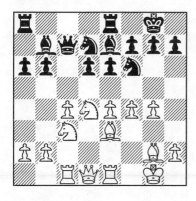

Black can be further squeezed by moves such as g5 and f5, sometimes combined with a knight sacrifice on d5 aimed at a breakthrough on c6:

a) B.Damljanovic-O.Annageldyev, Istanbul Olympiad 2000, continued

14...g6 15 g5 ♘h5 16 f5! exf5 17 ♘xf5 ♗f8 18 ♘d5 ♕d8 19 ♖c3 ♘c5 20 ♗d2 ♘e6 21 ♕g4, with a pull.

b) 14...h6?! 15 g5! hxg5 16 fxg5 ♘h7 17 g6! (significantly weakening Black's kingside) 17...♘hf8 18 gxf7+ ♔xf7 19 ♘d5! ♕d8 (or 19...exd5 20 cxd5 ♕b8 21 ♘c6!, intending 21...♗xc6 22 dxc6 ♘e5 23 ♕d5+ ♘e6 24 ♖f1+ ♗f6 25 c7 ♕c8 26 ♕xd6 ♔g8 27 ♗xb6) 20 ♘xe7 ♕xe7 21 ♘f3 ♘h7 22 ♘g5+ was excellent for White in R.Ruck-R.Markus, Calvia Olympiad 2004.

c) 14...♘c5 15 ♗f2 g6 16 b4 ♖ad8 (and not 16...♘cd7?! due to 17 ♘d5! exd5 18 cxd5 ♕d8 19 ♘c6! ♗xc6 20 dxc6 when White regained his piece with some advantage in A.Greenfeld-L.Cyborowski, Ohrid 2001) 17 ♗f3 h6 18 f5! e5 19 ♘c2 ♘cd7 20 ♘e3 was more pleasant for White in B.Damljanovic-B.Tadic, Pancevo 2006.

Returning to 14 f5:

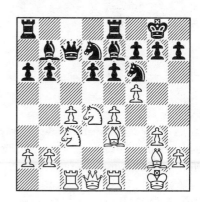

14...♗d8

This is not a pretty move but is probably best. Anticipating an exchange on e6, followed by ♗h3, Black prepares to defend e6, by ...♘f8, without having to play ...e5 and lose control of the central light squares. The natural retreat 14...♗f8 fails to prevent this plan, and after 15 fxe6 fxe6 16 ♗h3 ♘c5 17 b4! Black is worse. E.Kengis-M.Thesing, German League 2006, for example, continued 17...♘cxe4 18 ♘xe4 ♗xe4 and now 19 ♘xe6 wasn't bad, but Watson's 19 ♗xe6+!? ♔h8 20 ♗g5 may be even stronger.

15 fxe6 fxe6 16 ♗h3 ♘f8 17 ♗f2 ♘6d7

Black aims to occupy e5 with his knight. His pawn structure is good, but he still has quite a lot to do to sort out his jumbled piece development, while White's pieces are poised for attack.

18 b4

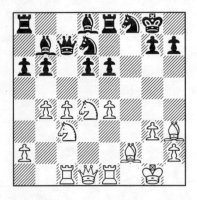

18...♗f6?!

This otherwise desirable developing move meets with an unpleasant counter. Critical may be 18...♘e5 (not, of course, 18...♕xc4? 19 ♘d5 ♕xa2 20 ♖e2 ♕a3 21 ♖c3, and White wins) 19 ♘ce2, and after 19...♕f7 (or 19...♗xe4?! 20 ♘f4) 20 ♘f4, while White still looks a little better, Black's game remains intact.

19 ♘d5!

This sacrifice isn't always correct, but it seems justified here because of the position of Black's knights. White can no longer expect much by playing 19 ♘ce2, as 19...♖ac8 20 ♘f4? ♗xd4 followed by ...e5 wins a piece.

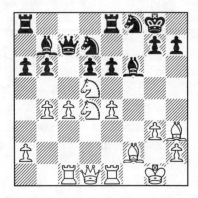

19...♕d8

The earlier R.Libeau-A.Stickler, German League 1993, had seen 19...exd5 20 cxd5 ♘c5 (White is much better too after 20...♕d8 21 ♘c6 ♗xc6 22 dxc6 ♘e5 23 c7 ♕e7 24 c8♕ ♖axc8 25 ♖xc8 ♖xc8 26 ♗xc8) 21 bxc5 bxc5 22 ♕a4 ♗xd4 23 ♗xd4, with some advantage.

20 ♘xf6+ ♕xf6 21 ♘f3 ♘g6 22 ♗g2 ♕e7 23 ♕d4

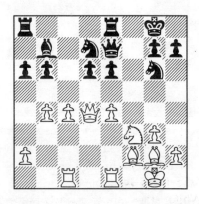

23...a5

Black still nominally controls e5, but he can't occupy it. After 23...♘ge5 24 ♘xe5 dxe5 25 ♕d2, White is better.

24 a3 axb4 25 axb4 ♖a4 26 b5 ♘c5 27 ♖cd1

Due to the weakness of his b- and d-pawns, Black is still unable to occupy e5 and after this and White's next move he finally gives up the battle to do so in exchange for some living space.

27...♖d8 28 h4 e5 29 ♕b2 ♖da8 30 ♗xc5 bxc5 31 ♕d2 ♖d8

Black has to stay on the defensive. After 31...♖xc4 32 h5 ♘f8 33 ♗f1, and if 33...♖xe4 (or 33...♖ca4 34 ♕xd6 ♕xd6 35 ♖xd6 ♖xe4 36 ♖xe4 ♗xe4 37 ♗c4+ ♔h8 38 ♘xe5) 34 ♖xe4 ♗xe4 35 ♗c4+ ♔h8 36 ♘g5, White is winning.

32 ♖a1 ♖xa1 33 ♖xa1 ♘f8

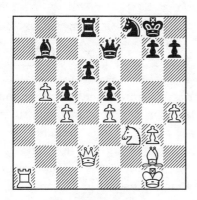

White still seems better, but Black hopes to get his knight to d4 which would clearly improve his chances. White decides on a sacrificial course to reach a better endgame.

34 ♖a7 ♕c7 35 ♗h3! ♕b6 36 ♕a5 ♕xa5 37 ♖xa5 ♗xe4 38 ♘g5 ♗b7!?

White stays ahead clearly against

this move. Perhaps 38...♗d3!?, and if 39 ♘e6 ♖b8! (39...♘xe6 40 ♗xe6+ ♔f8 41 ♗d5! looks good for White) 40 ♘xf8 ♔xf8 41 ♗e6 ♗e4, is a better try.

39 ♖a7 ♖b8 40 ♗g2 ♗xg2 41 ♔xg2 h6 42 ♘e4 d5 43 cxd5 ♖xb5 44 ♘d6! ♖b2+ 45 ♔f3

45...g6

White's piece activity is worth at least a pawn. He wins after 45...♖d2 46 ♘f5!, but now his d-pawn becomes a decisive factor.

46 ♘e8 c4 47 ♘f6+ ♔h8 48 d6 c3 49 d7 ♖d2 50 ♖c7 ♖d6?!

Black should have played 50...c2 51 ♖xc2 ♘xd7 52 ♖xd2 ♘xf6, with drawing chances, but not 50...♘e6? 51 d8♕+! ♘xd8 52 ♖h7 mate.

51 ♔e4 c2 52 ♖xc2 1-0

There's no defence in view of 52...♘xd7 53 ♖c8+ ♔g7 54 ♘e8+.

Game 26
G.Kasparov-M.Adams
Moscow 2004

1 c4 c5 2 ♘f3 ♘f6 3 ♘c3 e6 4 g3 b6 5

♗g2 ♗b7 6 0-0 ♗e7 7 d4 cxd4 8 ♕xd4 d6

Black prepares ... ♘bd7, followed by ...a6 and ...0-0. He can also play a set-up with ...♘c6. After the most common line 8...0-0 9 ♖d1 (White can also consider both 9 e4 ♘c6 10 ♕e3 and 9 b3 ♘c6 10 ♕f4) 9...♘c6 10 ♕f4 ♕b8 11 b3 ♖d8 12 ♗b2, White has a space advantage but Black has a solid position.

White seeks to complete his development, while restraining Black in the centre. Black seeks to play ....d5 but should be aware that this move may not always free his game completely. Overall, White's spatial edge and better development give him slightly the better long-term prospects. Practice has seen:

a) 12...a6 13 ♖d2!? ♖a7 14 ♕xb8 ♖xb8 15 ♘g5 ♗a8 16 ♘ge4 b5 17 ♘xf6+ ♗xf6 18 c5 ♗e7 19 ♘e4 f5 20 ♘d6 ♘b4 21 ♖ad1 ♗xg2 22 ♔xg2 ♘c6 23 e4 fxe4 24 ♘xe4 ♖bb7 25 a3, with a slight pull, was M.Stojanovic-U.Andersson, Banja Luka 2007.

b) 12...d6 13 ♖d2 a6 14 ♕e3 ♕c7 15 ♖ad1 ♖ac8 16 h3 ♗a8 17 ♘g5 h6? 18

♘xe6! fxe6 19 ♕xe6+ ♔f8 20 ♗d5 ♘e5 21 f4 ♘xd5 22 ♘xd5 ♕d7 was K.Georgiev-T.Markowski, Warsaw 2005, and now 23 ♕xd7 ♘xd7 24 ♗xg7+ looks good for White.

c) Andersson's first try was 12...♕xf4 13 gxf4 ♘a5, but after 14 ♘d4 d5!? 15 cxd5 ♘xd5 16 ♘xd5 ♗xd5 17 ♘f5! ♗f8 18 ♗xd5 exd5 19 ♖d3!, White again had a pull in A.Karpov-U.Andersson, Marostica 1989.

Returning to 8...d6:

9 ♗g5!

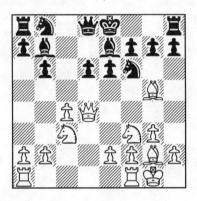

Kasparov first met this strong move as Black in a 1981 game against Anatoly Karpov. White prepares to exchange his bishop on f6, planning to lay siege to d6 and dominate play on the long light-squared diagonal. This is a good alternative to the older forms of the Hedgehog after 9 ♖d1 a6, which have a generally very solid reputation.

9...a6

White is also better after both 9...♘bd7!? 10 ♘b5 d5 11 cxd5 ♗xd5 12 ♘c3 ♗c6 13 ♖fd1 ♕c8 14 ♖ac1 ♕b7 15 b4 a6 16 a4 b5 17 axb5 axb5, as in D.Zifroni-A.Hauchard, Herzliya 1998, and now 18 ♘e1! ♗xg2 19 ♘xg2 supplies an edge, and 9...0-0 10 ♖fd1 ♘bd7 11 ♘b5 d5 12 cxd5 exd5!? 13 ♘h4 h6 14 ♗e3 ♗c5 15 ♕d2, with good chances in A.Huzman-M.Adams, Neum 2000.

10 ♗xf6

The most testing, although White can also consider retaining his bishop with 10 ♖fd1 ♘bd7 11 ♕d2 and now:

a) J.Gustafsson-M.Prusikin, Pulvermuehle 2004, continued 11...0-0 12 ♗f4 ♘e8 (or 13...♖c8 14 b3 ♘c5 15 ♘g5 ♗xg2 16 ♔xg2 h6 17 ♘ge4 ♘b7 18 ♕d3 f5 19 ♘d2 g5!? 20 ♗e3 f4?!, as in V.Ivanchuk-L.Nisipeanu, Warsaw 2005, and now 21 ♕g6+ ♘g7 22 gxf4 gxf4 23 ♗d4 e5 24 ♗xb6 ♕xb6 25 ♘d5 ♕d8 26 ♖g1! is dangerous according to Ivanchuk) 13 ♖ac1 ♕c7 14 b3 ♖c8 15 ♕e3 ♕b8? 16 ♘d5! ♗d8 17 ♗h3 ♔h8 18 ♘g5 b5 19 ♘xf7+ 1-0.

b) 11...♕c8!? 12 b3 0-0 13 ♖ac1 ♖d8 14 ♕b2 ♕c7 15 a4 ♖ac8 16 ♘e1 ♗xg2 17 ♘xg2 ♘e5 18 ♗e3 ♕b7 was roughly balanced in A.Karpov-L.Ftacnik, Thessaloniki Olympiad 1988.

10...♗xf6

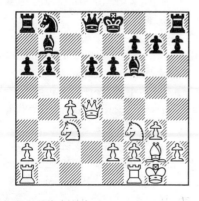

11 ♕f4

This is White's most active post, but Ribli's 11 ♕d3!? is also possible. Z.Ribli-F.Bilobrk, Sibenik 2006, continued 11...♕c7 (White also had the upper hand after 11...♖a7 12 ♖ad1 ♗e7 13 ♘d4 ♗xg2 14 ♔xg2 0-0 15 f4 g6 16 f5! exf5 17 ♘d5 ♖e8 18 e4 in the earlier Z.Ribli-I.Mandekic, Kastav 2002) 12 ♖fd1 ♗e7 13 ♘e4 ♗xe4 14 ♕xe4 ♖a7 15 ♘d4 0-0 16 b3 ♖d8 17 h4 ♗f6 18 e3 ♕c8 19 ♖d2 b5 20 cxb5 axb5 21 ♖c2 ♕d7 22 ♖ac1, with a clear advantage.

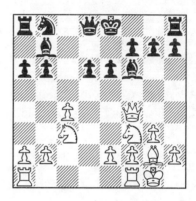

11...0-0

Black fails to equalize by exchanging either or both bishops. V.Kramnik-L.Ljubojevic, Monaco (rapid) 1998, continued 11...♗xc3!? 12 bxc3 ♗xf3 13 ♗xf3 ♖a7 14 ♖fd1 ♖d7 15 ♖ab1 ♕c7 16 ♕d4 0-0 17 ♕xb6 ♖c8 18 ♕xc7 ♖dxc7 19 ♖xd6 ♖xc4 20 ♗b7 ♖f8 21 ♖b3 ♖a4 22 a3, with good play, and White also held an edge after 11...♗xf3!? 12 ♕xf3 ♖a7 13 ♖fd1 0-0 14 ♖ac1 ♖d7 15 ♕e3 ♕c7 16 ♘a4! in D.Bunzmann-M.Duppel, German League 2005.

12 ♖fd1 ♗e7 13 ♘e4!

This is a key move. Black has to exchange his more active queen's bishop to eliminate this piece, leaving him increasingly vulnerable on the queenside light squares.

13...♗xe4 14 ♕xe4 ♖a7 15 ♘d4

White raises the uncomfortable prospect of b4, a4 and b5, followed by ♘c6, with serious light-square domination.

15...♖c7

Both players have been involved in other games at this juncture after 15...♕c8 16 b3:

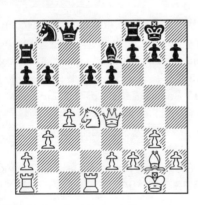

a) A.Karpov-G.Kasparov, Moscow 1981, continued 15...♕c8 16 b3 ♖e8 17 a4 ♕c5 18 ♖a2 ♗f6 19 ♖ad2 ♖c7 20 ♕b1 ♗e7 21 b4 ♕h5, and now 22 b5! a5 23

♘c6 ♗f8 gives White a 'tangible advantage' according to Karpov.

b) In his next outing with the double fianchetto, Adams preferred 16...♗f6!?, after which V.Anand-M.Adams, Sofia 2005, continued 17 e3 ♖d8 18 ♕g4 g6!? 19 ♖d2 h5 20 ♕e2 ♗g7 21 ♖ad1 ♕c5 22 h4 ♖ad7 23 ♗h3 ♖e7 24 ♕f3 ♖ee8 25 ♕e4

25...d5! (after 25...♕c8, White plays ♘e2-f4 or ♘f3-g5 – Golubev) 26 ♘xe6! dxe4 27 ♖xd8 ♕e7 28 ♖xe8+ ♕xe8 29 ♖d8 ♕xd8 30 ♘xd8 ♗f6 31 ♘b7 ♗e7 32 c5! ♗xc5 33 ♘xc5 bxc5, and now Stohl's 34 ♗g2 f5 35 f3 exf3 36 ♗xf3 ♔f7 37 e4 fxe4 38 ♗xe4 ♘d7 39 ♔f2 ♘f6 40 ♔e3 may retain an edge.

16 b3 ♖c5

Black must not only cover c6 but also watch the e6-square. V.Malakhov-L.Nisipeanu, Benidorm (rapid) 2005, varied with 16...♗f6 17 e3 ♘d7 18 ♖ac1 ♕c8 19 ♖b1, but after 19...♖c5?! 20 ♘xe6! fxe6!? (20...♖e5 21 ♘xf8 ♖xe4 22 ♘xd7 ♖e6 23 ♘xb6 ♕c5 24 ♘d5 is also in White's favour) 21 ♕xe6+ ♔h8 22 ♗h3 ♖d8 23 ♖xd6 ♘e5 24 ♕xc8 ♖xc8 25 ♖xb6, Black was struggling.

17 a4 ♕c7 18 ♕b1 ♘d7!

Now that Black can develop this piece, it makes sense to do so quickly. Instead U.Andersson-Y.Seirawan, London 1982, saw 18...♖c8 19 ♖a2 ♗f8 20 e3 ♕e7 21 ♖c2 g6 22 ♕a2 ♕g5?! 23 h4 ♕f6 24 b4 ♖5c7 25 b5 a5 26 ♘c6 ♘d7 27 ♖cd2 ♘c5 28 ♕c2 ♕g7 29 f4 ♔h8 30 ♗f3 ♖e8 31 ♔g2 f5 32 e4! e5 33 fxe5 dxe5 34 ♖d8, with a clear advantage.

19 e3 ♕c8

Black gives his rook a retreat square and prepares to play ...♘f6, with the idea of ...d5. After the immediate 19...♘f6!? White can play 20 ♗f1! threatening b4-b5, and 20...d5?! 21 b4 looks better for White.

20 ♖a2 ♘f6

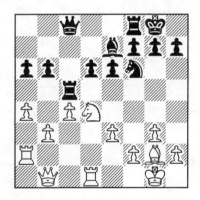

21 ♖c2

Kasparov is now threatening to play b4-b5. White might also try 21 ♖ad2 and if 21...d5 22 cxd5 ♘xd5 23 ♘f5 exf5 24 ♗xd5, with an edge (Stohl).

21...a5!

Black weakens b5, but due to the threat of 22 b4! he had no real choice. As it turns out, his defence is a robust one.

22 ♖dd2

Stohl considers that 22 ♖cd2!?, and if 22...d5 23 cxd5 ♘xd5 24 ♘f5 might be better. R.Cifuentes Parada-M.Van der Werf, Wijk aan Zee 1995, saw Black prefer 22...♖d8, although after 23 e4 (23 ♘b5!? and if 23...d5 24 cxd5 ♘xd5 25 ♗xd5 ♖dxd5 26 ♖xd5 exd5 27 ♕d3 might also be a little better for White) 23...♘e8 24 ♕d3 g6 25 ♕e2 ♘c7 26 ♘c2 ♖e8 27 ♘e3 ♖f8 28 h3 ♕e8 29 ♔h2 f5!? 30 f4 ♕f7 31 exf5 gxf5 32 ♖xd6! ♗xd6 33 ♖xd6, White had good play.

22...♖d8 23 ♘b5

Perhaps 23 e4 might have been tried. In the next few moves, Adams defends with great precision and White's initiative peters out completely.

23...g6 24 ♕d1 ♘e8 25 ♗f3 ♕d7 26 ♖d3 ♘c7

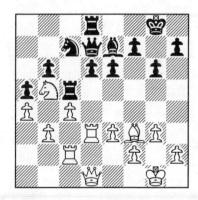

27 ♖cd2

White would like to keep knights on the board, but after 27 ♘c3 ♘a6, Black's knight heads for b4, and 28 ♘e4 ♘b4 29 ♖xd6 ♕xd6! 30 ♘xd6 ♘xc2 is level.

27...♘xb5 28 axb5 ♗f8 29 ♗c6 ♕e7 30

☖d4 ♛f6 31 ♔g2 h5 32 h3 ☖c8 33 ☖2d3 ☖c7 34 ♛f3 ☖f5 35 ☖f4 ☖xf4 36 exf4 ☖a7 37 ♛e3 ♛d8 38 c5

Kasparov does what he can, but he can no longer achieve any real advantage.

38...bxc5 39 ♛xc5 ♛b8 40 ♛e3 a4 41 b6 ☖a6 42 bxa4 ☖xb6 43 ♗b5 d5 44 f5 exf5 45 ☖xd5 ☖d6 ½-½

Game 27
V.Kramnik-L.Aronian
Turin Olympiad 2006

---

1 c4 c5 2 ♘f3 ♘f6 3 ♘c3 b6 4 g3 ♗b7 5 ♗g2 g6 6 d4 cxd4 7 ♛xd4 ♗g7 8 0-0

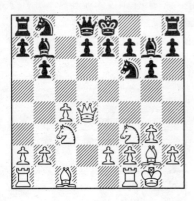

8...d6

This is generally considered to be Black's best move. He can also play:

a) The drawback to the otherwise natural 8...0-0 is that White can immediately play to exchange Black's important dark-squared bishop. White has a clear plan and a definite pull, often based on exploiting the vulnerable d5-square and his extra queenside space. White continued in aggressive style in

E.Agrest-V.Kunin, Griesheim 2003, with 9 ♛h4 d6 10 ♗h6 ♘bd7 11 ☖ac1 (White also gained a strong attack after 11 ☖fd1 ☖c8 12 b3 a6 13 ☖ac1 ♗xh6 14 ♛xh6 b5?! 15 ♘g5! ♗xg2 16 ♔xg2 bxc4 17 ☖d4!, in J.Gustafsson-V.Babula, German League 2004) 11...☖c8 12 b3 a6 13 ♗xg7 ♔xg7 14 ♛d4 ♔g8 15 ♘d5 ♗xd5 16 cxd5 ☖c5 17 b4! ☖xd5 18 ♛b2 ☖h5 19 h3 ♘e5 20 ♘d4 d5 21 g4, winning material.

b) Black's knight doesn't seem entirely comfortable after 8...♘c6.

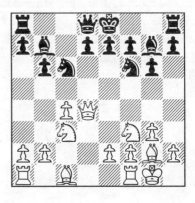

It struggled to find a useful role in F.Berkes-Cao Sang, Hungarian League 2004, which continued 9 ♛e3!? (more common and far from bad is 9 ♛f4, after which, for example, 9... ♘a5 10 b3 ♛b8 11 ♛e3 0-0!? 12 ♛xe7 ☖e8 13 ♛a3 d5 14 ♗f4 ♛c8 15 ☖ac1 d4 16 ♘d5 ♘c6 17 ☖fe1 saw White stand well in A.Flumbort-I.Radziewicz, Budapest 2006) 9...☖c8 10 ☖d1 0-0 11 b3 ♘b4 12 ☖b1 d6 13 ♗b2 ♛d7 14 a3 ♘c6 15 ♘d5! ♘g4 16 ♛g5 f5!? 17 ♗xg7 ♔xg7 18 h3 ♘f6 19 ♛e3 ☖ce8 20 b4 ♛c8 21 ♘xf6 ☖xf6 22 c5! dxc5 23 bxc5 ♘a5 24 ☖dc1 ♗xf3 25 ♗xf3 ♛e6 26 ♛d3 ☖c8 27 ♛a6

♖c7 28 ♖c3 ♕a2 29 ♖d1 ♕b2 30 ♖dd3, with a clear advantage.

9 ♖d1

White strengthens his grip on the d-file. White can also play 9 ♗e3 or 9 b3, but as he tends to develop his rooks to c1 and d1 in most games anyway, these moves usually just transpose.

9...♘bd7 10 ♗e3

This is currently the main line. Playing ♕h4 either on this or the previous move permits the strong reply ...h6. However, 10 b3 is a reasonable alternative. White can again expect to play an eventual ♘d5, with chances to exploit his queenside space and, in the event of an exchange of knights on d5, to exchange Black's more dangerous bishop. After 10...♖c8 11 ♗b2 0-0 we have:

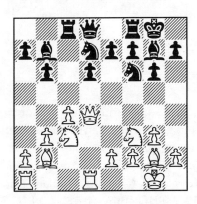

a) V.Anand-V.Milov, Biel 1997, continued 12 ♕e3 a6 13 ♘d4 ♗xg2 14 ♔xg2 ♖c5 and now Milov suggests 15 ♗a3, with a very slight edge.

b) 12 ♖ac1 a6 13 ♕d2 (C.Pritchett-D.Spence, British League 2004, varied with 13 ♘e1!? ♘e4 14 ♕e3 ♘xc3 15 ♗xc3 ♗xg2 16 ♗xg7 ♔xg7 17 ♘xg2 ♘f6 18 ♘f4 ♕c7 19 b4 ♕b7 20 f3! ♖c7 21 g4!

h6 22 h4 ♖fc8 23 g5 hxg5 24 hxg5 ♘h7 25 ♘d5, with a plus) 13...♖c5 14 ♗a3 ♖c7 15 ♘e1 ♕a8 16 ♗xb7 ♕xb7 17 ♘d3 ♖fc8 18 ♘b4 e6!? 19 ♕xd6 ♗f8 20 ♕d2 b5 21 ♘xa6 ♗xa3 22 ♘xc7 ♗xc1 23 ♖xc1 ♕xc7 24 ♘xb5, with slightly better chances, was B.Gelfand-L.Van Wely, Monaco (blindfold) 2005.

10...♖c8 11 ♖ac1 a6

11...0-0 12 ♕h4 a6 13 b3 usually just transposes, whereas White achieved little in V.Kramnik-G.Kasparov, World Championship (Game 14), London 2000, after 13 ♘e1 ♗xg2 14 ♘xg2 ♖e8 15 b3 ♕c7 16 ♗g5 ♕b7 17 ♘e3 b5, with an active game for Black.

12 b3 0-0

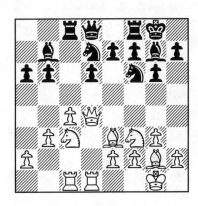

13 ♕h4

White keeps to the main line. Also playable is 13 ♕d2!? when White's grip is always likely to be an irritant for Black, even after minor piece exchanges. White retained an edge in V.Ivanchuk-L.Aronian, Morelia 2006, which continued 13...♘e4 (Black did better with 13...♖e8 14 ♗h3 ♖c7 15 ♗h6 ♖c5! 16 ♗xg7 ♔xg7 17 ♕d4 ♕c7 18 e4 ♔g8 19 ♕e3 ♕b8 20 ♘d5 b5, with a roughly equal game in B.Gulko-A.Grischuk, Beersheva 2005) 14 ♘xe4 ♗xe4 15 ♘e1 ♘f6 (15...♗xg2 16 ♘xg2 ♖e8 17 ♘f4 ♘f6 18 ♕b4 ♖b8 19 ♘d5 is also better for White, as is here 16...b5 17 cxb5 axb5 18 ♕b4) 16 ♗h3 ♖b8 17 ♘d3 ♗a8 18 f3 e6 19 ♗f2 ♖e8!? 20 ♘b4 a5 21 ♘a6 ♖c8 22 ♕xd6 ♕xd6 23 ♖xd6, with advantage.

13...♖c7

Now Black has the option of developing his queen to b8 or a8. Instead E.Kengis-R.Vaganian, German League 2002, continued 13...♖e8 14 ♗h3 ♖c7 15 ♘a4 (Pogorelov's sharper 15 g4!? ♕b8 16 g5 is another approach) 15...♗xf3!? 16 exf3 ♕b8 17 ♘c3 ♘e5 18 ♗g2 ♖ec8 19 ♗d4 ♘c6 20 ♗xf6 ♗xf6 21 ♕e4 ♗xc3?! 22 ♖xc3 ♘e5 23 f4! ♘g4 24 ♕e2 ♘f6 25 ♖e3 ♖e8 26 g4! e6 27 ♗f3 ♖c5 28 g5 ♘d7 29 ♕d2 d5 30 ♖d3, with a clear advantage.

14 ♗h3!

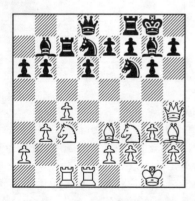

From h3, White's bishop may support g4-g5 ideas or plans involving piece play.

14...♕b8

Black plays his queen to b8 to main-tain contact with b6. Instead V.Anand-J.Gomez Esteban, Santurtzi (rapid) 2003, continued 14...♕a8 15 ♗xd7 ♖xd7 16 ♘a4! ♗xf3 17 ♘xb6 ♕b7 18 exf3 ♖c7 19 ♘d5 ♘xd5 20 ♖xd5, with advantage.

15 ♗g5

White puts indirect pressure on e7 and prepares ♘d5. He can also play to exchange the dark-squared bishops or launch a bayonet attack:

a) Veselin Topalov has been associated with 15 ♗h6, combined with the idea of ♘g5 and ♘d5.

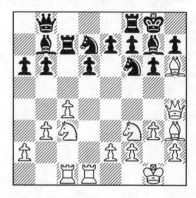

After some simplifying minor piece exchanges, White can hope to exploit his extra space:

a1) White played a testing gambit in V.Topalov-A.Grischuk, Monaco (rapid) 2006, which continued 15...♖d8 16 ♘g5 ♘f8 17 a4 ♖c5 18 ♗xg7 ♔xg7 19 b4 ♖c7 20 ♘d5 ♗xd5 21 cxd5 ♖xc1 22 ♖xc1 h6 23 ♘f3 ♘xd5 24 ♘d4 ♖e8 25 ♘c6 ♕c7 26 ♗g2 ♘f6 27 ♕c4 ♕c8 28 e3 ♘8d7 29 ♗f1 b5 30 axb5 axb5 31 ♕xb5, with a dangerous outside passed pawn.

a2) White was also better in J.Werle-K.Sasikiran, La Roche sur Yon 2006, after 15...♗xh6 16 ♕xh6 ♗xf3 17 exf3 b5 18 ♗xd7 ♖xd7 19 ♖d4 b4 (better is 19...e6, although 20 ♖f4 ♘h5 21 ♖h4 d5 22 cxd5 exd5 23 ♘e2 ♖c8 24 ♖d1 ♕e5 25 ♘d4 retained an edge in V.Topalov-L.Van Wely, Monaco (blindfold) 2005) 20 ♘d5 ♘xd5 21 cxd5 e5 22 dxe6 fxe6 23 ♕d2 a5 24 ♖c6 ♖fd8 25 f4 ♔f7 26 ♖a6 ♕b5 27 ♖axd6, with an extra pawn.

a3) 15...♗xf3 16 ♗xg7 ♔xg7 17 exf3 ♘e5 18 ♗g2 b5 19 cxb5 axb5 20 ♕b4!, gave White the better game too in V.Topalov-L.Psakhis, FIDE World Championship, Las Vegas 1999.

b) 15 g4!? is ultra-sharp and unclear. After 15...e6! 16 g5 ♘e8 we have:

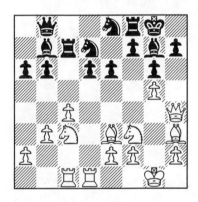

b1) 17 ♘e4 b5 18 cxb5 axb5 19 ♗d4 ♖xc1 20 ♖xc1 ♕a8!? 21 ♗xg7 was M.Sorokin-D.Sadvakasov, Moscow 2005, and now 21...♘xg7 is probably fine for Black.

b2) With colours reversed, an earlier Aronian-Kramnik clash (Saint Vincent 2005) saw 17 ♗g2 b5 18 ♘e4 bxc4 19 bxc4 d5 20 cxd5 ♗xd5 21 ♘c5 ♘xc5 22 ♗xc5 ♘d6 23 ♖b1 ♕xb1! 24 ♖xb1 ♖xc5, and Black held.

b3) John Watson suggests 17 ♘d4!? and if 17...♕a8 18 ♘a4 ♕d8 19 ♘xe6

fxe6 20 ♗xe6+ ♔h8 21 ♘xb6, with a plus, which may be critical.

Returning to 15 ♗g5:

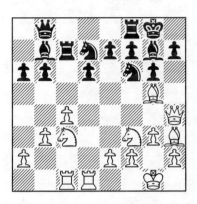

15...♗xf3?!

This is often a doubtful exchange and so it proves here. White's doubled f-pawns, supported by his active bishops, offer him prospects in the centre and down the f-file. Black chose a calmer option in R.Akesson-T.Nyback, Jyvaskyla 2006, which continued 15...♖e8 16 ♘d5!? ♘xd5 17 cxd5 ♘f6 18 ♖xc7 ♕xc7 19 ♖c1 ♕d8 20 e4 b5 21 ♖c2 ♘d7 22 ♗e3 b4, and now 23 ♗d4 ♗xd4 24 ♘xd4 may still give White a slight edge.

The consequences of the livelier 15...b5!? are also not entirely clear, though the straightforward 16 ♘d5, and if 16...♗xd5 17 cxd5 ♖xc1 18 ♖xc1 ♖c8!? 19 ♖c6!, looks like it may still cause some problems for Black.

16 exf3 b5 17 ♗xd7!

This appears to be White's strongest move. White can also retain a slight edge after both 17 cxb5 axb5 18 ♕b4 ♘e5 19 ♗g2 and 17 ♘d5 ♘xd5 18 cxd5 (Kramnik).

17...♖xd7 18 ♘d5

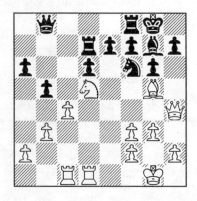

18...♘xd5

Now Black is always going to be in trouble because White dominates the c-file, particularly the c6-square. However, Black has no satisfactory alternative and he suffers tactically after 18...bxc4?! 19 ♗xf6 ♗xf6 20 ♕xf6! exf6 21 ♘xf6+ ♔g7 22 ♘xd7 ♕b7 23 ♘xf8 cxb3 24 axb3 ♔xf8 25 ♖xd6 ♕xb3 26 ♔g2 ♕a3 27 ♖c8+ ♔g7 28 ♖b6, with a winning endgame, as pointed out by Kramnik.

19 cxd5 ♖c7

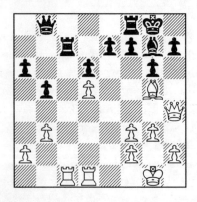

20 ♖c6!

White's kingside pawns may be mildly fractured, but his overall game bursts with energy. Occupation of c6 is pivotal. If Black exchanges on c6, White obtains a monster passed pawn on that square, but if Black leaves the rook on c6, his a- and e-pawns remain under fire, and White will strengthen his grip on the c-file after ♖dc1.

20...♖xc6!?

Black chooses to do battle with the c6-monster. As an example of how hard it is for Black to break White's bind, Kramnik gives the possibility 20...♖fc8 21 ♖xc7 ♖xc7 (or 21...♕xc7 22 ♖c1 ♕d7 23 ♖xc8+ ♕xc8 24 ♗xe7) 22 ♗xe7 ♖c2 23 ♕f4 ♗e5 24 ♕e3 ♖xa2 25 f4 ♗g7 26 ♖c1, with a clear advantage.

21 dxc6 ♖c8 22 ♖c1 e6 23 ♗d2

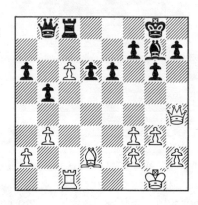

23...♕c7

Aronian didn't wish to allow White's bishop to reach a5, so holds back ...d5, though Kramnik considers that this would have been Black's lesser evil.

24 a4!

This excellent move loosens up Black's queenside, enabling White's queen to speed to that sector to increase his pressure.

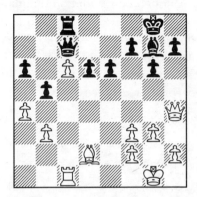

24...d5 25 axb5 axb5 26 ♕b4 ♖b8

Black has many weak dark squares. After 26...♕b6 27 ♕d6, White will soon play c7 with an almost certain win.

27 ♕a3 ♗d4

Everything hinges on White's battle to get his pawn to c7. Kramnik gives the line 27...♗e5 28 f4 ♗d6 29 ♕a6 ♖b6 30 ♕a1 ♕c8 31 c7 ♖b7 32 ♗a5, and White wins.

28 ♕a6 ♗e5?!

Black now clearly loses the battle for c7. He had to try either 28...b4 or 28...♗b6.

29 f4 ♗d6 30 ♗a5 ♕c8 31 ♕a7 ♖a8 32 ♕b6 ♖b8 33 ♕d4 b4 34 c7

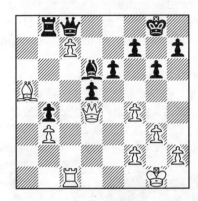

With White's pawn on c7, Black lacks sufficient defensive space and his game collapses.

34...♖a8

White also wins after both 34...♖b7 35 ♕f6 ♗xc7 36 ♕e5 and 34...♖b5 35 ♕f6 (Kramnik).

35 ♕b6 ♗f8 36 ♗xb4 ♗xb4 37 ♕xb4 ♕e8 1-0

Summary

This chapter concludes coverage of ...c5 and ...♘f6 defences with an examination of the Hedgehog.

When Black sets up a small centre (pawns on d6 and e6 with ...♗e7), White can either play indirectly for an early d4 break, based on 7 ♖e1, 8 e4 and 9 d4, or directly with 7 d4. Another popular black option is the double fianchetto. As Black hasn't played ...e6 in these lines, control of d5 becomes a key focus.

1 c4 c5 2 ♘f3 ♘f6 3 ♘c3 e6 *(D)*

      3...b6 4 g3 ♗b7 5 ♗g2 g6 *(D)*

4 g3 b6 5 ♗g2 ♗b7 6 0-0 ♗e7 *(D)*

      7 ♖e1 – *Game 26*

      7 d4 – *Game 27*

3...e6

5...g6

6...♗e7

Chapter Six

English-Indians

1 c4 ♘f6 2 ♘f3

As mentioned in the Introduction, I won't be covering the King's Indian, but here we will consider Black's attempts to play both the Grünfeld and the Nimzo-Indian directly against 1 c4 (or 1 ♘f3 ♘f6 2 c4). White needn't transpose to the main lines of those two openings and has good prospects of gaining a pull by keeping the game within English realms.

Game 28 considers **1 c4 ♘f6 2 ♘f3 g6 3 ♘c3 d5 4 cxd5 ♘xd5 5 ♕a4+**.

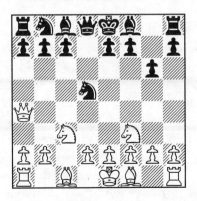

This is the main starting point for the English Grünfeld. Our coverage focuses particularly on the variation 5...♗d7 6 ♕h4 ♘xc3 7 dxc3 ♘c6 8 e4 e5 9 ♗g5 ♗e7 10 ♗c4,

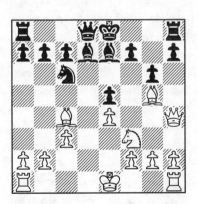

which offers White a risk-free, if modest pull, based on slightly better development, play down the d-file and chances on the queenside, based on moves such as b4 and (often) a4-a5. Game 27 also covers White's important 6th move alternatives, 6 ♕b3 and 6 ♕c2, which lead to more conventional Grünfeld-like play, based on eventually advancing White's pawns in the centre.

Games 29 and 30 consider the Nimzo-English which arises after **1 c4 ♘f6 2 ♘f3 e6 3 ♘c3 ♗b4**.

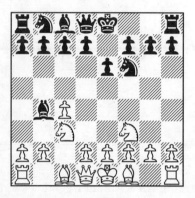

Black is prepared in most lines to exchange his bishop for White's knight on c3 in return for compensation in the form of doubled white c-pawns and/or a gain in time, such as after a3. Game 29 focuses on the main lines after 4 ♕c2 0-0 5 a3 ♗xc3 6 ♕xc3, and particularly on the variation 6...b6 7 e3 ♗b7 8 ♗e2 d6 9 0-0, followed eventually by b4 and d4, transposing into an active form of the Classical Nimzo-Indian Defence.

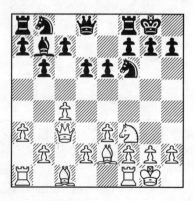

White has an edge, based on his prospects of gradually advancing his pawns, with the support of his bishops.

Game 30 considers the other main line, namely 4...c5 5 a3 ♗a5 6 g3, and particularly the variation 6...♘c6 7 ♗g2 0-0 8 0-0 d6 9 d3 h6 10 e3. The kingside fianchetto systems appear to offer White more against this line than e3 systems. Black fights to retain his dark-squared bishop, but a5 is not an ideal post, and Black sometimes voluntarily exchanges this piece later (with no gain in time) rather than struggle to get it back into play in the centre.

A radical, but playable alternative is 4 g4!?.

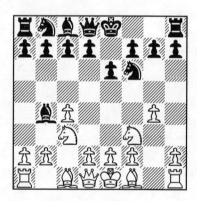

This double-edged bayonet thrust has recently become fashionable. White threatens g5, achieving a space advantage. Originally developed independently by Vadim Zvjaginsev and Mikhail Krasenkow, it has since been taken up by some of the world's best players. No guarantees can be given if you play this line, but a well-prepared, enterprising player might win many games and thoroughly enjoy it.

Often taken by surprise, Black has tried many defences after 4 g4:

a) 4...h6 is Black's 'most annoying reply' according to Krasenkow in an excellent article in *NIC Yearbook*:

a1) 5 ♖g1 has been played the most often, but Krasenkow currently considers that Black has 'no problems' after the solid 5...b6 (he also quite likes 5...g5!? which is akin to similar blocking lines played in the Sicilian Defence) 6 ♕c2 ♗b7 7 a3 ♗e7 8 g5 (or 8 e4 c5!) 8...hxg5 9 ♘xg5, which he suggests is 'highly unclear' (though this view could do with more testing).

a2) White's best may be 5 ♕c2!?, so that if 5...b6 6 a3 ♗e7 (or 6...♗xc3 7 ♕xc3 ♗b7, as in J-P.Wallace-P.Schuurman, Hastings 2006/07, and now the immediate 8 ♖g1 followed by h4 might be best) 7 e4! he builds a strong pawn centre.

cording to Krasenkow) 9 cxd5 exd5 10 e5 ♘e4, and now Krasenkow suggests 11 ♗d3! ♘g5 12 ♗xg5 hxg5 13 e6 ♖h6 14 exf7+ ♔xf7 15 ♗g6+ (or 15 0-0-0) 15...♔g8 16 ♘e5 ♗f6 17 0-0-0 with a clear advantage.

b) 4...0-0 5 g5! ♘e8 6 ♕c2 c5 (or 6...d5 7 a3 ♗e7 8 d4 c5 9 dxc5 ♗xc5 10 e3 ♗e7 11 h4 dxc4 12 ♗xc4, with advantage in V.Zvjaginsev-A.Riazantsev, Moscow 2003) 7 a3 ♗a5 8 ♘e4 b6 9 b4 cxb4 10 ♗b2 ♗b7 11 ♖g1 b3 12 ♕d3 ♗xe4 13 ♕xe4 ♘c6 14 ♖g3 f5!? (14...♘d6 15 ♕d3 is a little better for White) 15 gxf6 ♘xf6 16 ♕d3 ♕e7 was A.Kosten-C.Balogh, Austrian League 2004, and now Kosten suggests 17 ♘g5 e5 18 ♗g2, with good chances.

c) White is also very comfortable after 4...d6 5 g5 ♘fd7 6 ♕c2.

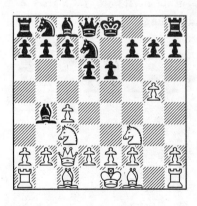

M.Krasenkow-M.Mchedlishvili, Warsaw 2005, continued 6...♘c6 7 a3 ♗xc3 8 ♕xc3 e5 9 b4 b6 (or 9...♕e7 10 d4 a5 11 b5 ♘xd4 12 ♘xd4 exd4 13 ♕xd4 0-0 14 ♖g1, with an edge – Krasenkow) 10 d4 ♗b7 11 ♖g1 ♕e7 12 d5 ♘d8 13 ♘h4 g6 14 f4 f5 15 e4, with advantage.

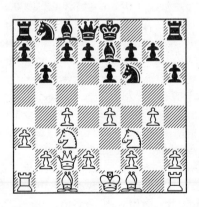

M.Krasenkow-W.Spoelman, Wijk aan Zee 2007, continued 7...♗b7 8 d4 d5 (8...♘xg4!? 9 ♖g1 f5 10 h3 ♘f6 11 d5! fxe4 12 ♘xe4 ♘xe4 13 ♕xe4 ♗f6 14 ♘e5 ♗xe5 15 ♕xe5 ♕f6 16 ♕h5+ ♕f7 17 ♗e2 gives White good compensation ac-

d) 4...♗xc3 5 dxc3 d6 6 g5 ♘fd7 7 ♗g2 e5 8 ♗e3 ♕e7 9 ♘d2 f5 (Palliser suggests 9...♘c6!?, not allowing White to favourably alter the structure) 10 gxf6 ♘xf6 11 ♘e4 ♘xe4 12 ♗xe4, gave White an edge in M.Krasenkow-E.Lobron, Subic Bay 1998.

e) V.Zvjaginsev-J.Piket, Tilburg 1998, continued 4...d5!? 5 g5 ♘e4 6 h4! ♘c6 7 ♕c2 f5 8 gxf6 ♘xf6 9 a3 ♗xc3 10 dxc3 ♕e7 11 ♗g5 ♗d7, and now the sequence 12 cxd5 exd5 13 0-0-0 is better for White.

Game 28
E.Ghaem Maghami-H.Odeev
Asian Championship,
Calcutta 2001

1 c4 ♘f6 2 ♘f3 g6 3 ♘c3 d5 4 cxd5 ♘xd5 5 ♕a4+

From a4, White's queen has many active prospects, including a possible transfer to h4, with kingside threats.

5...♗d7

Black's bishop isn't well placed on d7, but his other options also have some downside:

a) 5...♘c6 blocks Black's c-pawn and invites a dangerous pin with 6 ♘e5! and now:

a1) 6...♘db4 7 a3! gives White good prospects. He established a strong pawn centre in H.Steingrimsson-V.Sakalauskas, Tallinn 2006, after 7...♗g7 (7...♘c2+ 8 ♕xc2 ♘xe5 runs into 9 d4! with some advantage) 8 axb4 ♗xe5 9 b5! ♘b8 10 e3 0-0 (White also had an edge after 10...♘d7 11 d4 ♗g7 12 ♗e2 0-0 13 0-0 ♘b6 14 ♕c2 ♗f5 15 e4 in S.Kustar-J.Pribyl, German League 2004) 11 ♗e2 c6 12 0-0 cxb5 13 ♕xb5 ♘c6 14 d4 ♗g7 15 ♗f3 a6 16 ♕b3, with a definite edge.

a2) 6...♘xc3 7 bxc3 (7 dxc3 is also quite reasonable) 7...♗g7!? (or 7...♗d7 8 ♘xd7 ♕xd7 9 ♖b1 with a pleasant pull) 8 ♘xc6 bxc6 9 ♕xc6+ ♗d7 10 ♕c5 0-0 11 g3 ♖b8 12 ♗g2 didn't give Black enough for his pawn in A.Shariyazdanov-A.Kneutgen, Oberwart 2000.

b) The passive 5...c6 fails to stem White's initiative. A.Shariyazdanov-M.Duesterwald, Izmir 2004, continued 6 ♕d4 (the straightforward 6 ♘xd5 ♕xd5 7 e4 ♕d8 8 d4 also seems good) 6...f6 7 e4 e5 8 ♘xe5! ♘xc3 9 ♕xc3 ♕e7 10 ♘f3 ♕xe4+ 11 ♗e2 ♘d7 12 d4, with advantage.

6 ♕h4

As well as this lively switch to the kingside, White has two other challenging moves:

a) 6 ♕b3 more or less obliges Black's knight to retreat and after 6...♘b6 7 ♘g5!?, White induces a slight dark-square weakening in Black's game.

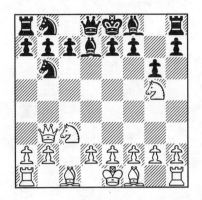

V.Korchnoi-J.Rowson, Port Erin 2004, continued 7...e6 8 d4 ♗c6 9 ♗e3 (9 ♗f4!?, intending 9...♕xd4? 10 ♘xe6! fxe6 11 ♕xe6+ ♗e7 12 ♗e5, may be better) 9...♗g7 10 ♖d1 ♘8d7 11 ♘f3 ♕f6? (11...0-0 is correct) 12 d5! ♘xd5 13 ♘xd5 ♗xd5 14 ♖xd5 exd5 15 ♗d4, with a clear advantage.

b) The deceptively modest 6 ♕c2!? is also testing:

b1) The critical lines arise after 6...♘b4. P.Wells-S.Kristjansson, Calvia Olympiad 2004, continued 7 ♕b3 c5 8 ♘e4 ♕a5!? (8...♗f5 9 d3 b6?! 10 ♘eg5! ♗e6 11 ♘xe6 fxe6 12 a3 was promising in the earlier P.Wells-J.Rowson, Scarborough 2004) 9 a3 (the tempting 9 ♘fg5!? ♕a4 10 ♕xf7+ ♔d8 11 b3 ♘c2+ 12 ♔d1 ♘xa1 13 bxa4 ♗xa4+ 14 ♔e1 ♘c2+ 15 ♔d1 ♘e3+ may be no more than a drawing variation) 9...♘8c6!? 10 ♕c3!? (10 e3 may give White a pull), and now 10...♗f5! is probably fine for Black.

b2) 6...♘b6 7 d4 ♗g7 8 e4 sees White build a sound pawn centre. A.Volzhin-V.Baikov, Elista 2001, continued 8...0-0 9 ♗e3 ♘c6 (9...♗g4!? 10 ♘e5! is also a little better for White according to Volzhin) 10 d5! ♘e5 11 ♘xe5 ♗xe5 12 ♖d1 ♕e8 13 ♗e2 c6 14 0-0, with an edge.

Returning to 6 ♕h4:

6...♘xc3 7 dxc3

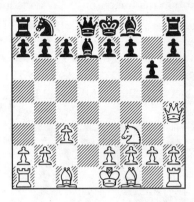

White abandons any thought of establishing an extra pawn in the centre, but can hope to play for an edge based on his better-placed pieces, good play down the d-file and queenside prospects.

7...♘c6

Black usually plays this move to support ...e5, seeking to exchange queens and simplify. Plans based on ...c5 are unconvincing. R.Cifuentes Parada-D.Komljenovic, Benasque 2005, for example, continued 7...c5!? 8 e4 h6 9 ♗c4 b5 10 ♗e2 ♗g7 11 0-0 ♕c7 12 ♗e3 a6 13 a4 bxa4 14 ♗d1 ♕b7 15 e5 g5 16 ♕c4, with good play.

8 e4 e5

Black has occasionally preferred 8...h6, but this gifts White time. After 9 ♗f4 (9 ♗e3 and even 9 e5!? are also promising) 9...♗g7 10 ♕g3 ♖c8 11 0-0-0 e6 12 ♔b1 0-0 13 h4 h5 14 e5! ♘e7 15

♕h3 ♘d5 16 ♗g5!, White's aggressive play had brought him a clear advantage in M.Ashley-C.Tsai, Boston 2001.

9 ♗g5!

This move puts most pressure on Black's game and enables White to maintain his queen on its active square (h4) for a little longer. Instead Black defended well in M.Turner-J.Rowson, Southend 2000, after 9 ♕g3 ♗d6 10 ♗c4 ♕e7 11 ♗h6 f6 12 0-0 ♘d8 13 ♖fd1 ♘e6 14 ♗e3 ♘f4, with at least equality.

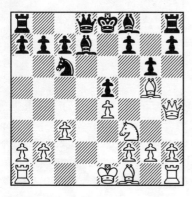

9...♗e7 10 ♗c4

Although exchanging the queens and dark-squared bishops leads in principle to endgames where White can probe a little, it is premature to exchange these pieces now. Indeed, Black held comfortably in E.Bacrot-A.Shirov, Odessa (rapid) 2007, after 10 ♗xe7 ♕xe7 11 ♕xe7+ ♔xe7 12 ♗b5 f6 13 0-0-0 a6 14 ♗xc6 ♗xc6 15 ♖he1 ♖ad8.

10...h6

Black tries to force White into exchanges. The most accurate way to do this may, however, be to play Alon Greenfeld's 10...h5!? which threatens 11...f6, followed by 12...g5, playing to

trap White's queen:

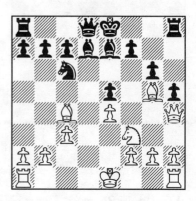

a) The ending after 11 ♗xe7 ♕xe7 12 0-0-0 ♕xh4 13 ♘xh4 ♖f8 is at best only very slightly better for White. J.Piket-V.Mikhalevski, Belgrade 1999, continued 14 ♗d5 0-0-0 15 ♖d3 ♘e7 16 ♗b3 f6 17 ♖hd1 ♗g4, and Black held. White's best may be to play the ending with Black's king in the middle of the board after 12 ♕xe7+ ♔xe7. Then, as well as the 13 ♗d5 h4 14 h3 f6 15 0-0-0!? of F.Vallejo Pons-V.Ivanchuk, Monaco (rapid) 2005, White can consider both 13 b4!?, intending 13...h4 14 h3 f6 15 a4 a6 16 a5 ♖ad8 17 ♔e2 ♗e6 18 ♗xe6 ♔xe6 19 ♘d2, with good prospects for White's knight and possible b5 breakthroughs, and 13 0-0-0, intending 13...♗g4 14 ♖d3 ♖ad8 15 ♗d5! which should be compared with the positions reached in the notes to White's 12th, below.

b) White can also keep the queens on the board with the rather convoluted 11 h3 f6 12 ♗e3 g5 13 ♕g3 h4 14 ♕h2, as he did in K.Sasikiran-E.Sutovsky, Paks 2005, but it is doubtful whether all the time involved in getting White's queen back into play in the centre will allow him to play for any real advantage.

11 ♗xe7 ♕xe7 12 ♕g3

With Black's pawn on h6 and not h5, White's queen can't be troubled by ...h4. White can therefore happily keep queens on the board and this retreat is commonly held to be the most troublesome. He can again head too for an endgame with 12 ♕xe7+ ♔xe7 when 13 0-0-0 (13 b4!?) 13...♗g4 14 ♖d3 ♖ad8 15 ♗d5!...

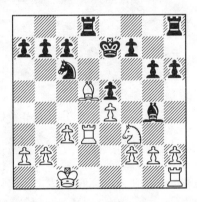

...offers a small pull. R.Vaganian-V.Jasnikowski, German League 1993, continued 15...♖d6 16 ♖hd1 ♘d8 17 ♖1d2 ♗xf3 18 ♖xf3 ♘e6 19 ♗xe6 ♔xe6 20 ♖xd6+ cxd6 21 ♔d2 b5 22 ♖d3 ♖c8 23 b4 ♖c4 24 ♖d5 a6 25 f3 f5 26 ♔d3 ♖c8 27 a4! ♖b8 28 c4! fxe4+ 29 fxe4 bxc4+ 30 ♔xc4 ♖c8+ 31 ♔b3 ♖c1 32 ♖a5! ♖b1+ 33 ♔a3 ♖e1 34 ♖xa6, with good winning chances.

12...0-0-0 13 0-0!

White risks little by castling on the opposite side of the board from Black and can hope to gain by heightening the cross-board tension. Both sides can launch pawnstorms against the enemy king, but White's pawns enjoy the support of better-placed forces. White stands particularly well on the d-file, where he can expect to take advantage of the strong d5 outpost to tie Black down and act as a block against too many exchanges. Black's kingside pawns are moreover slightly weaker than White's and may become long-term targets.

13...g5!?

Black plans to advance his g- and h-pawns to his fifth rank. He can also play for ...f5, but that takes time. S.Savchenko-V.Mikhalevski, Berlin 1997, continued 13...♖h7 14 ♗d5 ♖e8 15 ♖fe1 ♖g7 16 a4 f5 17 ♘d2 f4 18 ♕d3 g5 19 a5 ♘d8!? (19...g4!? may be a better chance) 20 b4 ♖g6 21 b5 g4 22 b6! a6 23 bxc7 ♔xc7 24 ♖ab1, with good play.

Practice has also seen 13...♕f6 and after the 14 ♖ad1 ♖he8 15 ♗d5 ♖e7 16 ♘d2 ♕f4 17 ♘c4 of V.Kramnik-V.Ivanchuk, Las Palmas 1996, Kramnik suggests that 17...♗e6 18 ♗xe6+ ♖xe6 19 ♖xd8+ ♘xd8 20 ♕d3 restricts White to an edge.

14 ♖fd1 f6 15 ♘d2 h5!?

Black continues aggressively on the kingside. He can instead maintain his kingside pawns in their current formation and seek exchanges in the centre, but White can then still play to exploit Black's weak light squares and exposed kingside pawns. A.Kharitonov-Y.Nepomniashchy, Cheboksary 2006, for example, continued 15...♗e6 16 b3 ♖d7 17 ♗xe6 ♕xe6 18 ♘c4 ♖hd8 19 ♕f3 g4 20 ♕e2 h5 21 ♘e3 ♘e7 22 ♖xd7 ♖xd7 23 ♖d1 ♖xd1+ 24 ♕xd1 ♕c6 25 ♕d3 a5 26 g3 b6 27 h3!, with an ongoing pull.

16 ♕e3 ♔b8 17 ♗d5 h4 18 b4

18...♖df8

Both sides push on with their respective plans as Black prepares a retreat square for his knight on d8. Postny suggests that 18...♕e8!?, and if 19 ♘b3 ♘e7, attacking White's powerful bishop, might be better, though 20 ♗c4, and if 20...♕h5 21 ♘c5, still looks a bit better for White.

19 b5 ♘d8 20 a4 g4

Black must react sharply. White's attack looks the better after 20...♘e6 21 ♘b3, with c4-c5 a dangerous threat.

21 ♘b3 g3 22 ♘c5!

Now a5, followed by b6, is in the air. White's attack still seems more concrete than Black's.

22...gxf2+ 23 ♕xf2 ♗g4!? 24 ♖db1 f5 25 a5! fxe4 26 ♕e3 ♖f6?

This move fails to stop b6, after which Black is probably lost. Postny's 26...♕d6 27 ♗xe4 ♕h6 28 ♕xh6 ♖xh6 was better, though after 29 ♖f1, White still has a definite edge.

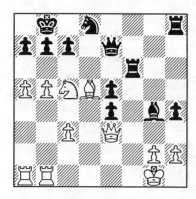

27 b6! cxb6 28 axb6 ♖xb6

Or 28...a6? 29 ♘xa6+! bxa6 30 ♖xa6, with a winning attack.

29 ♖xb6 axb6 30 ♘a6+!

This fine knight sacrifice wins.

30...bxa6 31 ♕xb6+ ♘b7

White wins simply after 31...♔c8?! 32 ♕xa6+ ♔d7 33 ♕b5+.

32 ♖xa6 ♗c8

Black has no good defence. White wins too after 32...♕c5+ 33 ♕xc5 ♘xc5 34 ♖a8+.

33 ♕a7+ ♔c7 34 ♖c6+ ♔d7 35 ♕b6 ♕d8 36 ♗e6+ ♔e7 37 ♕b4+!

After this precise check, Black loses his queen.

37...♘d6 38 ♖xc8 ♔xe6 39 ♖xd8 ♖xd8

40 ♕b3+ ♔f5 41 ♕d5 e3 42 ♔f1 ♔f6 43 ♔e2 ♘f7 44 ♕f3+ ♔e7 45 ♕xe3 ♖g8 46 ♕e4 ♔e6 47 ♕c4+ 1-0

Game 29
V.Kramnik-A.Kogan
French League 2005

1 c4 ♘f6 2 ♘f3 e6 3 ♘c3 ♗b4 4 ♕c2 0-0

This is Black's most flexible reply. His main alternative is the 4...c5 of our next illustrative game. Instead 4...d5 5 a3 ♗e7 (5...♗xc3 6 ♕xc3 0-0 transposes to the notes to Black's 6th move, below) 6 cxd5 exd5 7 d4 reaches a main line of the Queen's Gambit with a useful extra move for White (a3).

There's also 4...b6, which will usually just transpose into lines with ...b6 below, although it can lead to some distinct g3 systems should White prefer such a set-up:

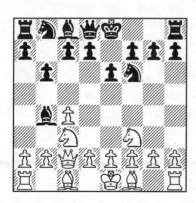

a) With 5 g3 White leaves Black's bishop hanging on b4 in the hope that Black may eventually have to retreat it or exchange it on c3 with loss of tempo. After 5...♗b7 6 ♗g2 0-0 7 0-0 ♖e8 (or

7...d5 8 cxd5 exd5 9 d4 ♖e8 10 ♗f4 ♘a6 11 ♖fd1 c6 12 ♘e5 ♖c8 13 a3 ♗d6 14 ♘d3 ♘c7 15 e3, with a comfortable form of the Queen's Indian in the game E.Kengis-V.Kunin, Schwaebisch Gmuend 2003) 8 d4 (probably more testing than the preparatory 8 ♖d1) 8...d5 (the more solid 8...♗xc3!? 9 ♕xc3 d6 10 b3 ♘bd7 11 ♗b2 ♗e4 12 ♖ac1 ♖c8 13 ♖fd1 c6 was preferred in M.Illescas Cordoba-A.Karpov, Linares 1994, and now 14 ♗f1!? d5 15 ♘h4 might be White's best) 9 ♘e5 (9 cxd5 exd5 10 ♗f4 is also good) 9...c6 10 ♗g5 ♗e7 11 ♖fd1 ♘bd7 12 e4 h6 13 ♗f4 ♕c8 14 ♖ac1 ♘xe5 15 dxe5 ♘xe4 16 ♘xe4 dxe4 17 ♗xe4 c5 18 ♖d2, White had a pull in A.Khalifman-J.Hjartarson, Tilburg 1994.

b) 5 a3!? ♗xc3 6 ♕xc3 ♗b7 7 g3 sees White first obtaining the bishop-pair and this may be stronger.

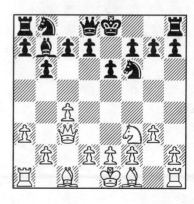

K.Sakaev-S.Azarov, Moscow 2006, continued 7...0-0 8 ♗g2 c5 9 0-0 ♘c6 10 b4 d6 11 d3 e5 12 e3 ♖e8 13 ♗b2 ♖c8?! (13...a6! is better according to Kramnik) 14 b5! ♘a5 (varying from the 14...♘e7!? of V.Kramnik-J.Ehlvest, Vienna 1996, when Kramnik suggests 15 e4 ♘g6 16 ♘d2 ♘f8 17 f4 ♘e6 18 ♖ae1, with advantage) 15 e4 ♘d7 16 ♗h3! ♖c7 17 ♗xd7 ♖xd7 18 ♘h4 f6 19 ♘f5 ♗a8 20 ♘e3 ♘b7 21 f4 ♕b8 22 f5 a5 23 ♖f2 ♘d8 24 ♕c2 ♔f7 25 g4, with good breakthrough chances.

Returning to the flexible 4...0-0:

5 a3

5 g3 is less popular at this juncture as Black has more options, including the solid 5...d5.

5...♗xc3

5...♗e7 can be played but White's extra move (a3) is useful. V.Chuchelov-T.Pioch, Eupen 2000, for example, continued 6 e4 d6 7 d4 c5 8 dxc5 dxc5 9 e5 ♘fd7 10 ♗d3 ♘c6 11 ♗f4 ♕c7 12 ♕e2 ♖e8 13 ♕e4 g6 14 h4 a6 15 h5 ♗f8 16 hxg6 hxg6 17 0-0-0, with an attack.

6 ♕xc3

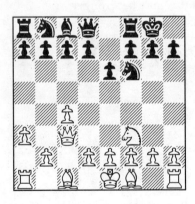

6...b6

This system is highly popular. Instead 6...c5 leads to note 'b' to Black's 5th move in Game 30 and after 6...d5, White was always ahead in A.Greet-A.Grant, Hastings 2006/07, which continued 7 e3 b6 8 b4 ♘bd7 9 ♗b2 ♗b7 10

d3 c5 11 ♗e2 ♕c7 12 0-0 ♖ac8 13 cxd5 exd5 14 ♖fc1 ♖fe8 15 bxc5 bxc5 16 ♖ab1, with a pleasant advantage.

7 e3

Kramnik delays b4, a move which is also testing straight away. After 7 b4!? Black must decide whether or not to counter with a quick ...a5:

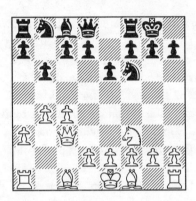

a) After 7...d6 8 ♗b2 ♗b7 9 e3 play is likely to transpose to lines considered in our main game. However, 9 g3 c5 (White had an edge after 9...♘bd7 10 d4 ♘e4 11 ♕b3!? a5 12 ♗e2 axb4 13 axb4 ♖xa1+ 14 ♗xa1 ♘df6 15 0-0, in V.Kramnik-A.Karpov, Dos Hermanas 1997) 10 ♗g2 ♘bd7 11 0-0 is also possible and has been used by both Kasparov and Kramnik. After 11...♖c8 12 d3 we have:

a1) 12...♖e8 13 e4 a6 14 ♕b3 b5 15 ♘d2 ♖b8 16 ♖fc1 ♗a8 17 ♕d1 ♕e7 was G.Kasparov-A.Karpov, World Championship (Game 24), Lyon 1990, and now Karpov suggests 18 ♖ab1 cxb4 19 axb4 bxc4 20 dxc4, with the slightly better game.

a2) 12...d5 13 cxd5 ♗xd5 14 ♕d2 ♕e7 15 ♖fc1 h6 16 ♗c3 ♖fe8 17 ♕b2 e5

18 e4 ♗b7 19 ♘d2 ♕d6 20 ♗f1 ♕e6 21 b5 gave White a plus in V.Kramnik-P.Nikolic, Monaco (rapid) 1997.

a3) White pressed after 12...♖c7 13 a4 d5 14 cxd5 cxb4 15 ♕xb4 ♘xd5 16 ♕a3 a5 17 ♖ac1 ♘c5 18 ♖c4 ♘b4 19 ♗e5, in M.Illescas Cordoba-E.Berg, Turin Olympiad 2006.

b) E.Agrest-V.Gashimov, Antalya (rapid) 2004, saw White build on his spatial edge with 7...♗b7 8 ♗b2 a5 9 b5 d6 10 e3 ♘bd7 11 ♗e2 e5 12 ♕c2 ♘e4 13 d4 ♕e7, and now 14 c5! bxc5 15 dxe5 dxe5 16 0-0 ♘g5 17 ♘d2 a4 18 ♘c4 was a promising positional pawn sacrifice.

c) Black also failed to equalize after 7...a5 8 ♗b2 axb4 9 axb4 ♖xa1+ 10 ♗xa1 c5 11 g3 d6 12 ♗g2 e5 13 b5 ♖e8 14 0-0 ♘bd7 15 d3 ♗b7 16 ♗b2 ♘f8 17 ♖a1, with an edge in L.Van Wely-V.Anand, Monaco (blindfold) 2005.

Returning to 7 e3:

7...♗b7 8 ♗e2

Kramnik continues to mask his intentions, rather than again advance with 8 b4.

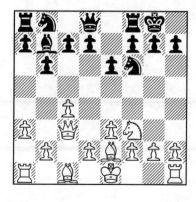

8...d6 9 0-0 ♘bd7

Play transposes after 9...c5 10 b4

♘bd7 11 ♗b2.

10 b4 c5

Now White can reach lines of the Classical Nimzo-Indian Defence that have an active reputation for him. The tough middlegames and especially endgames resulting used to be considered far more easily defensible than they are now. This shift has been due to recent achievements by Kramnik and others, in games such as this one.

However, Black can't easily equalize after other moves either:

a) 10...e5 11 ♗b2 a5?! (11...c5 looks better) 12 d4 ♘e4!? 13 ♕c2 ♕e7 14 c5! bxc5 15 bxc5 dxc5 16 dxe5 was promising in P.H.Nielsen-K.Lahno, Hastings 2003/04,

b) V.Kramnik-V.Anand, Dortmund 2000, saw 10...a5 11 ♗b2 ♕e7 12 d4 axb4 13 axb4 ♖fc8 14 ♖xa8 ♖xa8 15 d5!

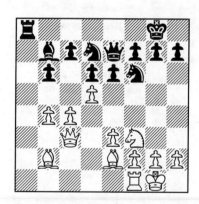

15...♘f8 16 ♖d1 ♗c8 17 ♘d4 e5 18 ♘b3, with an edge.

c) Yet another noted theoretician failed to equalize in J.Gustafsson-A.Khalifman, German League 2003, which continued 10...♕e7 11 ♗b2 c5 12 d3 ♖fc8 13 b5 ♘f8 14 a4 a5 15 ♖ae1 ♘g6

16 ♘d2 d5 17 cxd5 exd5 18 d4 ♘h4 (no better is 18...c4!? 19 f3, allowing White to play long-term for an e4-break), and now Ribli's suggestion 19 g3 ♘f5 20 dxc5 bxc5 21 ♕e5 is better for White.

11 ♗b2 ♖c8

V.Kramnik-Zhang Zhong, Wijk aan Zee 2004, had previously gone 11...♖e8 (or 11...e5!? 12 d4! exd4 13 exd4 ♖e8 14 ♖ae1 cxd4 15 ♕xd4 ♘e5, as in K.Sasikiran-E.Rozentalis, Bled Olympiad 2002, and now 16 ♘d2 would have retained a clear edge) 12 d4 ♘e4 13 ♕b3 ♖b8, and now 14 ♖fd1 was the best way to retain a pull.

12 d4

The switch to d4 systems is testing for Black. But it is also possible to play for a pull in more restrained style, as White did in L.Portisch-M.Najdorf, Wijk aan Zee 1978, which continued 12 d3!? d5 13 b5 ♖e8 14 a4 e5 15 cxd5 ♘xd5 16 ♕b3, with advantage.

12...♘e4 13 ♕d3!

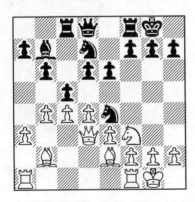

This is a common, modern theme in such positions. From d3, White's queen supports d4 and joins in the immediate battle to expel Black's knight from e4.

13...♕f6!?

White's simple plan is to play ♘d2, followed by f3, obtaining control of e4 and mobile pawns supported by a powerful bishop-pair. As this can't be prevented, Black seeks to find the best way to keep active. Kogan's queen heads for g6 to support play on the b1-h7 diagonal, whereas Black went disastrously wrong in J.Werle-E.Rozentalis, German League 2006, with 13...♕e7 14 ♘d2 f5 15 f3 ♘ef6 16 ♖fd1 e5?! 17 dxc5 bxc5 18 ♕xf5 ♘b6 19 ♕g5 h6 20 ♕h4 ♕e6 21 e4, and White won.

14 ♘d2 ♕g6 15 f3 ♘xd2 16 ♕xd2 d5?!

Opening the centre runs the serious risk that it will only benefit White, whose forces are generally more active. It is doubly doubtful here with Black's queen distant from the main action in the centre. Perhaps 16...♖fd8, followed by trying to get Black's queen back to e7, might put up more resistance.

17 dxc5 bxc5 18 ♖ac1 ♖fd8 19 cxd5

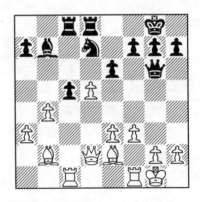

19...♗xd5!?

White can now open the entire queenside while Black's queen remains a virtual spectator on the other flank.

But the alternative 19...exd5 20 bxc5 ♘xc5 is strategically dire, and would clearly be a high price to pay to get Black's queen into some sort of contact with the rest of her forces along the third rank.

20 e4 ♗b7 21 ♖fd1 ♘f8 22 ♕e3 ♖xd1+ 23 ♗xd1 cxb4 24 ♖xc8 ♗xc8 25 axb4 a6 26 ♕c5 ♕h6

Black had to see this clever move at move 19. After either 26...♗b7 27 b5! axb5 28 ♗a3 ♘d7 29 ♕c7 or 26...♗d7 27 b5! ♗xb5 28 ♗a3, he loses.

27 ♗c1

Not, of course, 27 ♕xc8 allowing 27...♕d2!, threatening mate on e1 and White's bishops.

27...♕h4

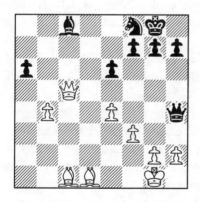

Black exploits the mating threat on e1 a second time, gaining the tempo necessary to allow his queen to get back to d8.

28 g3 ♕d8 29 ♗e2 h5?!

Still in trouble, Black decides on a doubtful gambit. He should probably have preferred 29...♘d7 and if 30 ♕d6 (30 ♕c3 is also possible) 30...♕b6+ 31 ♕xb6 ♘xb6, hoping to hold an inferior

endgame. White has real winning chances after 32 ♔f2, and if 32...♔f8 33 ♔e3 ♔e7 (or 33...e5 34 ♗b2 f6 35 f4) 34 ♔d4 ♘d7 35 e5 f6 36 f4, but would still have to work hard to deliver the full point.

30 ♔f1 h4 31 gxh4 e5 32 ♕xe5 ♕xh4 33 ♗c4

White still faces significant technical problems, but his extra pawn is now a safe and telling factor.

33...♕h3+ 34 ♔f2 ♕h4+ 35 ♔e2 ♘e6 36 ♗e3 ♔h7 37 ♕b8 ♕d8 38 ♗d3 ♕d7 39 f4

White must advance his kingside pawns to drive back Black's minor pieces and help harry Black's king.

39...♘c7 40 f5 ♘b5 41 ♕e5 f6 42 ♕c5 ♕e8 43 ♗f4 ♔h8 44 ♔e3 ♗b7 45 ♗g3 ♗c6 46 e5

After this final breakthrough, White's bishops and queen combine to create mating threats which quickly win the game.

46...fxe5 47 ♗xe5 ♘c7 48 ♕d6

White now threatens 49 ♕h6+ and Black could resign.

48...♘d5+ 49 ♔d4 1-0

Game 30
R.Vaganian-R.Dautov
Reggio Emilia 1995/96

1 c4 ♞f6 2 ♞f3 e6 3 ♞c3 ♝b4 4 ♛c2 c5

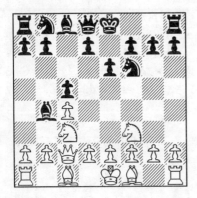

5 a3

Although this move is virtually standard, it is also worth considering the immediate 5 g3, which leaves Black's bishop to stew a bit on b4, unsure as to whether its role is to be exchanged on c3 or to try to find a way back into the game via a5. There's still plenty of room for experiment here and after 5...0-0 6 ♝g2 ♞c6 7 0-0 d5, White has tried:

a) A.Czebe-A.Jankovic, Steinbrunn 2005, continued 8 cxd5 exd5 9 h3 (or 9 a3!? ♝a5 10 ♞a4 c4 11 b4! ♝c7 12 ♝b2 a6 13 d3 cxd3 14 ♛xd3 ♞e4 15 ♖fd1 ♝e6 16 ♖ac1, with good play for White in C.Pritchett-E.Gausel, Gausdal 1993) 9....♝e6 10 d3 h6 11 a3! ♝xc3 (11...♝a5!? 12 ♞a4 looks a bit better for White) 12 bxc3 ♖e8 13 ♔h2 ♝f5 14 ♞h4 ♝h7 15 f4 ♛d6 16 ♛d1 ♖e7 17 a4 ♖ae8

18 ♖a2 b6 19 e3 ♛c7 20 f5, with a pull.

b) F.Berkes-C.Balogh, Hungarian League 2006, varied with 8 d3 ♝xc3 9 ♛xc3 d4 10 ♛a3 ♛d6 (10...♛e7 is better) 11 e3 ♞b4 12 exd4! ♞c2 13 ♝f4 ♛xf4 14 ♛a4 ♛d6 15 ♛xc2 cxd4 16 c5 ♛d7 17 ♛c4 ♖d8 18 b4 ♛d5 19 ♖fe1! ♖b8 20 a3, with a clear, Réti-like advantage.

5...♝a5

Uncommon but playable is 5...♝xc3. After 6 ♛xc3 play can easily transpose into lines with ...b6 and ...c5, considered in Game 29, but this move order can also give rise to some distinct alternatives:

a) White's bishops told on an open board in V.Kramnik-'Centrale Nantes', Paris simul 2006, which continued 6...d5 7 cxd5! ♛xd5 8 b4! ♞bd7 9 ♝b2 b6 10 g3 ♝b7 11 ♝g2 ♛d6 12 0-0 0-0 13 d3 a6 14 e4 ♛e7 15 ♞d2 ♖ac8 16 ♖fc1 ♖fd8 17 ♞c4 b5 18 ♞a5 ♝a8 19 ♛e1 e5 20 ♝c3 ♞b6 21 ♝h3, with a clear advantage.

b) 6...0-0 7 b4 (7 e3 and 7 g3 are also fine) 7...b6 8 ♝b2 d6 9 g3 ♝b7 10 ♝g2 ♞c6 11 0-0 e5 12 e3 e4?! (12...♞bd7 would restrict White to an edge) 13 ♞g5 ♞e5 14 d3! was favourable for White in L.Ftacnik-L.Aronian, German League 2002.

6 g3

White can play g3 or e3 systems. The principles are much the same. White ensures that he meets Black head on in the centre and tries to exploit the slightly awkward position of Black's bishop on a5. If Black exchanges his bishop on c3, White gets the bishop-pair. However, if it remains on a5, it may become a target, or if it retreats, this costs time.

After 6 e3!? practice has seen:

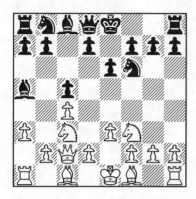

a) 6...♘c6 7 ♗e2 0-0 8 0-0 h6 9 ♖d1 ♗c7 10 ♖b1 d5 11 cxd5 exd5 12 ♘b5! was good for White in R.Buhmann-O.Romanishin, Hockenheim 2006.

b) V.Malakhov-A.Sokolov, French League 2004, went 6...0-0 7 d4 b6 8 ♗e2 d5 (Tal's 8...♗a6!? is probably better) 9 0-0 ♗xc3 10 ♕xc3 ♗a6 11 dxc5 bxc5 12 b3 ♘bd7 13 ♗b2 ♖b8 14 ♖ab1, again with a typical bishop-pair edge.

c) Black should, though avoid 6...d5?! 7 ♘a4!, after which M.Tal-M.Romero, Seville 1992, continued 7...b6 8 ♖b1 b5?! 9 cxb5 c4 10 b3 cxb3 11 ♖xb3, and White won.

6...♘c6

Black can also consider the tricky 6...d5!?. This move seems to invite ♘a4, but it isn't easy to time this reply well, particularly while Black's knight can still play to a6. White has struggled to prove anything after both 7 ♘a4 ♘a6! and 7 cxd5 exd5 8 ♘a4 c4. Perhaps 7 ♗g2 0-0 8 cxd5!? exd5 9 0-0 ♘c6 10 ♘a4

(or 10 h3), transposing to slightly more promising lines discussed in note 'a' to White's 5th move, is the best that White can do.

7 ♗g2

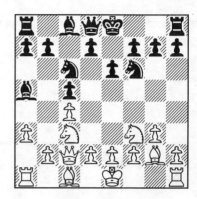

7...0-0

Now 7...d5?! 8 ♘a4! does seem to work for White. L.Ftacnik-Z.Rigo, Martin 2003, continued 8...♘d4 9 ♘xd4 cxd4 10 b4 ♗c7 11 cxd5 ♘xd5 12 ♗b2 0-0 13 0-0 ♘b6 14 ♘c5, with some advantage.

8 0-0 d6

Black prepares the blockading plan ...e5. He can also consider:

a) 8...♕e7 defends c5 in preparation for ...d5, but this is a little slow, and White can respond actively in the centre. A.Shchekachev-R.Berzinsh, Basle 2002, continued 9 e3 d5 (or 9...♗xc3 10 ♕xc3 a5 11 b3 d6 12 d4 ♗d7 13 ♗b2 b6 14 ♖ad1 ♖fc8 15 d5 exd5 16 cxd5 ♘a7 17 e4, with an edge in S.Savchenko-R.Bouhallel, Bethune 2006) 10 ♘a4! dxc4 11 ♕xc4 ♘d7 12 d4 ♘b6 13 ♘xb6 ♗xb6 14 dxc5 ♕xc5 15 ♕xc5 ♗xc5 16 b4 ♗e7 17 ♗b2, with good chances.

b) 8...d5 again seems a little suspect

after 9 ♘a4!. R.Pogorelov-A.Rizouk, Ibiza 2006, continued 9...♘d4 10 ♘xd4 cxd4 11 b4 ♗c7 12 ♗b2 dxc4 13 ♕xc4 e5 14 ♖ac1 ♗d6 15 ♘c5 ♖b8 16 f4!, with good prospects.

9 d3

As Black intends ...e5, this precise move induces ...h6 to prevent ♗g5, winning a kind of half tempo. The sequence 9 e3 e5 is also possible when White's most interesting move is the complex 10 d4!?:

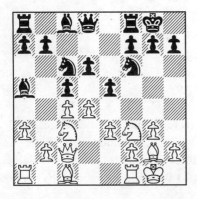

a) L.Pantsulaia-J.Gustafsson, Turin Olympiad 2006, saw the cagey 10...♗xc3 11 ♕xc3!? e4 12 ♘d2 cxd4 13 exd4 d5!? 14 c5!? a5 15 b3 b6 16 ♗b2 ♗a6, with unclear play.

b) 10...cxd4 11 exd4 exd4 12 ♘b5 ♗b6!? 13 ♗f4 ♗g4 (better is 13...d5! and if 14 c5 d3 15 ♕c1 a6 16 cxb6 axb5 17 ♗c7 ♕e7 18 ♖e1 ♘e4) 14 ♘xd6 ♕d7 15 ♘e5 ♘xe5 16 ♗xe5 ♗c7 17 c5 ♘e8 18 ♕e4, with advantage, was J.Granda Zuniga-A.Naiditsch, Wijk aan Zee 2004.

9...h6

Black might try 9...a6!?, as mentioned in Palliser's *Beating Unusual*

Chess Openings. Fairly testing is 10 ♖b1 ♖b8 11 ♘a2 ♘d4, but White appeared to show the way forwards in S.Krivoshey-E.Postny, Bad Wiessee 2006: 12 bxc3!? h6 13 ♗xf6 ♕xf6 14 ♘d2 ♗d7 15 a4 ♖ab8 16 ♖db1 ♕d8, and now 17 ♖b2 followed by ♖ab1, may still press.

10 e3

White retains his options and controls d4. He can play for a quick b4, but Black gets counterplay as he did with 10 ♖b1 e5 11 e3 ♗e6 12 ♘a2 ♕d7 13 b4 ♗d8 14 ♘c3 ♖c8 15 bxc5 dxc5 16 e4 ♗g4!, with chances for both sides in G.Kamsky-A.Karpov, Reggio Emilia 1991.

10...e5 11 ♘d5!

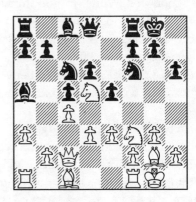

Vaganian plans ♘d2, followed by b3 and the pawn break f4. Other plans are also possible, but this is the most direct.

11...♗e6

Black continues his development. After 11...♘xd5 12 cxd5 ♘e7 13 ♘d2, and if 13...♘f5 14 ♘c4, White retains two possible (f4 and b4) pawn breaks and Black's bishop continues to look awkward on a5. Instead L.Pantsulaia-A.Istratescu, Turin Olympiad 2006, saw 11...♗d7!? 12 ♘d2 ♖b8 13 ♖b1!? (13 b3, and if 13...b5!? 14 cxb5 ♖xb5 15 ♘c4 looks simpler) 13...b5 14 b4 cxb4 15 ♘xf6+ ♕xf6 16 cxb5 ♘e7 17 a4 ♖fc8 18 ♕d1 a6, and now the critical test may be 19 ♘c4!?, and if 19...♗d8 20 bxa6 d5 21 a7 ♖a8 22 ♘d2.

12 ♘d2 ♖c8 13 b3 ♘h7

Black finds it difficult to drum up counterplay and gradually drifts into a position that looks better for White.

14 f4 ♕d7

Dautov must tread carefully. After 14...♘e7 15 ♘xe7+ ♕xe7 16 f5! White has obvious kingside attacking chances and Black faces long-term defence.

15 ♗b2 f6!? 16 ♘e4 f5

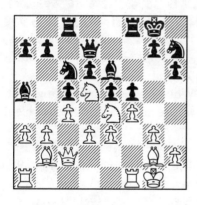

Black once and for all prevents f5 by White, but White still has control of the central light squares and an edge.

17 ♘ec3 ♘f6 18 ♖ab1 ♗d8

Black's bishop continues to struggle to find a useful role. Meanwhile White manages to get in b4, with further space gain.

19 b4 b6 20 ♗a1 exf4!?

Cramped for space, Dautov finds it difficult to co-ordinate his forces. This exchange is a necessary preparation for Black's next move and a plan to ease the pressure on his game by further exchanges, but it also significantly strengthens White's centre.

21 gxf4 ♘e7 22 bxc5 dxc5 23 e4!

Vaganian has the better game due to his powerful concentration of forces in the centre.

23...♔h8 24 ♘xe7 ♗xe7 25 ♘d5 ♖f7 26 a4

White seeks to weaken Black's queenside pawns.

26...♖cf8 27 ♖be1 ♗d8 28 ♕d1 ♘g8 29 ♗e5 ♗f6 30 ♕a1 ♗xe5 31 ♕xe5 ♘e7!

Black defends tenaciously. He threatens ...♘c6-d4 and ...♘g6 with pressure on f4, forcing further exchanges.

32 ♘xe7 ♖xe7 33 exf5 ♖xf5 34 ♕e4 ♖ff7 35 a5 ♗f5?!

The game starts to slip decisively away from Dautov about here. It isn't clear whether White can claim any advantage after 35...bxa5! and if 36 f5 ♗xf5 37 ♕a8+ ♔h7 (37...♕c8? 38 ♕xc8+

♗xc8 39 ♖xe7 loses) 38 ♗d5 ♗xd3 (or 38...♖xe1 39 ♖xe1 ♗xd3) 39 ♗xf7 ♖xf7 40 ♖xf7 ♕xf7 41 ♕d5 ♗xc4.

45...♗d3 46 ♔f2 ♔f6 47 ♔e3 ♗b1 48 ♖c1 ♗h7 49 ♖c6+ ♔f5 50 ♔f3 ♗g6 51 ♖c5+ ♔f6 52 ♔g4! ♗e4 53 ♖b5 ♗d3 54 ♖b6+!

36 ♕a8+ ♔h7 37 ♗d5 ♖xe1?!

Now Black should have played 37...♗xd3! 38 ♗xf7 ♖xf7 (not 38...♕g4+? 39 ♔h1 ♖xf7 40 ♖f3! and if 40...♗xc4? 41 ♖e8 ♖xf4 42 ♖h8+ ♔g6 43 ♖g3 and wins) 39 ♖f2 ♕d4.

38 ♖xe1 ♗xd3 39 ♗xf7 ♕xf7 40 ♕d5! ♗xc4 41 ♕xf7 ♗xf7 42 ♖e7!

White reaches an endgame an exchange ahead with good winning chances.

42...♗c4 43 ♖xa7 bxa5 44 ♖xa5 ♔g6 45 ♖xc5

White still faces technical problems, but Vaganian finds a way to drive Black's king into passivity.

Black's king now has to retreat and White's king journeys to e5 to increase the pressure.

54...♔f7 55 ♔f3 ♔f5 56 ♔e3 ♗c2 57 ♔d4 ♗f5 58 ♔e5! ♗d3 59 ♖b7+ ♔f8 60 ♖b3 ♗c4 61 ♖b4 ♗f1 62 ♖d4 ♗h3 63 f5 ♔f7 64 ♖d3 ♗g4 65 h3! ♗e2 66 ♖d7+ ♔g8 67 f6!

White's rook and king totally dominate and Black must lose his final pawn or be mated.

67...gxf6+ 68 ♔xf6 ♗h5 69 ♖d5 1-0

The win becomes clear after 69...♗f3 (or 69...♗e8 70 ♖d8 ♔f8 71 ♖a8) 70 ♖d8+ ♔h7 71 ♖d7+ ♔g8 72 ♔g6.

Summary

In practice Black often meets 1 c4 ♘f6 2 ♘f3 by playing either 2...g6 3 ♘c3 ♗g7, reaching the King's Indian, or 2...c5, returning play to Chapters Four and Five. White can, however, frustrate attempts by Black to reach a Grünfeld Defence by playing 2...g6 3 ♘c3 d5. After 4 cxd5 ♘xd5 5 ♕a4+ (Game 28) White's good centre and active development give him decent chances of securing a long-term edge.

White can also pleasantly bypass transposition into the Nimzo-Indian Defence after 2...e6 3 ♘c3 ♗b4, by playing 4 ♕c2 (Games 29 and 30), which is a good try for an edge. White either gains a bishop-pair pull after an exchange on c3 or Black finds his dark-squared bishop facing a problematic retreat after an eventual challenge on b4, usually by a3. More enterprising souls may well, though, prefer the radical alternative, 4 g4!?.

1 c4 ♘f6 2 ♘f3 (D) **2...e6**
    2...g6 3 ♘c3 d5 (D) – *Game 28*
3 ♘c3 ♗b4 4 ♕c2 (D)
      4...0-0 – *Game 29*
      4...c5 – *Game 30*

2 ♘f3

3...d5

4 ♕c2

Index of Complete Games